FORRY

FORRY

The Life of Forrest J Ackerman

DEBORAH PAINTER

Foreword by Joe Moe

McFarland & Company, Inc., Publishers
Jefferson, North Carolina

The present work is a reprint of the illustrated case bound edition of Forry: The Life of Forrest J Ackerman, *first published in 2011 by McFarland.*

LIBRARY OF CONGRESS CATALOGUING-IN-PUBLICATION DATA

Painter, Deborah.
Forry : the life of Forrest J Ackerman ;
Deborah Painter; foreword by Joe Moe.
p. cm.
Includes bibliographical references and index.

ISBN 978-1-4766-8517-5
softcover : acid free paper ∞

1. Ackerman, Forrest J. 2. Book collectors — United States — Biography. 3. Authors, American — United States — Biography. 4. Collectors and collecting — United States — Biography. I. Title.
Z989.A33P35 2021 920—dc22 [B] 2010039553

BRITISH LIBRARY CATALOGUING DATA ARE AVAILABLE

© 2011 Deborah Painter. All rights reserved

No part of this book may be reproduced or transmitted in any form or by any means, electronic or mechanical, including photocopying or recording, or by any information storage and retrieval system, without permission in writing from the publisher.

Front cover: Forrest J Ackerman (photograph by Mark Berry).
Back cover: (left to right) Sid Koss, Tor Johnson, Verne Langdon, Forrest J. Ackerman, and L. Strock Rupert, president of *Stunt Stars from Screenland* and creator of Unimart Touring Don Post Monster Show (Don Post Studios)

Printed in the United States of America

*McFarland & Company, Inc., Publishers
Box 611, Jefferson, North Carolina 28640
www.mcfarlandpub.com*

To my father, Floyd Eugene Painter,
who made everything possible

Table of Contents

Acknowledgments — viii
Foreword: Marching to the Beast of a Different Dreamer by Joe Moe — 1
Preface — 5

1. Forry's Background, Family and Early Years — 11
2. "I Couldn't Sleep with Marlene Dietrich!" — 26
3. Sergeant Ack-Ack — 41
4. The 1950s — Forry's Rise to Fame — 49
5. The 1960s — Forrest J Ackerman, Movie Actor — 64
6. The 1970s — Colleges, Conventions and Creatures — 86
7. The 1980s — The Best of Times, the Worst of Times — 101
8. The 1990s — Pinnacles of Achievement — 117
9. The 2000s — Documentarian and Octogenarian — 151

Five Personal Reminiscences (Powell, Knight, Atkins, Hawk, Morrow) — 181
Chapter Notes — 201
A Brief Bio-Bibliography — 203
Bibliography — 207
Index — 209

Acknowledgments

The following persons have made significant contributions to this book: Tadao Tomomatsu, archivist of the Los Angeles Science Fantasy Society, Joe Moe, Rick Atkins, Lee and Jana Harris, Mary Ellen Daugherty, David Hawk, Terry and Anita Pace, Mark Layne, Daniel Kirk, Alex Paige, Arlene Domkowski, Dennis L. Phelps, Jaclynn and Ron Chaney, Michael Ramsey, John Deall, Verne Langdon, Jim Morrow, Buddy Barnett, Sean Fernald, Bjo and John Trimble, Jeffrey Roberts, Dennis Druktenis and Beth Robinson, granddaughter of Murray Leinster.

This book was written for my cousin, Dennis Pipkin, because he is interested in history.

Foreword: Marching to the Beast of a Different Dreamer

by Joe Moe

There is a faction in fandom that will not, under any circumstances, allow themselves to love Forrest J Ackerman. I've met some of these people in person. There are not many of them and truthfully, they seem like extremely good people inside and out. A few are actual genre pros with impressive bodies of work that might lead you to assume they'd be first in line to give Forry his due. Nope. Can't bring themselves to do it. Why? Well, having lived with the Ackermonster for nearly two decades and being considered his "best pal" has made me intimately familiar with his halo and devil horns. I've come to some theories about this.

First, you should know that as much of a tireless cheerleader as Forry was, he was also socially awkward, not the natural public speaker people supposed. Forry was, and remained until his death, "painfully shy" (his own words). Yes, he overcame his paralyzing fear to push through to get up and speak. But it never came easily to him. I remember him agonizing over detailed lists of stories and names for many a speech. He'd often start scrawling this list with red Flair felt pen on napkin, envelope or scratch pad the moment we boarded the plane to take us to an event. Many times, when it seemed to some that Forry was on autopilot, spinning monster yarns as if they were on cue cards, he was simply too modest to talk about himself or any "real world" subjects. His well-worn anecdotes were the shoe he wedged in the door to gain entry. Puns were also a lubricant to conversation. But as a result of Forry's dissertations, some fans dismissed Forry as, well, self-centered. These fans craved Forry's acknowledgment and validation. When they didn't get it to their satisfaction during a brief encounter, they harbored some resentment. Sadly, in most cases, if those same fans had just hung around for a little while longer, or gone to House of Pies for lunch, Forry would have eventually opened up.

My life with Forry may have started in much the same way as many of you. I was grateful for his oblivious mentorship of my childhood life and dreams through the

Foreword by Joe Moe

pages of *Famous Monsters of Filmland* magazine. But my life ended up being linked to Forry's in profound ways that I never could have imagined. The alchemy of Forry's incredible, eccentric personality coupled with my openness and need to pay back my "uncle," made for a great friendship. He grew to trust me and I never betrayed that trust. Aside from all of the fantastic stuff we shared like sci-fi and monster cons, old and new movies, faraway lands, celebrities, priceless props and artwork, we weathered some profound setbacks together as well. The death of Forry's wife, Wendayne. A notorious conflict with a malicious publisher. Catastrophic illnesses and injuries. The increasing loss of old friends.

Through the triumphs and tragedies, I was lucky to get to know the "real" Forrest J Ackerman. I wasn't shocked to learn that he had not designed his magnificent life through ambition or strategy. Forry simply loved what he loved and did what he did. In my opinion, his biggest and most noble acts of intention were facilitating others to become involved in the genre he loved and risking the things he collected so that other fans could get near them. He didn't pay for a young Ray Bradbury to attend sci-fi functions just to be a hero. He knew Ray had talent and vision and Forry wanted to help sow those seeds and luxuriate in the exotic fruits that blossomed from them. It was no accident that the iconic art and objects in the Ackermansion were never under lock and key. God knows I constantly begged him to lock it up! Forry insisted that fans experience these treasures in the same way he did; up close and personal. Intimately. When I reflect upon the smiles, joyful tears and inspiration created by the act of touching a Willis O'Brien *Kong* dinosaur, I know in my heart of hearts Forry was absolutely right all along.

I'm sorry more people couldn't know the Forry Ackerman I was privileged to know. Particularly those fans and peers who dismiss Forry and his eccentricities as aloof, detached or arrogant. The fact is, those people would have loved Forry most of all it they had just gotten a peek into the true soul of the man. They also would have benefited the most from his presence in their lives just as Forry's quality of life would have been greatly enhanced by their presence in it. Ironically, one particular fellow has publicly and eloquently described his disappointment that, on their first meeting, Forry didn't seem to acknowledge or care that the fellow had published his own genre magazine. Well, because I dismantled the 18-room Ackermansion when Forry and I moved to the smaller Ackerminimansion, I happen to know for a fact that, behind a panel near Forry's desk sat a full run of that fellow's magazine, proudly collected and assembled. Forry *did* care. He just couldn't always express it in conventional terms or on cue.

Forry may have left us. But he left us with so much. He left us with each other. Dear Debbie Painter (dubbed "D'bee by 4E) has done a monumental job of encapsulating her broad knowledge of our "Dr. Ackula" in the pages of this book. She could probably add ten more volumes to this one and still have more to tell. There will never be another Forry. He was a haphazard, magical occurrence. But his spirit of generosity and passion for the things he loved will live beyond him and continue to make a positive impact.

Foreword by Joe Moe

Our punning muse may be gone, but the fateful pebble of inspiration he rolled down the hill continues to snowball and influence the shape of pop culture today. You can see it in movies, art and literature everywhere. We fans perpetuate it in the way we nurture a sense of wonder in one another and in our children. In these ways, Forrest J Ackerman Shall Not Die!

Joe Moe is a third generation Polynesian entertainer; a studio vocalist; screenwriter; FX artist; and designer of dark rides for international theme parks. He cared for Forrest J Ackerman for many years. His job has him occupied in developing and shooting such movies as Red Velvet, Wasted Space *and others.*

Preface

This is a book about Forrest J Ackerman for everyone. It is not written for the science fiction aficionado only or the classic horror film enthusiast exclusively. I am writing for them, too, those who enjoy a good yarn about interstellar adventures on planets revolving around Sirius, and who marvel over the wonderful performance of Basil Rathbone as Wolf Frankenstein, making the unfortunate decision to try to outdo his dad, Henry, and bring back the monster as a nice, civilized sort in *Son of Frankenstein* (1939) for I am in the same league of classic horror admirers. Rather, this is a book for anyone who enjoys reading about great Americans who accomplished marvelous things and improved life for hundreds of thousands, if not millions. Forrest J (No Period) Ackerman is one of those great Americans.

What makes someone great? Are great persons just fortunate people who are born in the right part of the world or the right part of the country in which they are born? I have heard others say that this is what makes people great. I heard one person say that being a person of means makes all the difference and lack of wealth equals lack of accomplishment.

Forry never owned a yacht or even a small boat, and even though he and his wife, Wendayne, had a maid for some years, and secretaries who came in twice a week for a few hours to handle his mailings, he certainly never owned a large estate or a fleet of cars. His and his wife's "mansion," though large by some people's standards, was not the biggest or finest mansion in the neighborhood, or even on the block. For most of his life he only had a few thousand dollars in the bank at any given time. His family was never wealthy and everyone had to work; his mom worked to raise the children, his dad and his brother and he had to make a living in the workaday world, and his wife worked. One can, then, rule out being born with a silver spoon in his mouth as the reason for his success.

There is more to being a successful person who influences others the way Forry did. I believe that even if he were born in a small town in Mexico, he would have found his way. Guillermo del Toro, famed director of *Pan's Labyrinth*, was born in a town in Mexico and was not from a well-to-do family. Del Toro found his way.

Some people can be placed in the path of opportunity and yet their response is to just sit still while opportunity flutters over their heads and vanishes from sight. Yes,

Preface

Forry was born in Los Angeles where he could easily make the right connections in film and in science fiction, but he had the insight and intuitive ability to recognize a good thing when he saw it and to make the most of every opportunity that came across his path.

He created opportunities for himself. When he was a boy he showed up unannounced at the homes of local science fiction authors and asked them for autographs. In most instances he ended up becoming friends for life with the authors. He formed a literary agency from his connections with people in the field when he was still a young man. Once he began to acquire some fame, he promoted himself and became even more famous. His name-dropping was legendary. Through his agenting work and his work as editor of *Famous Monsters of Filmland*, he made the acquaintance of almost every important director, star, scriptwriter and special effects provider in the field of science fiction, fantasy and horror films. Forry then used this to propel himself and his works toward more fame, which translated to more demand for his knowledge to be showcased in documentaries. He coined various phrases and catchy terms to promote his work and the work of his literary clients. At 65, even after the age when many people would have retired, Forrest J Ackerman worked from about 7 o'clock in the morning until mid-afternoon when he would have a short nap, then, back to work until about 6 P.M., when he grabbed some dinner and then sat down to watch a game show on television or perhaps a drama, and then it was back to work on some project until bedtime, which was usually 11:00 P.M. He felt that he could not just sit and entertain himself when there was someone out there somewhere who wanted something from him.

I became aware of the man in 1976 when in college and reading my first issue of a recent *Famous Monsters of Filmland* magazine, a Warren Publishing Company periodical which he edited at that time. The magazine was very informative about films and filmmakers and had a certain charm and corny sense of humor. I quickly learned that this corny sense of humor and this charm was the editor's unusual style. He also wrote much of the magazine uncredited. I began reading the magazine regularly and later became a subscriber because I loved classic fantasy and horror films since childhood. I also began to write for *Famous Monsters* in 1979 (yes, perhaps I, too, was in the right place!) and by doing so began to receive correspondence and even phone calls from the editor, mostly to chat. I was in college and very new at the publishing scene, having previously done cartoons for my father's archaeology journal, *The Chesopiean, a Journal of North American Archaeology*. Because of my lack of experience, I did not know that it is not an everyday affair for an editor of a magazine to call a freelancer to chat. I also sensed, but did not know, that it is even more uncommon for a magazine editor to invite freelancers to his Hollywood birthday parties! I received a party invitation printed on stationery with the *Metropolis* robotrix in a burnt sienna hue, as far back as 1981, before I even met the man in person. I had that privilege in 1983 when I attended the World Science Fiction Convention in Baltimore, Maryland, primarily to have a chance to meet him and see him speak on various panels. Forrest J Ackerman was extraordinarily

Preface

friendly and remembered me from my correspondences with him. I listened to his panel on trends in science fiction, shared with a fellow author, a filmmaker and a young person. He was a highly educated and sophisticated fellow, not just a punster. I was impressed. Like my own dad, he was a well-educated, articulate, self-made man who read and wrote as much as possible and made important contributions to the field that he had chosen. I have kept every "missive" Forry ever sent me about his many adventures and I in turn sent him a copy of every single thing I ever had published ... many of which were about him! After 26 years of knowing "The Ackermonster" and trying to be a good friend, and accumulating knowledge about Forry, it is about time I did something a little more consolidated for the history of Forrest J Ackerman than simply the few dozen magazine articles I have written about him. Many years ago a very young fan of *Famous Monsters of Filmland* wrote to Forry and asked for a photo and gave him a penny. "I send you this penny out of my love." Well, this book is my penny, Forrest J Ackerman, which I send you out of my love.

When one is researching someone as incredibly versatile and complex a person one naturally finds material. The author's material came from joining the Los Angeles Science Fantasy Society, from reading hundreds of books and magazine articles about and by Forrest J Ackerman, from viewing half a hundred films in which he had cameos and small roles, from studying the many documentaries he appeared in and narrated, from interviews with notables in the fields of fantasy, horror and motion pictures, and from just being a friend for more than 26 years.

Much has been written about Forry Ackerman by many people within and without the science fiction and classic horror film and television field over the past 55 years, for it was in 1955 that he began his rise to prominence.

Forry has written about himself as well, perhaps feeling that it is best to get your own thoughts about yourself committed to paper before someone else beats you to it and gets it wrong! Since Forry surrounded himself with writers it seems natural that people wanted to write about him, some negatively, the rest positively, but always passionately. Since the man took credit for so many accomplishments and gave away so many of his own accomplishments to others, and has aroused the jealousy of some while reaping the benefits of the undying devotion of others, working on his biography is just like carbon dating a piece of tapestry. To carbon date a substance it is necessary to take a bit of it apart and subject it to the chemical tests. Thus, I subject the tapestry of Forry's life to the chemical test.

Few people have brought a smile to my face as quickly and as naturally as did Forrest J Ackerman. I saw and felt the core of goodness, patience and youthful good humor he radiated. I think that is what made me smile so much. Seeing a photo of the guy brings a smile. Forry Ackerman radiated joy and continues to do so. He was famous, but what one does with one's time, energy and resources to make the world a little better is more important than mere fame.

Forry was a jumble of self contradictions. He was thrilled to be the winner of the first Hugo award in the category of the # 1 Fan Personality, and then, in his moment of glory on the podium at the 1953 World Science Fiction Convention, promptly gave it to a man who he felt deserved it more than he, Ken Slater. He loved adulation and yet, when pushed into a corner by all the attention and made uncomfortable, would become quiet.

Forry Ackerman was a tireless promoter of science fiction and he made it known to all who knew him or read extensively about him that if circumstances permitted he would die with the words "science fiction" or "sci-fi" on his lips. Though a supporter of science, Forry was not a scientist and did not study any scientific endeavor.

Forry made it well known that he had no belief in an afterlife or soul or in gods, angels or other metaphysical deities, and yet he was proud of a short story he wrote entitled "Letter to an Angel." It was about a little boy named Timmy O'Toole who, in 1930, writes a letter to the just-deceased Lon Chaney in Heaven, and sends it care of God. The boy then dies of pneumonia and meets God, mistaking Him for one of Chaney's amazing characters. The story was made into a short 1996 film with Forry as the storyteller and Ron Ford and Paula Pointer-Ford as the grieving parents. The film was shown at Forry's 65th birthday party in 1981. In "The Lure and Lore of 'The Blind Spot,'" published in *Expanded Science Fiction Worlds of Forrest J Ackerman and Friends PLUS*, he wrote of a strange Ouija board communication he was party to. By way of background, Homer Eon Flint had been a favorite author of his and had died at a young age as the result of a tragic automobile crash. His body had been found under the car in a canyon. During the séance Forry was asked if he wanted to hear from anyone and he said "H.G. Wells,—and Homer Eon Flint."

The medium asked, "Is there anyone who would like to say something to us?"

"FLINT" was the response received. The medium asked the ether, "Describe your fatal accident."

"NO ACCIDENT — ROBBERY."

"Did you have any unfinished manuscripts?"

"YES — THE LAST GODLING."

Later communication with the family of the deceased Flint revealed that he had indeed written a book whose title and plot would either be "The Child of the Southwind" or "The Hidden Empire" and would have to do with a child destined for greatness. In addition, Flint's family was to later find out that nails and a cord were found in the car that were later connected to a bank robbery in Fresno County, California, six weeks previously, which implicated some criminals in the mysterious and suspicious accident.[1] If he had been curious about metaphysical things Forry would have delved a little deeper after such an experience, but Forry had his own blind spots, and it merited little more than a mention in his preface to the book *The Blind Spot*, by Homer Eon Flint.

This man, Forrest J Ackerman, was larger than life. But who was Forrest J Ackerman, really? Was he as fascinating and accomplished as so many people have maintained? Or was that some carefully constructed public persona?

When you read this book you will know that he was every bit as big a person as

Preface

he was rumored to have been. It is the author's intent to convey proof that he was even bigger than his public persona.

Forry's first look at literary science fiction, and the inspirator of his careers in science fiction, was the magazine *Amazing Stories*. Enjoy this book on the amazing story of Forrest J Ackerman.

1

Forry's Background, Family and Early Years

Forry Ackerman often said he picked the right pair of maternal grandparents. His grandmother had a distinguished father. Belle Wyman's father was a landscape painter, portrait photographer and advocate for the rights of the oppressed.

Thomas W. Cridland was born in Leichestershire, England, on October 1, 1811, according to Ohiohistory.org. He immigrated to America in the 1830s looking for prosperity. He was apprenticed to a gilder and a looking glass maker until 21 years of age, at which time he married Amanda Looker, and moved first to Charleston, South Carolina, and then Philadelphia. In Philadelphia he worked as an artist and there met Samuel F.B. Morse, the inventor of the telegraph. Morse was, as it happened, interested in many new devices, among them the daguerreotype.

Cridland wisely took an interest in the new technology and realized its commercial possibilities. Morse had discovered the method of reproducing an image on a piece of burnished silver. This limited the photography to that of still life because of the iodide process that required that the subject sit very still for about an hour lest the photo be blurred.

Chemistry professors Morse and John Draper, then at New York University, found that by using a bromide process a picture could be made in about three minutes. Professor Draper made the first photograph or reproduction of a live person, his daughter.

Cridland, having learned the art and practical application firsthand from its inventors, moved wife and child to Kentucky on a flat boat plying the Ohio River, and set up a portrait studio. He was the first man in Kentucky to make a daguerreotype. An artisan, he had many side businesses as a maker and seller of picture frames and looking glasses, and as a cabinet maker. He also painted landscapes and designed and made outdoor terracotta ornaments. Because of his profession, he became acquainted with wealthy persons who came to his studio for portraits.

The house occupied by T.W. Cridland overlooked a slave pen and market and from his window he could see slaves being sold. He was often present when families were being broken up and when wives and husbands were being separated, which often happened upon the death of a slaveholder and the sale of his or her estate and property.

Cridland even saw children being taken from their mothers, and heard the anguished cries of the families. This repeated spectacle galvanized him to action.

Cridland not only made the acquaintance and had the friendship of Henry Clay, but also his nephew, Cassius M. Clay. A member of the slave-holding class, Cassius changed his entire attitude about slaves as a young man and became an advocate of abolition. Thomas Cridland became one of the active workers in the abolitionist cause because of the influence of the Clays. He became a leader in the Underground Railway which began in Lexington, Kentucky, and actively distributed Cassius Clay's literature.

Clay's activities for the abolition movement so annoyed and angered the wealthy who formed the larger part of his associates that he was forced ("obliged" is a polite term) to leave Lexington entirely. Clay continued to publish his papers in Cincinnati, Ohio. Thomas Cridland, through his associations with Clay and because of his own efforts in moving slaves to freedom, found himself similarly ostracized, so he decided to move with his family to Cincinnati. He later moved to Dayton.[1]

Forry's great-grandfather kept company with some of the most famous names in abolition and women's suffrage. William Lloyd Garrison, Harriet Beecher Stowe, Susan B. Anthony, Elizabeth Cady Stanton and Wendell Phillips were some of the people he knew. Here again we see someone in Forry's family having close associations with famous figures. The above-named persons were most certainly major celebrities in the mid-to-late 1800s, both in America as well as Europe. Stanton and others were, in their time, superstars in the human-rights movements.

Cridland made the acquaintance of the most revered and at the same time most hated celebrity of America in the mid–1800s: Abraham Lincoln. In 1859 Abraham Lincoln came to Dayton and made a speech at the courthouse which was across the street from Cridland's Photograph Gallery. Cridland sought an introduction to Lincoln, which was given by Samuel Craighead, a prominent lawyer in Dayton at the time. Upon Cridland's invitation, Lincoln accompanied him to his photograph gallery. Here, several photographs were made. (Forry kept on display in his homes a very old chair which Thomas used in his portrait studio and which was alleged to be the chair upon which Lincoln sat for his photograph. Forrest J Ackerman was seated in this very chair for interviews in a number of documentaries.) All of the negatives of the Lincoln portrait were destroyed sometime around 1864 by a fire caused by the rays of a solar camera, and the few pictures finally disappeared through the years. A close friend of Forry, Kevin J. Burns, now owns a photograph of the portrait maker.

Cridland retired from the photography business about 1890. He died in 1892, in Los Angeles, where he had moved his family years before to continue his painting. He left a daughter, Belle Cridland, born in September 1862, a son, Edwin Cridland, and another son, Harry Cridland, who died in Pittsburgh in 1924. Forry must have had some great aunts and uncles with children even if his immediate family did not produce any offspring of their own. Somewhere in Pittsburgh may be relatives of Forrest J.

Belle married George Wyman in 1882. She was nicknamed Zululu by the family because on her wedding day she was asked by the minister for her middle name. Real-

1. Forry's Background, Family and Early Years

Thomas Cridland would have his customers sit in this chair for their portraits. Customers included Abraham Lincoln (Michael Ramsey).

izing that she did not have one, Belle made one up at the last minute. In 1892 young George met a man at his architectural designing firm by the name of Lewis Bradbury, a real estate and mining entrepreneur, who felt he had the talent to be the architect for a new building he wanted. Its construction cost would be $100,000, a monumental sum for 1892. George was not long out of college, having apprenticed for a time under his uncle Luthor Peters back in Dayton. Possessing little hands-on experience, he was very afraid that if he took this big project he would fail and the company would go bankrupt. George was thinking of using a futuristic building design which was described in the early science fiction novel *Looking Backward from 2000–1887*. In Chapter 10, the year 2000 had the fellow from 1887 going inside a retail store.

> It was the first interior of a twentieth-century public building that I had ever beheld, and the spectacle naturally impressed me deeply. I was in a vast hall full of light, received not alone from the windows on all sides, but from the dome, the point of which was a hundred feet above. Beneath it, in the centre of the hall, a magnificent fountain played, cooling the atmosphere to a delicious freshness with its spray. The walls and ceiling were frescoed in mellow tints, calculated to soften without absorbing the light which flooded the interior. Around the fountain was a space occupied with chairs and sofas, on which many persons were seated conversing.[2]

George was going to have to make a decision soon as to whether he would accept this challenge. The family was of the Protestant faith and was interested in spiritualism. On the night of February 6, 1892, Belle and Forry's grandfather George, when still young, held a séance at their home. They asked a lady over who began a process that those in the know call "automatic writing." In this practice a spirit is alleged to take the medium's hand and write with it. In this case, a planchette was used which had an opening through which a pencil was placed. Forry displayed in a frame in his home the scrawl on a slip of paper that the Wymans cherished ever afterward. It read, "Mark Wyman Take the Bradbury Building and you will be successful." The Wymans recognized the name Mark as that of George's deceased brother who had died at the age of eight. They were puzzled over the last word which looked like gibberish. "You have been looking at it upside down," a friend advised them. When they turned it right-side up, they saw the word "successful."

George did take the assignment and became renowned the world over as the architect of the Bradbury Building at 304 South Broadway in downtown Los Angeles, which features an unusual airy courtyard that has been seen in such films as *Blade Runner*, *Double Indemnity* and *The Indestructible Man*. The progressive looking Bradbury Building is described by architects as a unique combination of Victorian and early 20th century concepts. It features a cast-iron interior breezeway and atrium with a sandstone and masonry exterior. Later designs done by George Wyman were more traditional, such as the National Soldiers' Home at Sawtell, which unfortunately has been demolished.

All of the Wymans' children were girls. They were Carroll Cridland Wyman (Carrie, born in 1883) and Louise (known as "Beezee," born in 1885). After a brief courtship

1. Forry's Background, Family and Early Years

Carrie married William Schilling Ackerman in 1914. William was originally from Brooklyn, New York. Born in 1892, his mother's maiden name was Conkling.[3]

Rebecca D. Conkling, born in January of 1857, was kin to the famous Roscoe Conkling family, the great politician of the Republican Party who initiated many Reconstruction policies. She married into the Ackerman family when living in Bath, New York. The trip west to Los Angeles occurred sometime between 1900 and 1910.

Rebecca was listed in the census records for 1910 in Los Angeles, where she was the head of the household and William, then 17, was working as a clerk for an oil company. He moved up the company ladder quite rapidly. (No information was available to the author regarding why the father was not present.) It was not an easy life for William, lacking a father in the home for part of his young life, and he had to work hard from his early youth.

In 1914, William was a packing agent for the Wholesale Oil Company when he married a pretty blonde named Carroll Cridland Wyman. The couple first lived at 1115 E. 18th Street in Los Angeles, and after 1915 moved to 5327 Virginia Avenue.[4] Enter

This home at 5327 Virginia Avenue in Los Angeles, still standing in 2009, was Forrest J Ackerman's first base of operations when he discovered Hugo Gernsback's *Amazing Stories*, and when he discovered *One Glorious Day* and Lon Chaney (David Hawk).

Forry

Forrest Clark Ackerman.* Born on November 24, 1916, in Los Angeles, he was the elder of two boys, his brother, Alden Lorraine, to be born eight years later. Nicknamed "Forry," he resembled his father most closely but had his mother's blue eyes. Forry was a towheaded baby who, judging from the early photographs, had a bemused expression. When Forry was a baby, the United States was embroiled in World War I. The war was short in duration for American servicemen, and by the time Forry was two years of age, the Armistice was in effect, having been signed on November 11, 1918.

As a grown man, Forry kept a memento of something he did as a boy that was naughty. When just seven he chewed on the corner of the family piano because he hated his daily piano practice. He kept that piano leg even after circumstances compelled him to get rid of a good many other possessions. As a child, Forry referred to tapioca pudding as having "bumps" in it. Even then he had an active vocabulary.

Forry spoke and wrote little of his father's parents, it appeared that he knew little about them. Forry enjoyed being spoiled by grandparents George and Belle. Little Forry went to plenty of movies with his beloved "Zululu" and her husband. His grandfather built a little tunnel for him in his backyard complete with a camouflaged trapdoor. The two of them would share as much ice cream as they could hold.

Forry felt that the Wymans were two great lights in his life. His grandmother would read, often several times, entire issues of *Ghost Stories Magazine* to him. This magazine from Constructive Publications, which debuted in July 1926, has been out of publication since 1931. It was probably the Wymans' interest in spiritualism and Eastern philosophies that led them to read these issues cover to cover.

In those days the radio was new, television was still in the process of being invented, the telegraph was still in wide use and the printed word, the telephone, radio, the telegraph and the motion picture were the primary means (other than word of mouth) that information was spread. Forry's life straddled the beginning of the Information Age and the close of the Industrial Age. Science fiction was not an important part of his life then, but it soon would become so. Forry would become fascinated by imaginative fiction.

Why has science fiction become such an important part of mass culture in this world today? When did all of this start? Forry liked to call himself "The Sci-fi Guy." Forry said that he coined this term in the 1950s. Did he start science fiction, as some fans of science fiction have asked the author?

Forrest J Ackerman is known for having coined the term "sci-fi," and may well have done so. Those persons who ask if he created science fiction are confusing the term with the entire genre. Science fiction was not originated by his generation. It really had its start almost 100 years previously, in 1818 with Mary Wollstonecraft Shelley's *Franken-*

---

*The middle name "Clark" is an error even though cited by FJA as correct, according to an oft-published photograph of him at age 3 that identifies him as "Forrest Clark Ackerman." Author, artist, filmmaker and Forry friend Paul Davids became in 2009 the owner of Forrest J Ackerman's actual birth certificate, tucked away in one of Forry's personal notebooks: the name recorded on it is "Forest James Ackerman" (one r). His family began to spell it "Forrest" after a time but there was apparently no legal name change. See Al Astrella and James Greene, A Forbidden Look Inside the House of Ackerman: A Photographic Tour of the Legendary Ackermansion (Baltimore: Midnight Marquee Press, 2010).

1. Forry's Background, Family and Early Years

stein. *Frankenstein*, often considered Gothic horror, is actually a combination of these two literary forms, while being a seminal form of both. The "monster" or "creature" is not brought to life through magic or alchemy but through the use of chemicals.

The genre of science fiction was a very minor one until the mid–1800s, a time approaching the height of the Industrial Age, when inventions to improve medicine, industry, mining, textile production, agriculture and transportation were being developed and patented at an astounding rate. With less time spent in the fields tending crops there was more time to read. Novelists began to write more material to satisfy this growing desire. Jules Verne in his *Journey to the Center of the Earth* and *From the Earth to the Moon* as well as *20,000 Leagues Under the Sea* extensively used scientific concepts in his work, as did Edgar Allan Poe (the inventor of the short science fiction story, the horror short story, and the detective novel), and Mark Twain and his fingerprint-studying lawyer, Puddinhead Wilson. The novel *Looking Backward from 2000 to 1887* by Edward Bellamy, whose description of a building inspired George Wyman, was a tale of an upper-class man who goes into a trance in 1887 and wakes up in the year 2000. Bellamy wrote the novel in 1888. In the future socialist society of 2000, Americans use something modern readers would instantly recognize as a debit card. Bellamy made some interesting predictions, but did not have everything right, however; people in his utopia retire with full benefits at age 45!

The Industrial Age owed its very existence to applied science. Such things as ground and polished lenses, tempered steel medical instruments, hot-air balloons, improved horseshoes, diamond cutters, locomotives, and color book printing depended initially on some scientist somewhere putting knowledge to everyday use. A very popular form of entertainment among intelligent persons in the 1800s and the early 1900s was attending scientific lectures. Halls would be packed by ladies and gentlemen eager to learn about butterflies, seashells and geology. Science was understood to be the sustaining force for the age of the aeroplane, the ocean liner, the vaccination, and the smokestack.

Probably due to its generally technical nature, and the debut in the late teens of *Science and Invention*, which ran frequent science fiction scenarios, science fiction began to be known as a literature favored by young men and teenaged boys. A number of girls and women read it and even wrote it, although using masculine pen names. Children's literature occasionally contained science fiction themes. Frances Trego Montgomery wrote *The Wonderful Electric Elephant* and its sequel, *On a Lark to the Planets*, in 1904.

In 1917 the first American book series for boys with science fictional concepts, the Tom Swift series, debuted. The newspaper format of the teens' "boy's papers" such as *The Boy's Own Paper*, *Boy's Ace Library* and *The Wide Awake Library*, with tales of adventures aboard futuristic dirigibles and submarines, gave way later to the magazine format. In the early 1920s there were probably 100 pulp magazines, each with its own specialty. The publications provided hours of escapist entertainment to hard-working men, women and children with their western, detective, and fantasy stories. Most specialized in a particular genre. *Ghost Stories Magazine*, the one Forry's grandmother read to him, specialized in paranormal fiction — called "supernatural" fiction in those days.

Weird Tales, the Unique Magazine, edited by Dorothy McIlwraith, was a horror-fantasy magazine. *Spicy Mystery Stories* was of special interest to men, with its bombshell-in-distress format. *All-Story Weekly* had no particular specialty. Romance, western, detective and swashbuckling adventure were given equal space in its format. It was in *All-Story Weekly* that two of the most enduring fictional characters created in the past 300 years made their debut in the teens: Zorro and Tarzan.

Science fiction concepts readers might find familiar today had their beginnings in the cinema of the late teens and early 1920s. Science fiction in the cinema was becoming very popular, both in the United States and in Europe. Their plots would be very familiar to 21st century film and television audiences as they include lost worlds filled with prehistoric beasts, time travel, robots, alien visitation to Earth, chemical alteration of the human body, death rays, anti-aging serums and treatments, faster-than-sound travel in space, and accelerated growth of plant life.

Dr. Frankenstein's creation was the subject of a short Edison film as early as 1910. A ray that stops human movement is fiddled with by an eccentric scientist in the French short film by René Clair, *The Crazy Ray*. Aliens from Mars with large craniums and huge ears were the highlight of *M.A.R.S.* (1923). That same year an ecological disaster was precipitated when there was *Gambling with the Gulf Stream*. Unfortunately a majority of the science fiction that Forry and his contemporaries were seeing in the theaters in the early 1920s is undeservedly obscure now, or lost. One of these was the German film *Algol*, in which a charismatic man from another planet comes to Earth and becomes a dictator. Interestingly, there are more horror films than science fiction surviving today from that time period.

The home where Forry lived when he began to love going to the movies with his grandparents and parents was at 5327 Virginia Avenue (near Vermont Avenue), and is still in existence at the time of this writing. (The little one-story wood-frame home is being cared for by its current owners and has a large garden and two lemon trees in its front yard. All this vegetation partly obscures the porch and the front has a small vegetable garden and bower. Virginia Avenue is partly bisected by the Freeway system and some of the street is subjected to traffic noise and proximity of the large sound wall, but this tree lined section of the street is a little oasis.)

Five-year-old Forry was astounded by a fantasy film his grandparents took him to see, the 1922 Famous Players–Lasky production *One Glorious Day* starring Will Rogers as Ezra Botts. Ezra is a timid fellow who is always being picked on by the town bully, played by Alan Hale. The bully has designs on the same pretty girl Ezra likes (Lila Lee). Meanwhile, Ezra is spied upon by a mischievous little human spirit named Eck (John Fox) who is currently between lives. Eck, a strange-looking sprite, is so impatient to be in the land of the living that he wants to bypass the usual way and possess someone currently walking and talking. Since Ezra is a student of spiritualism and often goes into a trance-like state, he is ready prey for Eck, who slips into his body and makes Ezra appear more bold and athletic than he naturally is. Ezra wins the girl, defeats the bully and closes down the corrupt political organization that is running the whole town.

1. Forry's Background, Family and Early Years

Eck decides to enter the world in the conventional way, leaves Ezra, and is born in the body of a new baby. (This film is believed to have survived only in very fragmentary form in an archive in Europe, and is unavailable for screening.)

Forry really enjoyed such science fiction films as *The Young Diana*, starring Marion Davies, a woman who undergoes reverse aging. It is a lost film now. *Aelita, Queen of Mars*, was a 1924 fantasy set partly in the new U.S.S.R. and partly on Mars. A young Soviet engineer by the name of Loss is trying to create (in his spare time and with a borrowed hangar) a rocket that will take him and his assistant to Mars. Loss has marital difficulties and shoots his wife for a suspected affair. The story takes a strange twist when he and his technical staff blast off for Mars to escape the police and meet the haughty Queen of Mars (Yulia Solntseva) who falls in love with Loss. He tells her that he will help her win back the political power that the Guardian of Energy on Mars has taken from her. The whole trip to Mars, it is revealed, is actually Loss's daydream. Forry felt the film was a good one, filled with amazing images of an exotic society. But he had not yet seen *Metropolis*.

Forry became an instant fan of Lon Chaney when he saw *The Hunchback of Notre Dame* (Universal, 1923). Chaney starred as the bellringer Quasimodo, misunderstood by everyone except the kind gypsy, Esmeralda (Patsy Ruth Miller), and his caregiver, the monk Dom Claude (Nigel de Brullier). Then there was *A Blind Bargain* (MGM, 1922), now lost, which Forry saw the following year when it was re-released. The plot concerns a scientist who is carrying out glandular experiments with apes to cure various diseases and strikes a bargain with Claudius, a desperate young writer whose mother is very ill. Only an expensive operation will save her, something far beyond his ability to pay given his meager earnings. The scientist has been injecting a gorilla with a hormone that has turned it into a bestial man (Chaney).

Forry was entranced by Chaney in all his roles, from *The Blackbird* (MGM, 1926), the drama of a criminal who poses as his own nonexistent humanitarian brother to cover his crimes to the Gothic romanticism and splendor of *The Phantom of the Opera* (Universal, 1925). Forry often remarked later in life that he regretted that he never met Lon Chaney, Sr., although he certainly met most of the other stars of classic films, including Lon's son, Creighton Chaney, whose screen name was Lon Chaney, Jr.

Forry was able to see quite a number of fantasy and science fiction films during the 1920s. Jules Verne's *The Mysterious Island* was made as a Technicolor spectacle in 1929 and starred Lionel Barrymore as Count Dakkar (Captain Nemo's real name). His submarine is commandeered by a baron who wants to use it for war. But there are actually two submarines, and Dakkar and his crew plunge into the depths to assist the other submarine. In so doing they encounter weird fish like intelligent beings of the ocean floor.

High Treason was a Gaumont (British) production of 1929 which Forry enjoyed. A science fiction look at what would come to pass in 1950, it predicted tension between several Western European borders, a peace movement, and a sorely tested relationship between a pilot (Jameson Deane) and the daughter of the foremost leader of the peace movement (Benita Hume). Its terrorist plots masterminded by a corporation secretly plotting to instigate war so that it might thereby profit, and passive resistance protests certainly do seem as though they are torn from headlines of the early 21st century. *High Treason* faded into obscurity soon after the talkie era began, but it does, fortunately, still exist.

All of these films made an indelible impression on Forry.

Forry said that as a child he grew impatient with the vaudeville acts that he had to sit through in between film screenings. Through the perspective of nostalgia, however, he felt a little more fondness for them because he got to see not only Bing Crosby and his brother perform when they were just starting out, but he also saw Al Jolson and many other famous and not-so-famous performers. Jolson was the very popular Broadway singer turned motion picture phenomenon who made many songs famous, including "Blue Skies," "Let Me Sing and I'm Happy," "Waiting for the *Robert E. Lee*" and "April Showers." Jolson became a big film star in 1927 with the Warner Bros. Vitaphone sensation, *The Jazz Singer*. He was the young Forry's favorite singer and would prove to be his top entertainer throughout the years. When Forry was a young man he saw Jolson emerging from a theater after a performance and Jolson put his arm around him and called him "Sonny Boy"![5]

Forry would, in later life, travel to an Al Jolson festival in Florida with his friend Lee Harris, another Jolson aficionado.

At the Grauman's Egyptian Theatre in 1925 Forry thrilled to *The Lost World* and its stop-motion dinosaurs and flying reptiles. Outside the entrance to the magnificent theater was a stand with one of the dinosaurs used in the film. It even had little rubber bellows which were fitted with a small rubber fitting that the theatergoer could push; thus the model would breathe. Forry wanted one just like that but since there were none available for sale, he had to settle for just looking at this one marvelous little model. He wanted to swipe it but did not succumb to temptation.

His film going was not limited to horror and science fiction, called "scientifiction" in those days. The Wymans took him to a wide variety of films they thought were suitable for a boy, including north woods dramas starring Strongheart, an early canine star.

Forry's favorite film, and the most

Al Jolson was Forry's favorite entertainer.

1. Forry's Background, Family and Early Years

influential in his life, was the 1926 *Metropolis*, a German science fiction extravaganza from Ufa Film. *Metropolis* is the tale of a city of the future and the strange socially stratified society it contains. Forry saw the picture in 1927 in Los Angeles when it was released theatrically in the United States.

According to the film's plot, there are many megalopolises in the future. For example, there is Tarnopolis, in what we may recognize as Russia or the steppes of Asia. Metropolis is somewhere in the Western European world, possibly in Germany, although this is not disclosed in the film. Cities are literally stratified, and reach into the sky. The Heart Machine and the Brain Machine are the main components of the huge plant that cools, lights and heats the great city. The lower levels are where the plant continually operates, and this is where the workers — uneducated peasants — toil almost every day of their lives and have no dreams of a future other than unending slave labor until their dying day. The higher levels of the city are reserved for the engineering and administrative functions of Metropolis, and for the pleasure centers, such as Yoshiwara, a nightclub district.

Alfred Abel plays Joh Fredersen, the Master of Metropolis, and a kind of megalomaniac city manager. His handsome and athletic young son, Freder (Gustav Fröhlich), meets the lovely Maria (Brigitte Helm) who has brought some children clothed in rags up to see him in his pleasure palace. "Look, these are your brothers," she manages to say to him before she is told by the guards to leave. Entranced by Maria's beauty and purity, Freder feels he must see her again. But he has his own father and his father's uneasy alliance with the evil scientist Rotwang (Rudolf Klein-Rogge) to deal with. His father has fired Josaphat, his general administrative secretary, for not keeping him informed of the secret meetings the workers have been having, or of telling him of an explosion in the Brain Machine. Freder senses that Josaphat is utterly devastated and follows him to prevent him from taking his own life. He invites Josaphat to work for him instead.

Rotwang wants revenge on the entire Fredersen family. Hel, his former wife, had become Fredersen's lover and died after giving birth to Freder. Rotwang has created a shining metal robot in the image of his deceased Hel and Fredersen wants him to use it to start a worker's revolt so he can crush it. This works out well for Rotwang, for he also has his own secret agenda: to destroy the Fredersens.

Freder visits the factory level again and sees an exhausted worker operating a huge dial that controls the temperature of a device. He asks him to let him take over for him that day and wears his clothes. The youth finds a note in his pocket about an evening meeting with Maria, and a map of the catacombs. That afternoon, the workers attend their secret meeting. Freder finds that the person who holds secret meetings with the hideously oppressed workers down in the catacombs is none other than Maria. She counsels them on spiritual matters, not revolution. Using parables, she teaches them that revolt is not the answer. One day a mediator will come, someone who will communicate the needs of the workers to the elite, and vice versa. Freder realizes he is that mediator. He lingers afterward to speak to her and tells her who he is and that he will be the mediator Maria has been waiting for. They kiss and part and she returns alone to her quarters deep in the catacombs. Someone has been following her — Rotwang! He abducts her and uses his super-science to extract her form, thoughts and memories and implants them into the robot. Maria survives, unharmed, but is still his prisoner.

The false Maria goes to Joh Fredersen's splendid office. Freder happens to visit his father and sees "Maria" there, in a green dress, kissing him. She looks at Freder, and her look is as evil and as cold as any look can be. Freder faints from the shock, and the next thing he knows, he is in bed, with a physician in attendance. The false Maria then goes to Yoshiwara, the pleasure district of Metropolis, performs an erotic dance on a pedestal, and initiates fist fights among the elite and anarchy and revolt among the oppressed poor. Freder's fevered mind makes a comparison of Maria to the Harlot of Babylon.

The whole situation explodes dramatically at the climax as a tremendous flood, started by the workers' sabotage, threatens to kill their own children. (This visually stunning 1926 release is now restored digitally with its original Berlin premiere's symphonic score; the music was composed by Gottfried Huppertz. The score was rerecorded for the 2002 DVD release which Forry also viewed and owned on DVD. Berndt Heller conducted the Rundfunk-Sinfonieorchester Saarbrücken. For the first time since its Berlin release, filmgoers heard the original score. *Metropolis* was something Forry would see more than 60 times over the course of the decades, and collect everything he could find. Fortunately, because of dedicated fans, Forry was able to see the most recent [as of Fall 2008] restored version, a version missing about ten minutes of footage.)

Metropolis was a huge influence in Forry's life. He was to befriend its director, Fritz Lang, and attended his private interment in 1976. Forry's favorite *Metropolis* items in his collection were reproduction sculptures from the film, such as plaster reproductions of the busts of "Greed," "Lust," "Sloth" and others from the film, a small model of the gong used by Maria to summon the children of the workers and the "robotrix" full-scale models made by artists including Bill Malone, who is also a film producer (the 1999 *The House on Haunted Hill*). Forry also owned Fritz Lang's personal monocle. Forry did not own any original materials from the film, although he met a number of members of the cast who had played the workers' children and met Brigitte Helm. I would marvel at just how many times Forry would report that he had seen this film and how many trips he would take to film festivals to see "the best version so far."

Another fantasy film directed by Fritz Lang was the 1923 *Siegfried*, a Decla/Bioskop UFA release. This filmed tale of the German folk hero who was a real person whose life became intertwined with fantasy still exists. *Woman in the Moon* was Lang's last science fiction release from 1929.

The 1920s was a wonderful, exciting time for a film buff to live in Los Angeles in the days when access to movie studios was so much easier to obtain than now. Persons with aspirations and experience in the competitive areas of acting or set design or writing scenarios found their job search very hard, and many people came to Hollywood dreaming dreams that never came to be. However, if one had any practical skills in carpentry,

1. Forry's Background, Family and Early Years

cinematography, animal wrangling or costume design, success was almost assured. The movie fan magazines were sold at newsstands all over the world, their pages hungry for talented go-getters who were able to write an interview or showcase the stars' spacious abodes. These magazines were the primary way the fans could learn about their idols. The studios, under the tacit control of Will H. Hays, made sure that the magazines eschewed controversy and strove to paint the industry folk in the most polite and respectful light. Movie stars and producers were beautiful people, elegant, and with wonderful taste. What they wore, the sports they played, their favorite recipes, and the places they visited were of huge interest to the fans who read these magazines.

In those days one could walk down the streets and see movie industry giants and, if respectful, one might get a free autograph. The era of overzealous fans who want to mob movie stars and tear at their clothing, and the era of *paparazzi* who make careers of photographing a star in an embarrassing moment, had not yet begun. A contemporary of Forrest J, an unrelated fellow named Joe Ackerman, was born the same year as he and moved to Los Angeles from the Midwest during this golden age of Hollywood. He made certain he secured as many autographs from the stars as possible and literally hundreds are on display in the Hollywood Museum on Hollywood Boulevard near its intersection with Highland Avenue. It is said that he never paid a cent to get an autograph. What a change from this modern day, when motion picture actors sometimes charge as much as $40 for an autograph at a movie convention.

Forry's brother Alden came along in 1924. Aldy also took an interest in these subjects, although he was more inclined to like sports, such as softball. Alden Lorraine was taller than Forry and more sturdily built.

The city of Los Angeles was populous (100,000 in 1922)[6] but still had orange and lemon groves in abundance. Something called the Dominguez Slough flowed down the main portion of the city to drain it. We see this ditch in the movie *Intolerance* where Constance Talmadge as "The Mountain Girl" drives her borrowed chariot past it. The Dominguez Slough is gone, as are the orange groves. But many things still remain. Many of the old street lights are exactly as they were in 1922 and much of the old architecture Forry saw as a little boy is there.

Forry liked the postman, whom he called the "Post Toastie Man," after the cereal of the time, Post Toasties, and the kindly fellow let him accompany him on his route. Clearly, Forry's fondness for mail and correspondence was becoming evident at an early age.

There were very few comic books in the 1920s. Comics were something one read in the daily and weekly newspaper. Children Forry's age did not see *Batman* or *The Silver Surfer* emblazoning magazine covers. But there were other types of fantastic entertainment.

Hugo Gernsback published several magazines on popular science which were available on newsstands. Originally from Luxembourg City, Luxembourg, Gernsback had been a pioneer of modern radio, founding radio station WRNY in 1925. He helped develop television and worked in early broadcasting experiments. What Gernsback was most famous for in life were his publishing ventures. *The Electrical Experimenter*, begun in 1913, was renamed *Science and Invention* in 1920. The magazine often carried fanciful "what if" stories. His own 1911 novel, *Ralph 124C41+*, was a pun on the words "Ralph one to foresee for one plus." First serialized in *Modern Electrics*, this novel concerned a man who lives in the far future, surrounded by technological marvels. Some of these were quite prophetic. Newspapers were on a small card about the size of a postage stamp that one inserted into a projector; it was updated every 30 minutes. (It sounds somewhat like an Internet newspaper accessed with a CD-ROM or a memory stick, doesn't it?) Another interesting future invention was a small aircraft, the aeroflyer, which can reach speeds of 600 miles per hour. We now have commercial jet liners which easily attain that speed. Permagatol, a substance that preserves organic material indefinitely, was also mentioned. Thankfully, the weather control stations predicted have failed to come into existence ... so far.

Gernsback started out printing "scientifiction" stories and later changed this term on the mastheads to "science fiction." Gernsback encouraged readers to correspond with him through the letter pages in the front of the magazine. This way, he could see feedback on what the readers wanted. Gernsback's *Amazing Stories* was devoted entirely to fiction about science and its impacts on society.

One special day in the fall of 1926 always stood out in Forry's memory, and he recalled it in a 1953 interview for *Fantastic Worlds*. His parents had just taken him to the city zoo and his brain was awash with images of unusual-looking animals such as ostriches and elephants. They stopped off to pick up items at a local pharmacy at the corner of Western Avenue and Santa Monica Boulevard. Forry saw something on the newsstand that caught his eye. It was a magazine cover showing a lobster-like intelligent creature with plant stalk-like forelimbs standing on three legs, greeting a human polar explorer who had been the first of his fellow explorers to approach it from the ship that had set down on the creature's alien looking land beyond the Antarctic Circle icecap. It was the cover for the October 1926 *Amazing Stories*. Hugo Gernsback was the publisher and the cover artist was Frank R. Paul. The story it heralded was A. Hyatt Verrill's "Beyond the Pole." "What in the world is that thing?" Forry wondered.[7] No, he did not recall in a 1952 interview in which he recounted in print for the first time his first encounter with *Amazing* anything about the magazine jumping off the newsstand and saying "take me home, little boy, you will love me!" Yes, the author has shattered a bit of Forry mythology.

Little Forry didn't have a quarter for the magazine so he enlisted the aid of his grandparents. It turned out to be the one object in his collection that he prized most highly, even to the age of 92! Should there be a tornado or flood and he had to get out of the house quickly, this one old back issue, he said, would be the one he would grab. Frank R. Paul would be his favorite artist and Hugo Gernsback ... well, Hugo Gernsback was a real innovator. With the publication of this magazine, he became the publisher of the first science fiction magazine aimed at adults.

Forry's first science fiction reading experience was that story by A. Hyatt Verrill.

1. Forry's Background, Family and Early Years

He didn't really understand some of the sophisticated fiction he read in these magazines and he did not know terms such as "stellar," but as he put it, he wasn't afraid of the dictionary, and he managed to learn definitions of many words. He knew too that he had to have more and more. He found that no amount of pleading or threatening to hold his breath until he turned blue would induce his parents and grandparents to buy him every magazine that caught his interest. So he came up with a plan: "If I have a letter published in the letter columns of each of the magazines they will surely purchase those issues!" So he went to work. There were letters published in *Amazing Stories*, *Thrilling Wonder Stories* and *Air Wonder Stories*, among others.[8]

"A New Method of Evaluation" was the heading the editor gave this 1929 letter Forry wrote to *Science Wonder Stories*:

> This is my idea of Science Wonder Stories:
> Take every word that means excellent out of the largest dictionary in the world, multiply those words by the number of seconds in two thousand centuries, and add to that amount the number of stars in the heavens and the sum will give you a very slight idea of what I think of your magazine.
>
> Forrest Ackerman, San Francisco, California[9]

2
"I Couldn't Sleep with Marlene Dietrich!"

After 1928 Forry and his mom, dad and brother, Alden, had moved to 530 Staples Avenue in San Francisco, due to his father's transfer to another office of the oil company. William was now a statistician for what was then called Pacific Western Oil Corporation (later Getty Oil). Soon he would be promoted to assistant to the vice president.

Lon Chaney died in 1930 from cancer and the news was a shock to Forry. Without a doubt Chaney was the master of silent cinema, being its highest paid performer, and was on his way to mastering sound with *The Unholy Three* (MGM, 1930). Now he was gone.

Forry was taken by his dad to see Bela Lugosi performing the stage version of *Dracula*. Forry was as mesmerized as the female leads portraying Lucy Westenra and Mina Seward were supposed to be. He received an autograph from Lugosi, signed simply "Count Dracula."

The motion picture palaces, now equipped for sound, vibrated with the dialogue for *Frankenstein*, which was a sensation when it premiered during Christmas of 1931. Forry saw this Gothic masterpiece and became quite interested in the work of Boris Karloff, Colin Clive and Dwight Frye. He likewise was entranced by *The Invisible Man*, ably portrayed by Claude Rains, and directed by the director of *Frankenstein*, James Whale. *King Kong* rampaged through the streets of New York City in spring 1933 and Forry felt the thump of the Skull Island villager's drums in his heart. He saw some films that were less than classics too, such as *Maniac*, directed by Dwain Esper.

By now he was collecting every newspaper story and every advertisement he could find concerning his favorite films, and placing them in scrapbooks. Forry's collection of magazines and film stills had begun to grow quite a lot.

"Son, do you realize how many of these magazines you have?" his mother asked him. "I just counted them. Why, you have twenty-seven! By the time you're a grown man you might have *a hundred*!" She asked him to sell some of them to make some money. He reluctantly parted with them and sold them to a boy in his school, but his mother noticed that the pangs of deprivation were becoming too much for the young scientifiction fan. Carroll Ackerman telephoned the boy and asked if he would be willing to sell them back to Forry, and he consented.

2. "I Couldn't Sleep with Marlene Dietrich!"

On a day when he was home from school with a virus, Forry received a letter in the mail from a youngster named Linus Hoganmiller who was thousands of miles away in a small town in Missouri. Linus had seen Forry's name and address in one of the magazines and wanted to correspond with him. This excited Forry very much. He wrote a long letter to the youth and when he mailed it he thought of something else he forgot to say and then wrote a second letter. About six letters resulted in one week and when Linus wrote back this started a new hobby for Forry. In 1930 Forry wrote to Linus, "I think we should start a Boy's Sciencefiction Club for people ages 12 to 18. I will be President and you can be Vice President." Linus liked the idea and before they knew it, other boys were joining. Forry ran a small lending library of magazines contributed by some of the boys. Members traded snapshots of themselves as well as three consecutive issues of one of the magazines that had a serial in it, or they might send a hardcover book. "Pretty soon," said Forry, "it got to where I was staggering five or six blocks to the mailbox, just to send off the books or the magazines."

The next step in the development of the Boy's Sciencefiction Club was a small magazine of newsworthy items. Two fellows in New York, Mort Weisinger and Julius Schwartz, wrote to Forry with the idea that instead of typing up these newsletters individually, they could help him out with a wonderful device they owned. It was a mimeograph, and this fortuitous machine could be put to use for the Club. *The Time Traveler* was thus born. It came out in the early 1930s at around the same time other fans elsewhere were putting out their own mimeographed magazines. These were the first "fanzines." A fanzine is a magazine that is published either regularly or irregularly, and is written by amateurs and sold or traded to other amateurs. One does not have to have a journalism degree to edit and publish such a magazine.

A large photograph of Walter Daugherty working with the fabled mimeograph is on display in the Paul Freehafer room of the clubhouse of the Los Angeles Fantasy Society in North Hollywood.

Walt Daugherty became Forry's friend at about this time. They were the same age, having been born just a few days apart. Walt, a tall dark-haired boy, was the son of silent cowboy actor "Two Gun" Monty Williams and his wife, Lilly Mae Williams. His last name was changed to Daugherty when Monty died and Lilly married a man named Jessie Daugherty. At various times in his career, Walt worked as a photography instructor, an aircraft company production control manager, and a movie extra. His hobbies would grow to include Egyptology and science fiction.

Forry was writing to 116 fans around the world, including one in Soviet Russia. It was during this time that Francis Flagg (George Henry Weiss), a science fiction author, became one of Forry's correspondents. Forry was allowed to collaborate with him on a short story entitled "Earth's Lucky Day," and it was published in the very last issue of *Wonder Stories* in April 1936.[1]

At 19 years old, Forry had his first professional publication — in one of his favorite periodicals, yet! Forry felt like he was walking on air. That wasn't all. He had aspirations of becoming a science fiction author.

Today, young people who are interested in science fiction have web site forums, blogs and chat rooms where they can discuss their love for the genre. They also have the printed version of the fanzine, although such is becoming increasingly rare.

In the 1930s Forry founded something called *Voice of the Imagi-Nation*. It consisted entirely of letters to him from fellow fans, and his responses to them. They managed to communicate across the globe. Forry's *Voice of the Imagi-Nation* lasted for 40 issues total. One of the young people he communicated with was Jerry (Jerome) Siegel, who was publishing his own fanzine titled *Science Fiction*. Jerry Siegel based a character in his story "Reign of the Superman" on Forrest J Ackerman.

Chemistry professor Smalley has perfected a chemical that he thinks will give an ordinary human superhuman powers. He lures Bill Dunn, an impoverished man in the local bread line, to his laboratory with promises of food and clothing. Smalley administers the chemical which makes Dunn able to read minds, have super-vision, intercept radio communications emanating from the planet Mars, foretell the future with accuracy and even implant ideas in the minds of others. Seduced by his new abilities, Dunn runs amok, using his brain power to make a wealthy man by the name of Kornau write him a check for $40,000. Smalley learns of Kornau's police report and writes a letter to the city newspaper editor telling him that he loosed this horror on the world. The professor takes the chemical himself to become a superman and destroy Dunn. Unfortunately, Dunn destroys him.

Reporter Forrest Ackerman is assigned the curious task of visiting Professor Smalley's home and laboratory to get the scoop. "Sounds screwy," Forrest comments to his boss as he leaves his office. Blood-splattered papers and overturned furniture are all that he sees at the Smalley home. Reporter Ackerman then feels an irresistible urge to go to another building in a different part of town. There he finds Dunn, who confesses to having murdered Smalley. The superman bolts the young newsman to a chair and boasts that as soon as he has disrupted a vital peace conference in the city, he is going to start a total war, then come back and kill Ackerman.

Forrest Ackerman prays to the Creator to save the world. Dunn sees himself in his mind's eye, again wearing ragged clothes and standing in the bread line. The chemical wears off and the superman's own clairvoyant vision comes true.[2]

If the name Jerry Siegel seems familiar, it should. He, along with Joseph Shuster, created the Superman comic book stories in the late 1930s for *Action Comics*.[3]

In one issue of *Voice of the Imagi-Nation* Forry created a column entitled "Fantascience Filmart" and wrote a synopsis of *High Treason*. He ranked it with the top scientifilms of the past ten years, such as *Just Imagine*, *Things to Come* and *Deluge*.

In the mid–1930s, Forrest J noticed an advertisement in *Photoplay* magazine wherein Carl Laemmle, President of Universal Pictures Corporation, wanted reader feedback on films, both released and proposed. He ended up writing about 60 of these letters to Mr. Laemmle, and asked for any unused film props or posters he may have available. Laemmle wrote a memo to his secretary with the instruction, "Give this boy anything he wants."

2. "I Couldn't Sleep with Marlene Dietrich!"

It was because of this correspondence with Carl Laemmle that he was given the 33⅓ sound discs for *Murders in the Rue Morgue* and the 1931 *Frankenstein* and an invitation to visit the set of *Bride of Frankenstein*. While there, he saw Colin Clive on crutches. It was a big thrill for young Forry to see the stars of the film and the sets dressed for the film. Little did he know how celebrated a film *Bride of Frankenstein* would one day become. Sadly, only a few years later, Colin Clive passed away and Forry paid his respects to Clive at the mortuary in 1937. Colin Clive was a young man in his thirties when he died.

David Hawk, who was a friend to Forry in his later years, sums up the young (and older) Forry in this way: "He got to where he was by being a motor mouth." And it is, by George, the truth. When Forry was ten years old he was looking up the addresses of science fiction authors in the local Los Angeles telephone directory. Fortunately for him, a good many authors did live in Los Angeles. He would then carry his copy of *Thrilling Wonder Stories* or another magazine to their home, knock on the door and when the author or a family member came to the door, he introduced himself: "I'm Forry Ackerman, and I am a reader of your stories and like them all. I wanted to meet you and get your autograph." Almost always, he would be invited in for milk and cookies and, before too much time had elapsed, he had befriended the author and his family.

Forry doted on his younger brother, and felt that he needed to be a mentor. Said his friend Al Paige, "I found in a box of letters at the Minimansion (these were just sitting out on the back porch would you believe!) a letter Forry had written to his brother Aldy when Forry was a teenager and Aldy was, I don't know, about 11 or 12, He was gently telling him how he could help him in collecting research or info or something for his book reviewing activities (I think) and correcting Alden's grammar, punctuation, etc. It was quite funny, but the thing that was most interesting was it very clearly expressed how Forry was taking a very paternalistic, 'big brother knows best' protective attitude towards Aldy. I had actually never thought about the age gap between them, in fact I think I'd assumed Alden was the older brother. But clearly Forry was very fond of his brother back then, no wonder he was so upset to lose him."[4]

William Ackerman was by this time becoming frustrated with his son Forrest. He was not sufficiently like him in his interests in baseball and other sports. While younger brother Alden was interested in sports at an early age, Forry preferred to socialize with his like-minded friends, read, write letters and go to the movies. "You'll never amount to anything!" Forry's father once told him. He never forgot that stinging remark. When Forry was attending high school a gang of rough boys decided they would make him conform. He resisted their attempts to get him to smoke, so they tied him to a tree and forced him to smoke a cigarette. He went ahead and smoked it. Fortunately, he did not take this as a sign from the Cosmos that he was supposed to smoke. It was his last cigarette.[5]

One day a 15-year-old Forry was seated on his front porch and a dimpled little two-year-old darling, recently moved into the neighborhood, made her way with difficulty up the steps of the home and told Forry, "I have something to give you."

"Oh?" he asked. "What's that, honey?"

"Tiss!" she announced, and planted one on his cheek.

Shirley Wrede was his youngest female fan then, and the first of many fans who would "tiss" him. Many years later, he met her children and called them her "tisslets."[6]

Forry met Edythe Eyde in San Francisco. He nicknamed the pretty brunette "Tigrina" and she was interested in science fiction as well. She would go on double dates with Forry's brother and his girl.

Forry loved girls but had a terror in those days of being invited to the girl's home for dinner by her parents and then being expected to eat what was served. He was particular about the food he ate back then. Forry hated vegetable salads, but as a man he loved salads. Later in life, being a world traveler and seldom cooking his own meals, Forry adapted and learned to enjoy a variety of foods. Cooking, however, was not his forte. He was content to leave the mysteries of elaborate meal preparation to others.

Though he was not going to become a scientist, Forry did understand the scientific method, by which through careful observation, documentation and repeated experimentation with reliably constant results, we can learn much about the universe. Forry thought that science and rationality were the only hope for the human species to survive our violent tendencies. He believed in the future of humankind and studied a futuristic language invented by Ludovic Lazarus Zamenhof. The first book of Esperanto was published in 1887. The language was dubbed Esperanto because it was a sort of amalgamation of the Romance languages of Italian, French, and Spanish, with some German. Forry learned Spanish, French, German and Italian before he learned this language. He took an interest in it because in one of the scientifiction stories Esperanto was described as the spoken language of a future time. Esperanto was invented in the hope that it would catch on as a universal language for wide use, although this has not happened. Scientific nomenclature for species of living things is the closest we have come to a universal means of communication thus far. These are, of course, Latin and Greek in origin and were chosen because they are not spoken languages and will not evolve.

Hugo Gernsback started the Science Fiction League in the middle thirties. A group of west coast boys and one girl started the fourth chapter. Forry met with them in an adult science fiction fan's garage. After that meeting, nothing else happened for about a year. Finally, the club began in earnest, and that was because *Thrilling Wonder Stories* was sponsoring them. A fellow named Roy Test came to the meetings with his mother, Wanda, who, due to her gender, was considered ideal to be the note taker and general secretary. Need I mention that her minutes of each meeting became known among the club as "Thrilling Wanda Stories"?

The Fantasy Fan was a very early fanzine that had a professional appearance. Charles D. Hornig, a member of the club, impressed Gernsback and so was appointed, at the age of 17, to become the editor of *Wonder Stories*.

In the 1930s, if you wanted to do so, and your grades were good, you could choose when you turned 17 to spend another year in high school. You would get no credits toward college or trade school but you could just attend for your own edification. Forry wanted to do so because he was having a good time being one of the editors of the high school newspaper. After graduation from Balboa High with academic honors, eighth in his class of 256, he went on to college. He wanted to become a journalist so he attended at the University of California at Berkeley for a year, from 1934 to 1935. Forry was impatient with the idea that he had to take courses in unrelated subjects. He was focused on journalism and he did not want to take courses in anything else, especially military training, but he could not avoid them. His first paper was something about a film he had seen. He got his paper back from the professor with the grade of "A."

Forry felt that this meant that he had already reached the highest pinnacle of achievement: his first paper, and he had an A already? He went to his father just before the end of the second semester and told him that college was a waste of his money and Forry's time. Reluctantly, William Ackerman let him go to work. Forry wanted to please his father, who was the secretary to the vice president of Associated Oil, so for a while he worked for him. "My job was to add columns of numbers and then at the end of the month, subtract the same column. And Heaven help you if you didn't come up with zero at the end of that month. I hate numbers and love words." This was definitely not his forte so he went on to other jobs.[7]

Like the notion that college cannot do you any good if you get mostly A grades in your classes, the notion that there is no God or gods is an idea Forry came up with at a young age.

His attitude toward metaphysics was shaped by the concept of God as the one that the Sunday school teachers presented; an all-knowing all-good deity who loved all of us. Forry reasoned, "If He is all-knowing and all good He should be able to prevent the suffering that we see each day. Since God does not prevent violence, war, or hate from harming living beings, either He is bad, which the Sunday school teachers tell me is not so, or He does not really exist." Forry felt that God should also stop people from using Him or books said to be written by Him as a reason to wage war or intimidate others in any way. Since these human activities continue to this very day, without divine intervention to stop them, Forry believed that this meant that there is no beneficent God or gods to watch over the world and, in fact, there were no gods at all, good or bad. No religion found any particular favor with him. Christian theology and "mysteries" about resurrection, another idea taught in Sunday schools he attended, did not make sense to him. If God is all-powerful, why does the Devil seem to get the upper hand now and then? "Why didn't God save his own son, Jesus, by sending a volcano to stop his tormentors?" is a question he asked others in a humorous manner. Nor did he believe in devils — Pazuzu, Satan or Beelzebub, or Maya, or any of the negative deities of various cultures. Forry's attitudes were also shaped by the beliefs of such influential authors as Olaf Stapledon who was a believer in God.

Forry confessed in "Confessions of a Sci-fi Addict" that in his teens he was a terror. He was very forceful when coming up to a movie actor to get an autograph.[8] He was just as forceful in communicating his opinions. He would become angry if anyone at the LASFS club house smoked cigarettes. Forry felt that science fiction magazines should remain "pure" and free of fantasy literature.

His less-than-complimentary comments on a Clark Ashton Smith tale in *Wonder Stories* began a feud of sorts between him and the renowned horror and science fantasy author H.P. Lovecraft: The following information is from L. Sprague de Camp's biography, *Lovecraft: A Biography*.

In 1932, Clark Ashton Smith, a close friend of H.P. Lovecraft and a famed writer himself, published a tale called "Dweller in Martian Depths." This graphic story tells of human explorers on Mars who find a creature which has appendages for extracting explorers' eyeballs and then consuming them. Forry wrote to Charles Hornig's *Fantasy Fan*, complaining that a weird horror-fantasy had no place in a science fiction magazine. Lovecraft replied: "As for Ackerman's ebullition, I fear he can hardly be taken seriously in matters involving the criticism of imaginative fiction. Smith's story was really splendid, except for the cheap ending which the Editor [of] *Wonder Stories* insisted. Ackerman once wrote me a letter with a very childish attack on my work — he evidently enjoys verbal pyrotechnics for their own sake and seems so callous to imaginative impressions."

The first six issues of Hornig's fan magazine were almost filled with this quarrel between Forrest Ackerman and H.P. Lovecraft. FJA's remarks evidently annoyed Lovecraft more than a little, for during the next three years he called him a "little louse," "habitual pest," "Superficial Smart-Alleck," "insubstantial oaf," "insolent young brat," and "pompous little joke." Lovecraft finally lost interest in complaining about Forry. In 1937 he said: "I'm sure he must be a bright & delightful kid underneath the surface ... mellowing into something very different from the *enfant terrible* of three years ago.... I haven't a thing in the world against him!"[9]

With all these correspondents, everyone involved grew a little tired of writing "scientifiction" all the time so they shortened it to "sf."

In the 1930s Forry wrote the world's shortest science fiction story, for which he was paid $100 by *Vertex* magazine years later. The story was *Cosmic Report Card: Earth*. It suggested that aliens were orbiting various planets around the solar system and assigning grades. Poor, underachieving Earth got an "F" for its continuing war, prejudice and injustice.

As time progressed, the Science Fiction League's West Coast chapter decided to form its own club apart from the League. The original emblem was the same as the emblem on the May and December 1934 covers of *Wonder Stories*. The first official meeting of the Los Angeles Science Fantasy Society was on March 27, 1940. It sent letters to all the fanzines such as *Fantasy Fiction Field* to inform the other fans why there was a new club and to invite them to design a new emblem for the new organization. This new emblem had to include the motto for the old club, "De Profundis Ad Astra" which is Latin for "From Profound Depths to the Stars." As it happened, the only person to respond was Roy V. Hunt of Denver's Colorado Fantasy Society, so it was he who had the winning entry. The coat of arms depicts four stars in the center, symbolic

2. "I Couldn't Sleep with Marlene Dietrich!"

Los Angeles Science Fantasy Society members posed for this rare portrait by Walter J. Daugherty. Top row: fourth from left, Forrest J Ackerman, seventh from left, T. Bruce Yerke. Center row, fourth from left, future famed physicist Roland Dishington, sixth from left, Russ Hodgkins, eighth from left, Robert A. Heinlein, ninth from left, Walter J. Daugherty, tenth from left, E.E. ("Doc") Smith, twelfth from left, Ray Bradbury. Bottom row, fourth from left, Eleanor O'Brien, seventh from left, Myrtle Douglas ("Morojo"), eighth from left, Leslyn Heinlein (Mary Ellen Daugherty [Mrs. Walter J. Daugherty]).

of LASFS's previous status as Chapter Four of the Science Fiction League. The coat of arms is divided into three parts. To the left is a section depicting a microscope, symbolizing the profoundly small or deep, and opposite it is a starship traveling through space to symbolize the stars. In the lower third of the coat of arms two demons are stirring something in a pot. This was taken from the logo of the *Weird Tales* club and represents the fantasy fiction interests of the members. The topmost section symbolizes the Science Fictioneers, a club begun by author and magazine editor Frederik Pohl.[10]

Forry recalled in 1991 in the pages of *Forrest J Ackerman, Famous Monster of Filmland #2*, when printing a photo of his younger self in front of the Los Angeles Science Fantasy Society in 1941, "I have been its director, secretary, treasurer, club organ editor and publisher, angel and janitor, and have attended over 1500 meetings. I was present, of course, at the 50th Anniversary Fanquet of the organization I helped found but was not invited to give the keynote speech. In fact, I was not even introduced. I fare far better with you filmonster fans. Your appreciation is overwhelming and I am grateful to each and every one of you who writes to me or sends me a gift or remembers my brrrthday or comes to see me. I hope Ole Uncle Forry in the 21st Century ... will still be worthy of your attention."[11]

Forrest decided in 1934 at the age of 18 to move back to the movie capital of the world and stay with the Wymans. What he wanted most of all was to have some sort of career in the movies. He wanted to get a job as a personal assistant to a star, preferably Marlene Dietrich. He did meet her, as well as Cary Grant. He never did work for Dietrich, unfortunately, nor did he serve in this capacity for any actor. In a 1985 taped interview with Comic-Con organizer Shel Dorf, Mr. Dorf suggested that Forry might have a bestselling autobiography if he titled it *I Slept with Marlene Dietrich*. He corrected Shel. "I couldn't sleep with Marlene Dietrich!" Forry was so thrilled just to meet her. He also got her autograph.

Forry was one of the earliest members of the Los Angeles Science Fantasy Society, which was then a small group of teenagers and adults who read and wrote science fiction. He claimed to have been the first to publish a fanzine, *Voice of the Imagi-Nation*. Refutations of this fact have surfaced and Ray Palmer's *Cosmology* may have, in fact, been the first and, if not, Allen Glasser, Julius Schwartz and Mort Weisinger's *The Planet* and *The Time Traveler*.

The *Los Angeles Science Fantasy Society* coat of arms has a rich history.

In volume one, number one of *The Time Traveler* there is a list of the science fiction films that had been produced to date, compiled by Forry Ackerman. He believed that this was the first such list ever compiled. The list included *Radio-Mania, Avalanche, By Rocket to the Moon, Metropolis, Mystery of Life*, the serial *The Unknown Purple*, and many others both extant and lost. Some of the films were not truly science fiction. For example, Forry recalled later in life that he should not have included a film such as the Universal *Dracula* since it was obviously a supernatural fantasy.

A youth named Donald

2. "I Couldn't Sleep with Marlene Dietrich!"

A. Wollheim was very active in the fanzines. He was later appointed head of the committee for the first World Science Fiction convention. *Science Fiction Digest* was another fanzine of the late 1930s that Forry worked on with Ray Palmer, who would go on to considerable fame as a publisher. These fanzines often were short lived. Fanzines were an early invention of these young men (and several young women) who yearned for self expression and networking with other fans of science fiction. Fanzines were mailed widely around the English-speaking world beginning in the 1930s and continuing to this day. The Amateur Press Association was instrumental in encouraging the growth of these APAs, or Amateur Press Association publications. The famed Los Angeles Science Fantasy Society still mails its own APA—L as well as e-mail alerts and updates. Forry was as active as possible in these pursuits. Forry used a rather eccentric way of writing for these fanzines. Paragraphs ran over, sentences spilled onto one another, and odd spellings — laced with generous puns — was the style he employed. This was Ackermanese. He may not have been the originator of these quirky ways of writing but he was to continue to occasionally use them in the pages of his writings for magazines, such as *Famous Monsters of Filmland, Forrest J Ackerman's Monsterland* and a number of others.

He popularized the idea for fanzines of shortening spellings of words to their *extrme abbrviations, a methd thot best for use in quck messages for evryday life.* Forry also invented the word "egoboo," which means an ego boost (sometimes obtained as a result of inventing odd spellings that become widely used!).

We now have Twitter and we have abbreviations that have been invented expressly for the Internet, with abbreviations like LOL (Lots of Luck), IMHO (In My Humble Opinion) and "What r yu doing?" text messages on one's cell phone. In answer, we write, "I'm @ the drug store gtting suntan lotion!"

This interesting venture in writing using abbreviations in no way implies that Forry only wrote using this colorful style. He wrote "Dwellers in the Dust" in 1934 and showed signs at the age of 18 of being a quite talented fiction writer. This tale is the story of a man who befriends a brilliant scientist who tells him he can go back two years in time using an invention of his, and prevent the tragic drowning of his "baby" sister. It was the winner of a story contest, and was to be published in *Marvel Tales*, but the magazine folded before it could be published. In the 1950s, it was picked up by *Fantasy Book* and reprinted.

Forry, by this time, was trying to obtain a real job, as he had decided not to continue on with college, and his idea of being a mail-order book proprietor was not working out. Neither were his attempts at securing public relations work for a movie studio.

Forry befriended a certain Los Angeles–based teenager named Ray Harryhausen, who made his acquaintance through the giant ape of Skull Island, King Kong. Ray was very interested in stop-motion animation, having seen First National's *The Lost World* and RKO-Radio Pictures' *King Kong* and wanting to do that sort of special effects work himself. Ray had been doing his own short films in his backyard; these early ones starred a cave bear. He knew he was new at this and wanted to learn all he could about this

Because of the photography hobby of a young Walt Daugherty, he has preserved for posterity this very early production shot of a young Ray Harryhausen working on one of his very first stop-motion short films in his dad's workshop (Mary Ellen Daugherty [Mrs. Walter J. Daugherty]).

technique. He attended a late 1930s screening of *King Kong* in Hawthorne, a Los Angeles neighborhood. He noticed some nice black and white stills from the film in the theater lobby and asked the manager if he could borrow them to photograph them and have copies for himself. Ray was told that a young man named Forry Ackerman owned them and he would have to get in touch with him. That was the beginning of a friendship that would span the decades and be celebrated in documentaries such as *Ray Harryhausen: The Early Years* and *The Sci-Fi Boys*. But Ray Harryhausen and Forry Ackerman had no thought that one day their shared interests and their good times together would interest so many others. They were just teenagers living life.

Forry, Ray and Ray Bradbury (a young fellow originally from Waukegan, Illinois) would meet with other friends in the Little Brown Room, a wood-paneled banquet room at Clifton's Cafeteria in downtown Los Angeles, in the Broadway theater district. There, they would chat about all sorts of things, including, as Ray Harryhausen recalled, space platforms.[12] Not too many people in Los Angeles were discussing space platforms in those days and if one did one got some strange looks.

A film that made a huge impression on Forrest J Ackerman premiered in 1936: the Alexander Korda film *Things to Come*. Based on a book by H.G. Wells, it was one of the few serious science fiction films ever made. In 1940 Everytown (a city in England) is trying to celebrate Christmas when it is bombed by an unnamed enemy. Friends Pippa Passworthy (Edward Chapman) and his friend John Cabal (Raymond Massey) and their families' lives are forever altered. The war drags on, not for years, but for decades. Society in England regresses to a semi-feudal state. At last, when a terrible plague called the Wandering Sickness, bred from the rubble and decay of war, runs its course, humanity can rebuild. The year 2036 sees a clean whitewashed underground city on the site of Everytown and a wondrous new scientific society where John Cabal's grandson and Pippa Passworthy's grandson, members of the minority elite, are planning a launch to the Moon. Some members of an artist's movement vehemently oppose the launch, believing that man has no business doing such a thing.

On October 30, 1938 — the night that America was under the erroneous impression that it was being invaded — Forry was working his night job. The *Mercury Theater on the Air* dramatization of the *War of the Worlds* by H.G. Wells was broadcast in the early evening hours on the East Coast. When he picked up the newspaper the next morning he saw the words "Gas Raid from Mars," "Scare Is Nationwide." "Nation May Act." A Martian invasion? And he missed it?[13] Fortunately, it turned out to be young Orson Welles and his radio troupe being a tad too realistic in their dramatization. Not long afterward the federal government cracked down on broadcasting stunts that proved hazardous, as this one had become.

The summer of 1939 was a big one for Forrest J Ackerman. This was the year of the first World Science Fiction Convention, the first science fiction convention in the history of the planet. Donald Wollheim of the Futurians, the other science fiction club of any size that existed at that time, was tasked with chairing it and professional attendees included Nelson S. Bond, Ray Cummings, Mort Weisinger, Ross Rocklynne, L. Sprague de Camp, John W. Campbell, Jr., the emerging author Isaac Asimov, Otto Binder, and Manly Wade Wellman. Forry had heard about the convention through the pages of *Thrilling Wonder Stories*. Attending it was a necessity. As soon as he disembarked from the train, Forry saw Donald Wollheim and about a half-dozen others waiting to greet him. He was pretty thrilled at first to have a reception committee, but as it happened, it wasn't the sort of reception he would have wanted. When he approached the group smiling, an overweight teenager said to him, "So *you're* the Forrest Ackerman who has been writing those ridiculous letters to the science fiction magazines!" And after that assessment, its originator, young author Cyril Kornbluth, proceeded to punch Forry in the stomach!

Forry proceeded to the convention and hoped things were going to improve. The guest of honor at the World Science Fiction Convention was *Amazing Stories* artist Frank R. Paul, and this was great news to Forry, as Paul was his favorite artist. The attendance was estimated to be 200. Attendees included not only Forry but Myrtle Douglas (nicknamed Morojo, Forry's girlfriend of the time), Robert D. Swisher, Harry Harrison, Oscar Train, Will Sykora, Julius Schwartz and Ray Bradbury. Ray arrived courtesy of Forry. As Ray later remembered, he was too poor to afford a bus ticket to

New York City so Forry gave him the money for the fare. His friend also paid for his meals while there and made it possible for Ray to go to the World's Fair where they bought lapel pins reading "I Have Seen the Future."

There was a banquet at the convention and Forry was able to attend. It was a very expensive dinner — one dollar. Forry sat next to the famed rocket expert Willy Ley. He also recalled that science fiction author L. Sprague de Camp attended and sat nearby.

Julius Schwartz was the agent for Stanley Weinbaum, famed author of *A Martian Odyssey* and other acclaimed stories. Weinbaum did not live to see the convention, having died at the young age of 32. Julius had a manuscript with him — Weinbaum's unpublished manuscript, *The Mad Brain*. Forry was supplying some editing for him and had taken the manuscript to the home of a friend in New York City to finish it. He had too much to do at once, because there was an auction at the convention and they were auctioning off a Weinbaum manuscript. So Forry hurried back to the convention with his friends and found that he had missed the bidding. The manuscript was eventually edited. Years later, Forry spoke with Weinbaum's widow, Margaret, who told him that Stanley had told her that when he was having a particularly good day, he called it an "Ackerman day." Forry was amazed and did not know that Weinbaum was so fond of him. And they had not even known each other very long.[14]

Forry and Myrtle made heads turn at the World Science Fiction convention by arriving in costume. A skilled seamstress, she had made both their costumes to resemble a combination of *Things to Come* and *Buck Rogers* outfits, a sort of generic "futurian" raiment. Forry's had 4SJ embroidered on the chest, so there would be no mistaking him for some other fan. As he recounted later, he thought that at a science fiction convention everyone was supposed to show up in costume. It happened that only he and Myrtle wore costumes.

They walked down the streets of New York in their costumes and heard children exclaim "Flash Gordon!" and "Buck Rogers!" While he, Ray, and some other friends were at the World's Fair, Forry noticed that there was a podium with a microphone provided for visitors who had come from other nations. They could stand at the podium and speak into the microphone, greeting people in their native tongue. A proponent of Esperanto, that "futuristic" language, Forry had the idea to go up in his costume and greet everyone in Esperanto. He recited a line from *Things to Come*.

While in New York, Forry and some fans wanted to meet A. Merritt, the author of *The Moon Pool* and *Seven Footprints to Satan*, but Merritt was busy at his day job as Sunday editor of *The American Weekly*, and would entertain fans in his office. So, the day after the convention a group of about eight fans visited him in his newspaper office. A chance meeting with artist Virgil Finlay (who worked for *The American Weekly* and science fiction magazines) occurred when Finlay brought some art for Merritt to approve for an upcoming edition.

Forry was aghast when he learned of a huge schism that formed in fandom at that very first convention in New York. Donald A. Wollheim and Cyril Kornbluth, the kid who punched Forry in the stomach at the train depot, were told to stand outside the

2. "I Couldn't Sleep with Marlene Dietrich!"

hotel. A similar tiff between fans was to form some time later at the headquarters of the Science Fiction League, later called the Los Angeles Science Fantasy Society. Fortunately, the rift was healed through the efforts of Paul Freehafer, a young man who had a knack for smoothing over disputes and getting people to work together. The LASFS' Freehafer Hall was named for his contribution to keeping the club from falling apart early in its development.[15] Paul Frehafer died at a very young age from a heart condition; as Forry put it, he went off for a summer vacation in a Western state and never came back.

The early meetings were held at the Pacific Electric Building in Los Angeles and later, Clifton's Cafeteria. Paul Frehafer is remembered through the name Freehafer Hall, the main meeting hall where the club members see films, play board games and have parties. Building 4SJ is the first small building one enters when one visits the headquarters. It houses the library and the computer center.

In Chicago some fans formed a committee for the next convention and Forry was part of that committee. Many big names were being tossed about as potential guests for the next one. Edgar Rice Burroughs was one, and Olaf Stapledon another. Finally, Forry suggested Robert A. Heinlein. Heinlein had recently moved to Hollywood and met Forry, who had even had a chance to read his manuscripts that he was readying for publication at that time, including *The Roads Must Roll*. Heinlein did, in fact, become the guest of honor for the next convention.

Seldom did Forry, who shared credit for being half of the first science fiction convention costumed pair, ever wear another costume to a convention, and one of those occasions was the second Worldcon, Chicon in Chicago in 1940. At this convention Forry brought along his old *Things to Come* style "futuristicostume," as he called it, and he and some other people in costume walked to one of the Chicago newspaper offices to visit the night editor. It was probably a scene worthy of a 1940s comedy. Teenagers and young adults in wacky space costumes converged upon the editor's office to announce with dramatic flair (and no small amount of chutzpah) that they were time travelers who picked up the paper and saw a photo of themselves in it being interviewed, so they had to come there to remember how it felt!

The Denvention, the 1941 Worldcon, was a special one for Forry. Here he won a prize for his "Hunchbackerman of Notre Dame" costume, the mask of which was designed and made for him by none other than Ray Harryhausen.

Forry wore various costumes for other occasions, such as the film roles he played, as well as dressing as Superman as a young man and going to several movie producers' offices trying to interest them in doing some fantasy films utilizing scripts written by a client. He dressed as a character from *Things to Come* for a 1991 video Ray Ferry produced entitled *Forrest J Ackerman's Amazing World of Science Fiction and Fantasy*, and as a vampire for *Hooray for Horrorwood*. However, as far as conventions were concerned, Forry ceased to appear in costume very early on.

Forry recalled for *Mimosa* magazine and for this author some memories of that convention where Heinlein was to be the guest of honor, the 1941 Denvention. By now the conventions and their organizing bodies were in full swing. Forry had named the first one the Nycon, the second, the Chicon, and this, the third convention, since it was held in Denver; it seemed perfectly natural to name it the Denvention. He felt that the speech that Robert A. Heinlein gave was the most extraordinary one he had ever heard at any science fiction convention. (Even in the 1990s, Forry had never heard a more remarkable speech.) Titled "The Discovery of the Future," it was so good that Forry asked friend Walt Daugherty to record it. The ever-obliging Walt had a machine that recorded the speech on a phonograph record. Forry, the chronicler, took the record home to transcribe it onto paper. He then stenciled it, mimeographed it and mailed it to 100 interested parties for ten cents a copy. Many decades later he learned that at an auction, one of his mimeographs was sold to a dealer for $1300.[16]

There was not a fourth Worldcon until the end of World War II when domestic life could resume for returning servicemen and servicewomen.

In the early years of the science fiction conventions, the programming consisted of lectures about scientific subjects, perhaps a play, and always panels and discussions. Sometimes someone would arrange with a film publicity department to bring posters and movie theater displays from current science fiction films. Art rooms consisted of posters taped to the walls of the main programming room. The programming would frequently include an auction. What they did not usually include were costume contests. This did not begin in earnest until the 1960s. Costume contests and presentations became more elaborate with more expensive materials and intricate workmanship. By the 1980s some even included tiny LEDs (light-emitting diodes) sewn into the fabric! The modern 21st century evolution of convention costuming is the Japanese cosplay, from the words costume and play. What hath Forry wrought?

Nineteen thirty-nine would prove to be a very sad year also for Forrest J Ackerman. That year his beloved grandfather, George Herbert Wyman, passed. Forry felt that one of the great lights in his life had flickered out.

3
Sergeant Ack-Ack

Forry actually saw H.G. Wells in person in 1938 — when he came to speak in a lecture hall and recalled that he was expecting a tall man with a booming voice, since his novels had always conjured up such an image, and Raymond Massey had seemed to be such a wonderful embodiment for Wells's ideas in *Things to Come*. Instead, he saw that Wells was a roly poly Englishman with a reddish complexion. Forry recalled a portion of the speech given by the famed author: "I am going to talk to you for about an hour. East is west and west is east ... and they are coming together ... with a bang."

Forry worked at various jobs, including one as a movie projectionist. He eventually got a job with the Academy of Motion Picture Arts and Sciences. One of his tasks was to guard the Oscars backstage before they were handed out to the recipients. He recalled that it was 1940, the year the Academy Award for Best Effects went to *The Rains Came*. He stayed with the Academy until he became embroiled in a big dispute where some disgruntled fellow employees organized and said they were going to quit because of a tyrannical manager. His immediate supervisor was a good-natured person, but the man over him was abusive. So, on an appointed day, the entire staff was supposed to show up at the offensive manager's office. Forry showed up and waited for all the others, who did not appear, and when Forry was asked what he was doing there, Forry gulped and said, "I was supposed to tell you that we — a lot of us — were resigning."

Forry's next place of employment was the Fluor Drafting Company. By this time the war was in full swing and he had tried to join the Navy, thinking that it might be a bit less hazardous to serve aboard a large destroyer. But the Navy had refused him because although he was very tall — six feet — he was very thin. Forry thought he might be able to avoid being drafted because he was the only person in the country who knew how to operate a varityper for the company. It had been developed especially for the Fluor Drafting Company and saved much time for draftsmen. However, his job security went down the drain when a girl was trained to operate the varityper. Off to the Army Forry went. Forry was of the opinion that he might just get killed since they were training him on how to fire a rifle. He made a will which left all of his books $1000 of his insurance money to endow a Fantasy Foundation.

Fortunately, Forry's fears were not realized, and he lived through the experience at Fort MacArthur in San Pedro, initially manufacturing dog tags. He was approached by someone one day who was working on the Fort's newsletter. The young sergeant in charge of the newsletter was struggling with it because he had no real aptitude for the task and figured that this Ackerman guy had some talent in that area since he had shown him his fanzine he was publishing. Forry was then put in charge of editing the camp newspaper, the *Bulletin/Alert*, with the assistance of cartoonist Virgil Partch, who was also stationed at Fort MacArthur. It was a bit of synchronicity that he was working with Partch because Partch had done illustrations for a magazine that had included *The Time Twister*, a Francis Flagg story collaboration.

During his World War II career as a staff sergeant in the Army, Forry realized some acclaim for editing and writing for the wartime newspaper. When Forry was editing this newspaper, it was annually judged second most-popular out of 2000 military publications. Forry acquired his well-known Warren William–style moustache and hairstyle during his Army years. Warren William was a debonair character player in the 1930s and 1940s for MGM and many others. Some of his better-known films are *Employee's Entrance* and *Strange Illusion*. Forry had also copied the distinctive style of prolific actress Kay Francis's signature. It had its own Forrest J Ackerman quality also, as he did not copy Miss Francis's signature exactly.

Metropolis director Fritz Lang, a recent émigré to the United States, visited Forry in the Army Hospital in the company of his lady friend Lily Latté when Forry was recuperating from the German measles. This was one of the big thrills of his young life, because *Metropolis* was one of his favorite films, if not his all-time favorite. Lang was just making the routine patriotic rounds at the hospital and saw one of his biggest fans.[1] Forry recovered more quickly after that visit.

Later on, he was to become a good friend to Fritz Lang. The German director had by the beginning of the war divorced his wife, Thea von Harbou, author of the *Metropolis* novel, because of her Nazi affinities. He had carved out a niche in the United States. One of his famous films of this time period was *M*, a noir drama that achieved critical acclaim for its depiction of a child molester, played by Peter Lorre.

When stationed at Fort MacArthur, Forry had occasion to be an extra in a musical. Columbia Pictures Corporation was filming *Hey, Rookie!* at the base. The *Hey, Rookie!* play that the soldiers put on each year at their base recreation center was so well known that Columbia decided to use the fort in some of the picture and played up the *Bulletin/Alert*, showing a photo of Ann Miller in an issue. The story is about a young officer (Larry Parks) who joins the Army to get away from stage productions and a betrayal by his ex-girlfriend (Ann Miller), only to find that he has orders to put on a big show on a tiny budget and *she* is going to be in it. Forry decided that he would like to be in a scene. The camera pans across several seated enlisted men in the recreation room and the uncredited Staff Sergeant Ack-Ack is seen in the background perusing the pages of the newspaper he edited. An astonishing bit of synchronicity is connected with this film appearance. Larry Parks, who played Al Jolson in both *The Jolson Story* and its sequel *Jolson Sings Again*, was the star in this pre–*Jolson Story* film.

The swimming pool for the enlisted men and women at the base was purchased with the proceeds from the show.

3. Sergeant Ack-Ack

Forry was an extra in *Hey, Rookie!*, starring Ann Miller, Larry Parks and Joe Besser, here getting his full spectrum of Army inoculations (Columbia Pictures).

Walt Daugherty was working as an extra on a film starring Loretta Young, *The Farmer's Daughter*, and asked Forry if he would be interested. Forry could use the money, so he appeared in a scene with a political rally, and was in the blurry background.

Forry made sure that his Army career did not derail his involvement with the Los Angeles Science Fantasy Society, and he attended as many meetings as he could manage, even though it meant driving all the way from San Pedro each Thursday night. He spent the entire war stateside. The same did not hold true for his younger brother, Aldie, who had enlisted. Alden did not survive the savagery of war, as he was sent to the European Theater. He was killed on New Year's Day in the Battle of the Bulge in Belgium, when he was serving in the 42nd Tank Battalion D company, 21th Armored Division. He was only 20 years old. His early death affected Forry greatly. He decided that he was going to try to be two people in one, to continue for his brother, Alden. This was indeed one of the most significant events in his young life. Forry wrote in *Voice of the Imagi-Nation* (number 39) in February 1945, reprinted in *Amazing Forries*,

Left: **Sergeant Forrest Ackerman edited the Fort MacArthur** *Bulletin/Alert* **for three years during World War II (Rick Atkins).** *Right:* **Forry inscribed this photograph of himself in uniform, "To Walt — a Great Guy (and that's no lie) from Forry Ackerman" (Mary Ellen Daugherty [Mrs. Walter J. Daugherty]).**

"My brother's death came at a very opportune time for me. A concatenation of events had conspired to beat me down 'spiritually' to very low ebb."

Forry wrote that he never appreciated being born in the first place, and he had been scorned by so many for his ideals and found to his dismay that despite society maintaining that virtue and goodness are desired, the fact was that many people seem to prefer "the man of easy conscience," as he phrased it. He did not want to live the way so many others would appear to want him to live. At the time of Alden's passing, Forry had been feeling that absolutely no one in his life was behind him and his efforts in life. No one totally believed in him. "So," he continued, "it works out this way, that I say 'OK, I'll dedicate myself to humanity thru my brother.' He was a good kid, but he died before he ever got much of a chance to do anything about it. Let his chance, then, be incarnated in me. I will be good and do good, as I see it, for his sake. By being true to his memory I will be true to myself. If nobody living vindicated me or cares for what I am doing, I can console myself that he would have approved.... Maybe it's a kind of screwy psychology, acting as if someone who's gone would have appreciated you, because there's no way now of proving he wouldn't have."[2]

We all need someone who will give us a helping hand when we are launching a career. Many a writer, special effects artist, producer and fan has spoken appreciatively of how Forry helped them and encouraged them when they needed it most. But who, other than his parents, spouse and grandparents, were the most encouraging and mentoring persons in Forry's own life?

The unnamed teacher who put him in charge of the Balboa High school newspaper had to be one of these mentors for Forrest J Ackerman.

The C.O. who gave him the Fort MacArthur *Bulletin/Alert* to edit gave him an opportunity to be an editor for the first time was a mentor; the bulletin was helping him hone his reporting skills.

Francis Flagg, the science fiction author who collaborated with him on several short stories and novelettes, and whom Forry regrettably never met, made it possible for Forry to have bylines in several magazines at a very young age. He also was a proponent of Esperanto and was the reason why Forry became interested in the language.

The young Forry was literally counting the days before he was discharged from the Army. He served three years, five months and 29 days and was glad to be out. Now, with an Honorable Discharge and some more writing experience, the youth was eager to be involved in some sort of editing work. He was staying with his grandmother at her home at 236½ North New Hampshire Avenue. He was very busy then with girls and dated many women but hadn't yet found anyone he wanted to settle down with. He also became friends with several lesbians due to their interest in science fiction and horror. Some of them had written lesbian-oriented science fiction, which he read avidly. Once he was voted "Honorary Lesbian" by the Daughters of Bilitis, an organization for lesbian rights which was founded in 1955 in San Francisco. He wrote under one of his pseudonyms, Laurajean Ermayne, for *Vice Versa*, a very early fiction and nonfiction magazine for lesbians. One of the Daughters of Bilitis remained friends with Forry for many decades.

Forry found out that the famed creator of Tarzan and of John Carter of Mars, Edgar Rice Burroughs, lived on a ranch within easy driving distance of his home in Los Angeles and it was high time he went to see him, he recalled in an article reprinted in James van Hise's book *Edgar Rice Burroughs' Fantastic Worlds*. Mr. Burroughs was older and was not going to be available for meetings at his ranch forever. Forry wrote him and asked for an appointment for himself and several other fans of his work to visit him. Burroughs kindly consented.

Even in the late 1940s, the San Fernando Valley community where he lived was known as Tarzana, as he had sold off portions of his ranch to developers for the construction of residential subdivisions. Amazingly, there was no street sign to indicate the address Forry had been given. The foursome stopped at a service station to ask directions. The attendant did not know where the legendary Burroughs lived. They then visited a drug store and asked the owner if he knew where the residence of their most famous citizen was. He also had no idea. They got back in their car and drove around more. The young men were looking for a big mansion and a huge ranch and found instead a small rural style mailbox along the road with the name "Burroughs" upon it. They drove down the driveway to a small six-room house with a garden and orchard.

Edgar Rice Burroughs greeted them and showed them to his living room. Surrounding them was a large vermillion jar decorated with elephants, a Japanese silk painting of a tiger, and a zebra skin beneath their feet. Statuettes of horses and a huge Indian chief's robe completed the décor. Forry asked Burroughs if it was in fact true that he had written his very first stories on envelopes. "No," Burroughs replied, "but I did use old letterheads that I printed when I went into sales many years ago, and did not continue with. I did not have much business acumen, unfortunately." Mr. Burroughs added that it was not true that he began to write because of insomnia, as some had alleged. "I wrote because I was hungry," he said. "I had a family to support." Burroughs had had quite a few interesting dreams which he used as foundations for his stories. He had worked as a policeman and a cowhand and nothing had ever really panned out.

It wasn't until he was 35 years old that Burroughs achieved his fame. As a salesman for a patent medicine company, he had been responsible for making certain that the advertisement copy for the magazines came out correctly and on time. He read the pulps in which they appeared, he told Forry and the other young men, and realized upon reading the stories that he could do as well as, or better than, the adventure tales in these magazines. His first story set on Barsoom (Mars), *Under the Moons of Mars*, was serialized in *All-Story Weekly*, in early 1912. He followed that one up with *Tarzan of the Apes*, and his success was assured. At the time of Forry's interview with the esteemed author, he had made substantial income from motion picture rights for Tarzan films, as well as Tarzan gasoline and Tarzan bread! Forry asked Burroughs if fantasy fiction like *She* and other novels of H. Rider Haggard had ever influenced him, and his reply was no. He did not read fantasy fiction as a boy. Burroughs had been disappointed at the slight critical and monetary response to his historical novel, *The Outlaw of Torn*, although the research that had gone into it was useful in the writing of *Tarzan, Lord of the Jungle*. He hadn't even seen all of Hollywood's motion pictures based on his most famous character. His own son-in-law, Jim Pierce, had starred in a Tarzan film in the late 1920s, *Tarzan and the Golden Lion*, and had played Tarzan the way he had always seen him: grim, at times savage, although well educated and able to read and write as well as would be expected of an English lord. Burroughs preferred Herman Brix's Tarzan to all the others, however, due to his displays of fearlessness.

The author of *The Land That Time Forgot* asked the young men to sign his own autograph book before they departed. "Not everybody is quite sincere," he told Forry and the others, "but I believe that you have been."[3]

In a May Company book aisle he was browsing during the late 1940s, Forry was approached by an attractive brunette store clerk. "May I help you?" she asked. He liked her at the very first meeting. And as he put it many years later, she helped him ever since!

He began flirting with her. "Where did you get that fascinating accent?" Forry asked, noticing her German/Polish accent.

"My ancestors from Europe," she replied.

"Who were they?"

"*My* ancestors were highly civilized while *yours* were still hanging by their tails from trees!" was her haughty reply.

3. Sergeant Ack-Ack

They began dating. Her name was Mathilde Wahrman. The daughter of Moses Aron Wahrman and Berta Wahrman of Poland, she had a son, Michael, from a previous marriage to Frederic Porjes, a customer representative for a lumber wholesaler. Michael was born in Israel on January 17, 1941.[4]

Mathilde's ex-husband, Frederic Porjes, was born in Pressberg, Czechoslovakia, in 1902, and was a customer-service representative for the lumber company. She divorced him in 1948. Forry found out that she had been all over Europe avoiding the tyranny of the Nazis, as she was Jewish. She had earned a degree in biology in Germany but had to flee. In 1933 Mathilde worked long hours as a midwife in France. She later moved to Israel, where she had met Frederic. Her parents decided to move to Los Angeles and she went with them. Here, in the United States, she hoped to make a new life with her son. Her parents settled in the United States and met Forry at around the same time and Forry befriended them. He wrote a piece of doggerel entitled "The Ballad of Berta" in which he described their lives and travails as the family traveled throughout Europe. He also expressed humorously in his poem that he was aware that Mathilde's plan to marry a Gentile was something that most of the people in her family had never done before.

Forry nicknamed Mathilde "Wendayne" and always referred to her thereafter as "Wendy." She was a few years older than he.

Forry took one alcoholic drink at the age of 30 and never drank again. He also never regretted that.

Fandom, as Forry discovered in those days, was in its financial philosophy rather mercurial — something like a piece of mercury that had fallen out of a broken thermometer — hard or impossible to persuade to sit still. For one fan convention, he wanted to bring over E.J. Carnell from England as a guest. It would have cost $500 to do this, and Ackerman thought that if 500 fans each contributed a dollar, the goal would easily be accomplished. This did not happen. He asked publishers to offer original illustrations, subscriptions and books. He even ran a lottery and contributed some of his own money and own girlfriend's as well. A handful of other fans gave a few dollars. He brought Carnell over to the United States but the total raised was only $127.

Forry was also disappointed by a handful of Los Angeles scientifiction fans that showed huge enthusiasm for the Fantasy Foundation idea that someone else had come up with and wanted him to work it. He was skeptical but they were adamant. But Forry had other priorities right now. The Pacificon was the fourth convention and the first Worldcon to be held after the war. It was also the last one to be given a nickname by Forry. Forry met Robert Bloch just prior to this convention and he is listed in the Program Book as an attendee. He was just getting started in his writing career. William S. Ackerman and his wife Carroll were in fact members of the 4th World Science Fiction Convention Society. On the second full day of the Pacificon Science Fiction Convention of 1946, the early morning's event was open house at the Ackerman's. The Pacificon I Program contains many paid ad space quotes from the family. "In memory of ALDEN ACKERMAN, one of the cleanest boys I have ever known — Dad" was William Ack-

Robert Bloch was an early member of the science-fiction fan community; his career took him to great heights as a writer (Mary Ellen Daugherty [Mrs. Walter Daugherty]).

erman's entry. Within the program book there was this advertisement from Belle Wyman: "I guess I made him WHAT HE IS TODAY. I hope you're satisfied." Mrs. Carroll Ackerman wrote her ad for the program thus: "Tell me, after 20 years, do you think my son's interest in scientifiction is just a passing FANTASY?"[5]

In 1948, Forry's beloved grandmother, Belle Wyman, died at the age of 86. Two years later, Forrest and Mathilde were married.[6]

4
The 1950s — Forry's Rise to Fame

"Forry," this author once asked him while we were attending a monster movie convention in the 1990s, "I wish you would tell some stories to the audience during your talks about your work as a literary agent representing the best writers in science fiction and selling their stuff to the movie producers. I am sure they would like to know about that. I know I would."

He grumbled something and said, "I don't think they would find it to be very interesting."

Au contraire, Forry, I think many people will and have considered it to be interesting. Among his clients were: A.E. van Vogt, Ray Bradbury, Jerome Bixby, L. Ron Hubbard, Rod Serling, Franklin Jones, Edward D. Wood, Jr., Charles Nuetzel and Murray Leinster. The Ackerman Science Fiction Agency brokered short stories and novels and sold motion picture rights. After the war ended Forry moved back to Los Angeles where he stayed with his maternal grandmother while starting his career as a literary agent. He specialized in science fiction properties: short stories, novels and even films. In the first year of operation, 1949, the Ackerman Agency made $50 in gross sales and spent $1,075. Fortunately, there was no rent or mortgage to pay and, after a year or so, business began to become established. During 1950 he had as many as 70 clients, including Isaac Asimov. He really began to see the business become a profitable venture, however, when A.E. van Vogt became a steady client and he made many sales.

Forry helped Ray Bradbury when he was poor and trying to support his new family on his tiny earnings as a writer during the late forties and early fifties.

"Forry would buy books from my personal library. He didn't want 'em." Bradbury said when honoring Forry at his 80th birthday party in 1996. "He bought them because I was broke. Later, when I had made it as a writer, I bought some of them back!"

Forry was remembering the promise he had made to himself that he would be two good men in one, to be the man his brother, Alden, would have wanted him to be. Forry's father, William, suffered a stroke and had "a miserable final few years," according to his son. But before he passed, he wanted to provide for his only surviving child, and he had approximately $100,000, so he had purchased a 13-room home for him on Sherbourne Drive. Forry was on his way to New Orleans for a World Science Fiction Convention when he received word that his father had died. It was August 30, 1951. He turned around and came back home immediately.

Forry takes notes while relaxing at home in his original Ackermansion on Sherbourne Drive in Los Angeles (Mary Ellen Daugherty [Mrs. Walter J. Daugherty]).

In the early 1950s Forry tried to run a mail-order book-selling business from his home but finally abandoned this idea because he never cleared any substantial profit. Forry was collecting all the current magazines and received them via air mail special delivery. He also tried to interest some television producers in a TV series. This did not come to fruition, either.

Science fiction in Asia at this time was in dire straits. The G.I.s who were stationed in Japan after World War II were burning many paperback books. A young man named Tetsu Yano saw one such instance and retrieved a science fiction book and magazine minutes before they could be destroyed. He wrote a letter that was published in *Thrilling Wonder Stories* in which he opined, "I'm just a poor know-nothing Japanese boy bitten by the science fiction bug. Could anybody conceivably send me an old cast-off magazine?"

Forry mailed some packages to Tetsu and so began a friendship that lasted for many decades. Yano's home had been bombed during the war and he and his family had been living with friends ever since. Forry mentioned to him in 1953 that the fans were going to have a Westercon science fiction convention. Forry received a very excited letter from Tetsu, which read, "Gee, if I could manage to get there, would I be permitted to attend?" And Forry wrote back, "*Permitted!* You would be the Guest of Honor! This would be grand! You could stay at my home!" Tetsu bought a ticket on a cattle boat. Twenty-nine days later, Forry and Wendy met him and the boat at the docks. "Tetsu couldn't sleep the first night he was with us, he was too excited," Forry recalled. He had intended to stay in America for two weeks but ended up staying for several months.

Tetsu had some hair-raising adventures while he was in the United States. Besides the Westercon, Forry and Wendy also took him to that year's World Science Fiction Convention, the 1953 Philcon in Philadelphia. Tetsu, Wendy, Forry, and H.J. Campbell (the editor of the British magazine *Authentic Science Fiction*), were an interesting band of travelers as they journeyed across the continent by automobile. Campbell was huge and had a long, black beard, resembling a mountain man or a Celtic warrior. Yano was short and slight of build. At one point the car was at the top of a mountain pass. Wendy was behind the wheel and the car was straining to make it and could not. Forry, Tetsu and H.J. got out of the car and pushed. When gravity took over, the men all ran after the car! Fortunately, it did not crash and Wendy was not hurt ... just scared.

In the 1950s, according to friend Lee Harris, Forry liked to visit the strip clubs to see the performances. Jenny Lee was one of his favorites. He wrote to one theater that one of the strippers was "flat where it flatters and round where it matters." The newspaper advertisement for the show had the line "Forrest J Ackerman says — she's flat where it flatters and round where it matters!"[1]

The year 1951 was a big one for Forry, as he was invited to be the guest of honor at the First International Science Fiction Convention in London, England, and *Life* magazine published photos of a very young Forry (then 35) posing with his personal library of *Thrilling Wonder Stories* at his home at 915 South Sherbourne Drive in Los Angeles. Forry must have felt that he was indeed becoming a celebrity.

In 1953 he attended the World Science Fiction Convention, Philcon II, in Philadelphia. That was the first year that Achievement Awards were presented to those in the field who had done exemplary work and the committee expressed in the Program Book for Philcon II that they hoped this would be successful enough to merit it becoming an annual event. These Achievement Awards were dubbed "Hugos" after Hugo Gernsback, the publisher of *Amazing Stories* and a host of other magazines. At this eleventh Worldcon, Forry was surprised when he was presented with a Hugo Award, the very first Hugo given that evening, for #1 Fan Personality, the first and only one with that name. He felt Ken Slater of England deserved it more than he. The reason he felt he did not merit the Hugo was because in the early 1950s he felt he was no longer a major fan personality. If it had been a lifetime achievement award for fannish activity, he felt, he would feel more comfortable about the award. But, he recalled to this author, it was an award for the Best Fan of the year that had just ended and Forry felt he was not the most active fan of that year. He said, "I appreciate the gesture, I really do, but I really believe that Ken Slater should have it." And then he left the stage. Wendy was very angry with him: "You have insulted the whole convention! They voted this to be awarded to you!" Forry now felt even worse about the entire affair. He was too embarrassed to attend the masquerade that night. Forry really hoped that he would not see anyone the next morning, and thought maybe he would sneak down to the hotel restaurant to grab some breakfast and then hide himself in his room for the rest of the convention, but Robert Bloch was there before him and he accosted him. "Forry!" he said. "That was certainly a fine gesture. Wow, you did a lot for international fandom."

Years later Ken returned the award to Forry after Forry was besieged by questions from various people who asked him, "What about that first Hugo ever bestowed upon anyone? Didn't you get it?" and Forry decided to write Ken and explain to him that he didn't intend to try to take back the award, but wanted to know how he felt about the award and if he had plans for it, whether it was going to be willed to his children or end up in a museum. If that was so, fine. But if he didn't have any such plans, Forry offered to preserve it. After that he worried that the letter might offend Ken and so First Fan David Kyle wrote Mr. Slater and explained the situation. When Forry next saw Ken in England, Ken cheerfully gave him the Hugo.

Forry was seeing his young friend Ray Bradbury achieving considerable success in the motion picture industry. Ray wrote the screenplay for Universal-International's *It Came from Outer Space* Most of the film was as he had conceived the original tale; Hollywood had not rewritten much of it. Bradbury had also written a short story, originally published in the *Saturday Evening Post*, entitled "The Foghorn," adapted into a motion picture, *The Beast from 20,000 Fathoms*. The special visual effects were supplied by their mutual friend, Ray Harryhausen. The three friends who, only 18 or so years previously, had met in Clifton's Cafeteria and talked of "things to come" were indeed seeing some amazing successes coming their way.

Forry knew a young boy named Richard Sheffield who had befriended actor Bela Lugosi through a mutual friend. Richard became a helper and errand runner. Richard went to Bela's modest apartment on Carlton Way near Sunset Boulevard many times each week to get money to pick up groceries for him at the nearby market. At this time, Bela was not physically very strong, but still managed to go to the corner delicatessen every night to pick up his newspaper. Divorced from Lillian Lugosi, the great Hungarian actor was working hard to pay the bills and rent. He was still appearing on television occasionally and had recently worked in an occasional film such as the British film *Old Mother Riley Meets the Vampire*, or an Edward D. Wood, Jr. programmer like *Glen or Glenda*. He had been in the hospital for his much-publicized treatment for morphine addiction, incurred through physician prescriptions to relieve his intense sciatica pains. When he regained some strength Lugosi remarried, this time to a young woman named Hope Lininger. Richard introduced Forry to Bela and the former star of famed classics such as *Ninotchka, White Zombie, The Body Snatcher, Son of Frankenstein*, Universal's 1931 *Dracula* and dozens of other films, visited Wendy and Forry at their Sherbourne Drive home. He wrote in Forry's guest book "Amazed!" when he saw the growing collection of fantasy and science fiction memorabilia in the home.

Forry recalled to this author that Bela seldom discussed his own films, preferring to talk about his adventures in his younger years, fighting for the rights of fellow actors back in Hungary. Lugosi was a well-read man who enjoyed talking about philosophy

4. The 1950s

and science. "I don't know why you young people are so good to me," he said to Forry and Richard. Forry remembered him as a gentleman who never swore, and whose main vice was smoking cigars, which he smoked often. Forry joined Richard in assisting Lugosi with ordinary errands. One day, Forry and some friends showed up at Bela's home to escort him to the theater for the Hollywood premiere of *The Black Sleep*, a horror film starring Lon Chaney, Jr., Basil Rathbone, Patricia Blair, Tor Johnson and Herbert Rudley. An older friend of Sheffield's wore a chauffeur's uniform and rented a limousine so that Bela would arrive appropriately. There was television news coverage of the event, and popular television horror host Vampira (Maila Nurmi), and star Tor Johnson were there.[2]

Bela had a small part in *The Black Sleep* as a servant to the obsessed character played by Rathbone, a doctor who is trying desperately to find a cure for his wife's brain injury, no matter how many people he has to cripple or deform to do it. Bela was in his seventies, in failing health and nearly blind, but his vanity would not permit him to wear glasses in public. "Point me in the right direction, fellas," he told Forry and Richard, and, as Forry recalled, the audience saw the wan, frail Lugosi slowly straighten up, fill up before their eyes and once more become the debonair, regal Count Dracula.

This was Bela Lugosi's final film unless one considers *Plan Nine from Outer Space* to be his last film, as he appeared in several sequences. Edward D. Wood, Jr. had done some generic shots of Bela which he had planned to expand upon for *Plan Nine*, and Bela died on August 16, 1956. Wood worked him into the film and used a double for some shots with Lugosi's unnamed character. (Similar awkward doubling was done in 1937 for Jean Harlow when she died during the making of MGM's *Saratoga*.)

Forry attended the funeral services at a Hollywood Boulevard funeral home for Lugosi and was the 101st person to file past his open casket.

In 1955 Forry was subpoenaed by the State of California for practicing agenting without first being licensed by the state. Forry obtained a license and the case was rapidly closed.

Wendayne by now was teaching biology in high school. She earned her master's degree and graduated magna cum laude in foreign languages.

In the 1950s Forry had some differences of opinion with Robert A. Heinlein over various issues. One visit for business purposes led to Heinlein making the statement to Forry that philanthropism is actually selfishness. Forry actually wrestled with this remark from someone he had always admired, and asked himself, "Am I really doing good things for people to help them or am I doing it for my own selfish reasons?" After thinking about this for some weeks he decided to continue to do well by others anyway. It was a vow to the memory of Alden Lorraine Ackerman, and he was going to keep it.

In the mid–1950s Forry was also busy writing for French magazines such as *V26*, and using his own real name as well as various pseudonyms, including Laurajean Ermayne, Chon Graystark, Spencer Strong, Dr. Acula, Weaver Wright, Carroll Wymack, Clair Helding, Jack Erman, and Mirta Forsto. Forry had a penchant for pen names. Paul Linden was a pseudonym he would use many years later in *Famous Monsters of Filmland*. Forry used dozens of pseudonyms. Mrs. Allis Kerlay and S.F. Balboa, a reference to his high school, Balboa High, were among the more peculiar ones. He wrote editorials condemning censorship such as "We Gotta Protect the Kiddies!" under female pen names. Forry also penned regular columns on the latest science fiction B pictures for *Nebula Science Fiction* back in the 1950s. He wrote reviews of such minor genre classics as *Invasion of the Saucer-Men* and *This Island, Earth*.

"Scientifilm Marquee" was a column that Forry wrote from 1955 to 1956 for the short-lived *Imaginative Tales*, a science fiction magazine which was published from 1955 to 1958. The artwork for "Scientifilm Marquee" was a pen-and-ink montage of iconic images from various films, including a brontosaurus from *The Lost World*, a sarcophagus from *The Mummy*, "Gort" from *The Day the Earth Stood Still*, and the executive tower where Joh Fredersen's offices were located in the great city of *Metropolis*. Forry was honing his skills at reportage on motion pictures. The following excerpt is taken from his lively column in the September 1956 issue.

> Richard Denning, who starred in the original, has been signed for an untitled sequel to *The Day the World Ended*.... Curtis Harrington, who produced and acted in his own fantasy film at the age of 14, and has steadily built a reputation in the surrealistic field, has scripted *The Girl from Beneath the Sea*, which Roger Corman will direct for Allied Artists.... Lon Chaney, Jr. will appear as *The Lizard Man* for the producers of *The Black Sleep*; he costars in the latter with Bela Lugosi, John Carradine, Akim Tamiroff and Tors [sic] Johnson.[3]

Forry befriended science fiction author and actor Fritz Leiber and the two of them decided one day in the early 1950s to make a humorous short amateur film at Leiber's home. The title was *The Genie*, and they needed a girl to play a belly dancer. Betty McCarthy, who adopted the nickname Bjo, was an active member of the Los Angeles Science Fantasy Society and in her early twenties, just the right age to play a belly dancer. She was also a talented seamstress and made her own costume. Bjo recalled to the author in 2009 that she met her husband of over 45 years when working in the fan film. John Trimble helped her adjust her costume, and that was certainly an unusual first meeting for them![4]

The Genie is about a man (Forry) who finds a magic lamp on a shelf of his home and rubs it. A genie (Fritz Leiber) appears and tells him he has one wish. "How about that!" Forry exclaims, playing this role to the hilt. Then he analyzes his options carefully. Maybe he can wish to have a million dollars. Oh, maybe he should wish for a beautiful girl. The genie gives him a sneak peek at a beautiful dancer. "If I wish for her, she would be mine from now on?" Forry asks.

"From now on," said the genie. "But you must decide soon. I grow impatient."

"Well, I can't decide so quickly. I — I need time to think. This is too much pressure! Make me a martini!"

There is a puff of smoke, and a martini appears in the chair where Forry was sitting. The genie drinks it, and the film fades out.

Bjo later married John Trimble and she became a famous science fiction fan. She

4. The 1950s

worked for Gene Roddenberry's Lincoln Enterprises, a mail-order *Star Trek* merchandise company, in the sixties. Bjo and John Trimble were instrumental during the late 1960s in organizing a successful letter-writing campaign to persuade Desilu to not cancel *Star Trek*. In more recent decades Bjo Trimble has authored *The Star Trek Concordance* and *On the Good Ship Enterprise*.

In 1954 Forry and Wendy were driving along a busy street listening to the car radio. Forry heard the term "hi-fi" and thought, "sci-fi." And a new term was created. He began to use it and it caught on quickly. In less than a year the term was becoming used all over the world. Forry did indeed create "sci-fi," as revealed by research of the official Heinlein Archives by Christopher Kovacs. Robert A. Heinlein had actully used the term "sci-fic," commonly in use in science fiction circles of the time, in private correspondence, instead of "sci-fi," as erroneously reported.

Forry traveled to New York City in 1956 to attend the World Science Fiction Convention and it was there that he received a phone call from George Orick, who wanted him to be the editor of a magazine called *Sci-Fi*. It was the dream of a lifetime for Forry and, naturally, he jumped at the chance to meet with Orick and his partners. Forry arranged with some artists of his acquaintance to do some mock covers. The company which wanted to publish *Sci-Fi* was, at that time, publishing a magazine entitled *Smart Money*. Unfortunately, *Smart Money* did not bring in enough money and it folded soon after. Forry's dream project of editing a science fiction magazine went out the window.

Reeling from this major disappointment, he remained busy with his agenting work. Forry and Robert A. Heinlein, formerly friends, had drifted apart and for some reason they could never agree on anything anymore when they spoke at club meetings of the LASFS. Forry wrote Heinlein a note in 1956 which explained that he was a huge admirer of his work but the two of them seemingly could not get along anymore and so may as well give up on each other. "You have your friends and I have mine and I'm sure we have plenty to do," he wrote. So, for years, they would only nod at each other when their paths crossed.

Forry had a big scare in 1957, as he liked to recount in one of his oft-told stories, when he received an angry telephone call from the famed author.

"Why did you accept my Hugo in absentia and never say anything to me about it?" Robert A. Heinlein asked him.

Forry was totally confused by the accusation and said, "I — I will look into it, but I don't remember taking your Hugo at all." He asked Wendy, "Honey, did I ever have Heinlein's Hugo?"

She replied in the negative.

Forry then telephoned Isaac Asimov and said in desperation, "Help! Save my life! Tell me I didn't take Heinlein's Hugo!" Isaac didn't remember any such incident. He did recall, however, that Robert Bloch was the master of ceremonies and he would have been the man who presented the Hugos. He should ask him. Bloch could not recollect, but told Forry to ask David Kyle.

Forry called David Kyle and woke him up, since David was in England at the time and it was early morning there. "Dave! Tell me I didn't take Heinlein's Hugo at last year's Worldcon! He says I did!"

Instead of being furious at him for waking him, David began chuckling.

"Dave!" Forry protested. "This call is costing me money! What is so funny?"

"Don't you remember?" David said. "That was the time the Hugos did not get delivered on time to the convention. We had nothing to give to anyone so you could not have taken the Hugo!"

Forry was not sure that Heinlein was going to accept this as anything but hearsay, but David Kyle remembered that a Franklin Dietz had taped the whole convention.

Forry called Dietz and said, "Save my life! Find those tapes and listen to see if I ever said anything like 'I accept this Hugo on behalf of Robert A. Heinlein!'"

Dietz was too busy to do that for many months and it actually took a year for him to find the tapes among the many recordings he had made. After that, Forry wrote Robert Heinlein and told him what really happened and asked him why he had the idea in the first place that he had his Hugo. Cyril Kornbluth, as it happened, was the party who had told him that Ackerman did not give it to him. Unfortunately, he had died quite young (in 1957) and so there was no way to confirm or deny the rumor. Things unfortunately did not improve between Forry and the author of *Have Spacesuit, Will Travel*, even after this discovery. Forry was to learn a valuable lesson soon thereafter.

The editor of a new magazine, with the title *Vertex Science Fiction*, called Forry and asked him if he could arrange for an interview with Robert A. Heinlein. Meanwhile, they had gone ahead and placed Heinlein's name on the cover because they were so certain he would consent. Forry was not sure that this was a good idea, especially since Heinlein had declined to give Forry his phone number. "Well," Forry said, taking a chance, "he was just interviewed by *Playboy*." Heinlein had only consented to the interview if the magazine had paid for it and this, Forry had been told, had been the first time that *Playboy* had ever paid for an interview. Forry advised the editor that Heinlein would probably only allow an interview if he received payment.

The editor called Forry again soon afterward and said that they had reached Heinlein, and he did not wish to be interviewed. Could Forry help them in some way? They already had his name mentioned on the cover.

Forry thought of the guest of honor speech, "Discovery of the Future," that the author had given in 1941, and he had a copy of it. He cautioned the editor that if it was published in their magazine, even though it was not copyrighted, they should pay Heinlein. Forry surmised that maybe Heinlein should have no objections, since if Walt Daugherty had not taken the trouble of recording it, there would be no record of it in any event. Forry would be paid and he would give 85 percent of the proceeds to Heinlein and it was a win-win situation for everyone. He was wrong. Heinlein wrote him when it was published a year later and after he had received his $230, and expressed his outrage at having something published without his consent. To make matters worse, he was not even paid the full $250 from the publisher!

4. The 1950s

Forry explained to him that he had hoped that the magazine would have paid Heinlein directly but they had paid him instead, assuming incorrectly that he was acting as agent. Forry had allocated $25 to Daugherty since he had recorded the original talk and thus was entitled to something. Forry, then, had actually lost money, but Heinlein was convinced that Forry had only sent him the money because he felt guilty.

Despite all of the problems, Forry still held the author in high regard and was impressed with his lack of racial bias. When Forry was in Heinlein's presence he had opportunities to see him several times express his displeasure when someone would make a racial slur or treat African Americans in a dismissive manner. The author of some of the greatest science fiction ever written always treated everyone with courtesy.

Forry began a correspondence with a German science fiction fan named Walter Ernsting of Germany back in the 1950s and helped Ernsting found the Science Fiction Club Deutchland. There was no German science fiction being produced during the fifties, and it appeared that American science fiction was most popular, so Ernsting used a pen name, Clark Darlton. He began to write a series on a hero named Perry Rhodan, a name derived from the name of a Japanese giant monster from a recent film.

Science fiction in the 1950s was a major genre in the movie theaters, with a new release every several weeks. Forry himself was becoming responsible for making some of this happen. The 1953 Hammer science fiction production *Four Sided Triangle*, as well as *This Island, Earth*, became realities because Forry acted as the agent for their original authors. He represented authors selling scripts to episodes of TV's *Science Fiction Theater* and *Four Star Theater*. Charles Beaumont, Kris Neville, Nelson S. Bond, and Emil Petaja were clients. Forry was also seeing some remarkable successes being made by his friends, Ray Harryhausen and Ray Bradbury.

The Beast from 20,000 Fathoms was the first full-length effort by Ray Harryhausen. The animator had previously done short wartime training films, some advertising films, his *Mother Goose* series and a good deal of the animation for the 1949 RKO production of *Mighty Joe Young*. *Earth Versus the Flying Saucers*, produced by Harryhausen along with Charles H. Schneer in 1956, was bringing the audiences to theaters to watch devastation wreaked by alien invaders. The monsters had come back to the motion picture screen, and instead of Gothic terrors like vampires, they were hostile Martians (George Pal's *War of the Worlds*), giant irradiated octopuses (*It Came from Beneath the Sea*) and huge mutated ants (*Them!*).

In the latter part of the 1950s, Gothic-style monster movies with werewolves and vampires returned to America. A similar craze had come to Mexico about four years previously and there had been a revival of classic-style Gothic monster films with titles like *The Resuscitated Monster*.

Many factors combined to create the monster boom.

Forry may not have realized it at the time, but he had connections with the return of the classic Gothic monster to the screen through his old high school. Forry's Balboa High classmate Jim Nicholson teamed up with attorney Samuel Arkoff to form American-International Pictures in 1955. They specialized in inexpensively produced films that were intended to appeal to a teenaged audience. One of their earliest films was entitled *Blood of Dracula*. The most famous of their early efforts was the cleverly titled 1957 release *I Was a Teenage Werewolf*. In this film, newcomer Michael Landon is a troubled teen who goes to a psychologist at the insistence of his teachers. Unfortunately, the psychologist is, shall we say, unconventional. He uses hypnotism and various treatments to turn him into a werewolf when he hears a bell ring. This picture was a very successful moneymaker for American-International, and they followed it up with such entertaining movies as *How to Make a Monster*.

The motion picture industry was becoming aware of a very interesting fact; teenagers had money and they wanted to spend it. They constituted a large portion of the moviegoing audience, and they liked thrilling, chilling melodrama. The time was becoming right for *Famous Monsters of Filmland* magazine.

Screen Gems, the distributors of Columbia Pictures' films for television, put together a syndication package in 1957 called *Shock Theatre*. Fifty stations purchased the *Shock Theatre* package in October of that year. Their general managers were amazed at how ratings soared for these films in their late-night time slots. Then, something different was added to help keep the audiences there.

Young Philadelphia TV personality John Zacherle was hired to be a comic host to introduce films in the syndication package at WCAU TV in 1957. He portrayed a "cool ghoul" by the name of Roland. Horror hosts were uncommon but not nonexistent prior to 1957. In 1953 a host named Bob Dalton of WTOP-TV (now WUSA) in Washington, D.C., did atmospheric live cutaways between the episodes of *Tales of the Black Cat*, a CBS-filmed television series. In general format, the WTOP-TV program was similar to a horror-hosted movie, although it did not involve monster movies.[5]

A very early and groundbreaking horror host by the name of Vampira had appeared for the Hollywood premiere of *The Black Sleep* several years before. Maila Nurmi had had a very short stint of only one year when she appeared on a Los Angeles television station from 1954 through 1955 as the alluring Vampira to introduce horror films in a format entitled *Nightmare* in the pre–*Shock Theatre* days. But the zany John Zacherle was the first to have staying power.

Famous Monsters of Filmland was in the making.

James Warren of Topton, Pennsylvania, was an ambitious and energetic young man working in advertising. He felt that his career as Assistant Advertising Manager of the Caloric Appliance Corporation was not taking him where he wanted to go. He had graduated from the Philadelphia Museum School of Art and had also studied at the Charles Morris School of Advertising. Warren's bachelor of arts degree was in advertising and he was getting bored with Caloric. The dark-haired, handsome bachelor liked the *Playboy* style expressed by Hugh Hefner and he wanted to publish a magazine like *Playboy*. He created his own company and called it Jay Publications, publishing *After Hours* magazine. The colorful red, white and black covers promised interesting men's material inside. Like *Playboy*, Warren's *After Hours* had articles on celebrities of the day as well as nude photo spreads. Magazines like this one were very common and prominent in

4. The 1950s

the late 1950s, a time when being a "swinging bachelor" with a "pad" to attract "chicks" was fashionable. Reading magazines like *Playboy* added to the mystique.

Forry was selling his clients' stories to the new magazine and writing them, too. Only four issues were printed, but not before Forry's own article "Scream-O-Scope Is Here!" ran.

It is a good thing Forry knew how to read French, because one day he was in France and something on a newsstand caught his eye. It was a magazine called *Cinema 57*. What attracted Forry's attention was no doubt the *Werewolf of London* headshot on the cover. He sent it to Jim Warren. As it happened, James Warren had also seen a copy of this magazine and he also read French. Warren called him on the phone and said that he had suspended publication of *After Hours*, as it had been a financial failure. He had enough assets to do a one-shot magazine on movie monsters because of the monster craze raking in the coin at the theaters and keeping kiddies' eyes glued to their television sets at home. Warren wanted to get permission to do an English-language version of *Cinema 57* for Central Publishing, Warren's new company. Forry and Jim Warren investigated the possibility and were discouraged from doing so when they realized that the text was scholarly and not at all something that a teenager would like to read. No one person owned the rights to the stills used in the magazine and they would have to contact dozens of collectors and owners of these photos. In addition, the magazine was devoted to film of all genres; this was its only horror genre issue.

James Warren asked Forry to assist. Forry said he could do more than just assist in the production of the magazine. He was quite knowledgeable about motion pictures of a fantasy and horror nature, had been collecting stills, lobby cards and posters since 1930, and knew a hundred or more people in the field of fantastic film and television. Forry was the agent for a hundred or more authors, and had tens of thousands of stills for use in the pages of the proposed one-shot. They would not run out of material; there would be material left over for 20 or 30 more such magazines!

"Well, Warren was skeptical, he wondered if this Ackerman fellow was just full of hot air, so he told me that he planned to fly out to Los Angeles to see all this for himself," Forry related in a 1985 interview with San Diego Comic-Con organizer Shel Dorf. "I met Jim Warren at the airport and took him to my house. As it turned out, I learned later that he had been too broke to fly all the way from his home in Philadelphia, so he had taken the Greyhound bus to Las Vegas and from there flew out to Los Angeles International Airport to impress me." The original title of the magazine was to be *Wonderama*, a title Forry had always liked. But Kable News, which was to be the distributor for the magazine, did not approve of the title and suggested *Fantastic Monsters of Filmland*. Warren and Forry did not like that but they settled on *Famous Monsters of Filmland*. Forry was not altogether happy with the title or the concept of adolescent ridiculing of quality films like the *Creature from the Black Lagoon* or *Dr. Jekyll and Mr. Hyde*, and wished he could have edited *Wonderama* instead.[6]

The next week was spent with Jim Warren holding a sign in front of himself as Forry typed. The sign read, "I am eleven years old and I am your reader. Forrest J Ackerman, make me laugh!" Forry was a tireless punster from his young days, so creating jokes and amusing copy was not difficult.

The cover of *Famous Monsters of Filmland* had a blood-red backdrop with James Warren wearing a Frankenstein Monster mask and business suit with his girlfriend of the time, Phyllis Farkas, looking back at him over her bare shoulder with a smile. "Welcome, Monster Lovers!" the front page read. "Did your last date call you a monster? Do your friends think you're horrible? On Halloween, do they say 'take off your mask, Frankenstein!' when you are not wearing a mask?"[7]

There was a letter-writing contest for teenagers to submit essays on their favorite monsters, in an effort to create a fun atmosphere.

Jim Warren arranged with the *Shock Theatre* promotional staff to run a plug for *Famous Monsters of Filmland* in their episodes, and in exchange, he would promote *Shock Theatre* in the magazine.[8] The first print-run of the new one-shot was to have a test market in Philadelphia and New York City. One hundred and fifty thousand copies were produced. The first issue of *Famous Monsters of Filmland* sold out under very adverse conditions. A blizzard had gripped the Northeast for its first week of sales. Despite this, sales were very strong. Letters came pouring into Warren's offices literally by the thousands. There were 117,305 issues printed for other cities across the nation, and the company was encouraged to come out with issue number two. This one had Warren on the cover, again wearing a suit and a different monster mask, sitting cross-legged on the floor. It was another big success, though not as huge as the first. It had a print run of 200,000 but only sold 95,000 copies, so the third issue had a print run of 150,000 copies. James felt that a new imitator, *World Famous Creatures*, recently appearing on newsstands (and, incredibly, distributed by Kable News) was the reason for the decreased sales of *FM*.

Warren sued the publishers for plagiarism but a judge ruled in favor of *World Famous Creatures*. The imitator magazine did not last long, in any event.[9]

James Warren himself painted the cover for the third issue, a vivid portrait of the Lon Chaney, Phantom.

Forry desired to carry on the tradition used by his favorite science fiction magazines he read avidly as a boy; namely, the letter columns. The letter column for *Famous Monsters of Filmland* was dubbed "Fang Mail."

Letters indeed began to come in from all over the world from eager readers wanting to know when issue number four of *Famous Monsters of Filmland* was due. It was a quarterly magazine for some years and in 1961 went to a bimonthly publishing schedule. The covers for issues number four through eight were by artist Albert Nuetzell, a client of Forry's for many years and a close friend. He was the father of author Charles Nuetzel, who had used Forry as his literary agent. Another well-regarded artist was Vic Presio. Basil Gogos did 16 covers for the magazine in the early days; these covers are among the most famous, striking and beloved of all *Famous Monsters* covers.[10] Later, he continued to paint more covers for *Famous Monsters*. He has since lent his striking artistic gifts to *Monsterscene* and to *Rue Morgue*.

4. The 1950s

Famous Monsters of Filmland made it possible for other Warren projects to come into being. James Warren put his marketing background to work and came up with various contests to attract the young readers to purchase the magazine. He also formed the Captain Company, which sold some interesting items in the back of *Famous Monsters of Filmland*. Giant rubber flies, just the thing to scare girls with on the playground, tiny movie projectors, and Frankenstein monster posters were popular items.

By 1958 Forry was also beginning to get very busy with editing other Warren periodicals. Forry had to write about film genres in which he was not interested for Warren's *Screen Thrills Illustrated* and *Favorite Westerns of Filmland*, renamed *Wildest Westerns*. *Wildest Westerns* only lasted for a half-dozen issues, and *Screen Thrills Illustrated* held on until 1965.

The articles he wrote for

Basil Gogos has been a popular convention guest at classic horror conventions around the world. Gogos painted some of the most memorable covers for *Famous Monsters of Filmland* (David Hawk).

the French magazine *V* were similar to what he was writing for Warren Publishing Company. Tadao Tomomatsu, North Hollywood–based television actor as well as archivist for the Los Angeles Science Fantasy Society, shared with the author a real gem of information — a photocopy of an article Forry wrote for this now-extinct periodical entitled "*V59.*" The emphasis on semi-nude females notwithstanding, the monster movie photos selected, the puns and the alliterations were very like the style Forry was using in *Famous Monsters of Filmland*.[11]

In the late 1950s Forry befriended an eccentric San Francisco–based musician named Anton Szandor LeVey (Howard Stanton Levey), who at that time was running a "salon" in his home that was dedicated to fantasy and science fiction and was popular among writers and fans. LeVey played the Wurlitzer at the Lost Weekend Cocktail Lounge in Alameda.

Walter Daugherty photographed Forry filing in his office at the 915 South Sherbourne Drive address where he and Wendy lived in the 1950s and 1960s (Mary Ellen Daugherty [Mrs. Walter J. Daugherty]).

Wendy visited the salon and was horrified when LeVey introduced them to his pet lion, Togare. And Forry petted it! It was not until 1959 or 1960 that LeVey apparently decided that more "devilish" fun could be available if he was the head of a church for Satanism. He became quite well known for his many books and for his TV appearances on *The Tonight Show* promoting Satan worship. Forry felt that LeVey was a harmless

4. The 1950s

entertainer and seemed to admire his interest in science fiction and his skill as a musician. Forry did not attend the Satanic ceremonies as he did not believe in Satan or devils, or any deities. He felt Satan was as fully fictional a character as Jehovah or Allah. Forry tended to make little mention in later years that he was ever friends with Anton LeVey.

The home at Sherbourne became so filled with props, books, stills and other memorabilia by the late 1950s that the Ackermans actually lived in an apartment and continued to own the home at Sherbourne. Michael Porjes, Forry's stepson, was beginning to have major conflicts with Forry. After one major blowup with the boy, Forry told Wendy that he had had it and gave her an ultimatum: either Michael went, or he went. She decided to leave and take her son. Forry and Wendy separated and divorced in the late 1950s.

The couple did not stay divorced for long, however. They began seeing each other again in various friends' homes, and began going to the movies together. It wasn't long after that Wendy and Forry remarried and began life together anew. She taught French and German at a nearby university and had real property elsewhere, which she rented. This, added to Forry's agenting and editing, provided them with a comfortable income.

As the 1950s drew to a close, Forry decided that science fiction fans should have their own award honoring them, not for professional achievements, but for the thoughtful things they did for fandom. The E. Everett Evans Big Heart Award was thus instituted. Some recipients since that beginning award of 1959 have included E.E. (Doc) Smith in 1959, Janie Lamb in 1969, Robert Madle in 1974, Andre Norton in 1988, and Filthy Pierre in 2004.[12]

5
The 1960s — Forrest J Ackerman, Movie Actor

Forry was writing well-illustrated "filmbooks" (including one on the 1925 *The Lost World*) for the early issues of *Famous Monsters of Filmland* with materials he had accumulated from a lifetime of collecting. No other magazine editor was doing anything else quite like this. Of a certainty, several publishers came out with very similar magazines after the word got out that *FM* was a top seller. In the late 1950s and early 1960s a number of magazines on the subject of movie and television monsters showed up on magazine stands all over the world. These included titles like *Horror Monsters, Castle of Frankenstein, Fantastic Monsters of the Films* (published by movie monster makeup and prop designer Paul Blaisdell) *Monster Parade, Gore Creatures* (later to become *Midnight Marquee*, the longest continually running classic horror genre magazine in existence) and *For Monsters Only*. Only *Gore Creatures/Midnight Marquee* lasted for many years although contributors to *Horror Monsters*, in particular, took pains to do research on the careers of various horror actors and include interviews and filmographies. The subject matter was considered unworthy by a good many people, including film scholars and sixth grade schoolteachers. The schoolteachers confiscated the horror film magazines in mass quantities. In reality there was little scholarly film study until the 1960s. Persons who were seriously researching the history of the studios and their products were usually doing catalogues as employees of studio vaults. There was the occasional book such as the German *Magic and Myth of the Movies* (1947) and Myne Publishing's *Peter*, a lengthy 1944 "biography" of the animal star Peter the Great, illustrated with stills from films starring the canine hero, films that would (with one exception) be lost forever.

In general, however, books on film and filmmaking were rare until the late 1960s and early 1970s. Anthony Amaral's 1967 *Movie Horses: Their Treatment and Training* was an early book for young people on the technical side of animal wrangling and training. Carlos Clarens' *Illustrated History of the Horror Films*, an essential in college libraries, was not to be published until the early 1970s. Another influential early book was *Tarzan of the Movies*, an illustrated history of all Tarzan films to 1971, written by Gabe Essoe. Forry actually assisted Mr. Essoe with research for this tome.

A visit to a small town library prior to 1970 in search of serious books and magazines on film would in all likelihood leave a person empty handed. What was a young person to do? If said young person chose the subject of film history or filmmaking technology for a school paper, he or she was not likely to find much material unless a relative happened to work in the movie theaters and gave them press kits, or knew someone in the movie industry who would sit down with them and explain how these things were done. The days of *The Boy's Cinema*, a British newspaper on motion pictures aimed specifically at young people, were decades in the past. The movie star magazines sold at newsstands in the 1950s and 1960s focused on the lifestyles of the prominent stars and starlets of the day and would not be of any help if a young person wanted even bare-bones information on how the effects were achieved to make Claude Rains appear transparent in *The Invisible Man* or how James Bond accomplished his amazing stunts in *You Only Live Twice*. To learn about such technical subjects the child would either have to rely on rare books like the Anthony Amaral horse training book mentioned above or would have to read *Famous Monsters of Filmland*, and the majority of the teachers and librarians disapproved heartily of the latter material. Most educators judged the book by its cover and these covers sported vivid paintings of slavering werewolves and man-eating plants. *Famous Monsters of Filmland* was the main source for movie mavens who wanted to know about the life stories of actors Christopher Lee or Edward Van Sloan. *Screen Thrills Illustrated*, Warren's magazine on serials and action films, could shed some light on how one stuntman appeared able to toss an entire barroom full of cowboys on their ears. These other magazines had their own staff writers, although Forry was occasionally called upon to write for this and for Warren Publishing Company's *Wildest Westerns*, although he took no interest in Westerns and was only somewhat interested in serials.

By now, an estimated 2,000,000 children and young adults were purchasing *Famous Monsters of Filmland* magazine. Mark McGee, Ron Haydock, Bill Warren, Joe Dante, and Paul Blaisdell all wrote for the magazine, although Forry wrote most of it.

In 1962 Forry recorded *Music for Robots* for Science Fiction Records. Side one is the 18-minute "The Tin Age Story" which he narrates. Side two is Frank Coe's electronic music which is presumably the sort of music robots will listen to when they begin to become sophisticated enough to listen to music. Forry's face, overlaid on a B-movie style robotic body, adorns the black-and-white cover.

The early 1960s brought amazing scientific breakthroughs to America and the world. The International Geophysical Year brought about unparalled cooperation between nations to explore the ocean floor and for the first time it was discovered that there were mountain ranges beneath the sea. The first living human being from Earth to travel in space was a Russian named Yuri Gagarin. He was the first living being to go into space and safely return. Several animals had been sent into space and never had a chance to return. In 1961 American astronaut Allan Shepard was sent into orbit and spent a short time in space.

"Telstar," a hit instrumental recorded by the British group The Tornados, was on radios all over the world in 1962. It was an ode to the first communications satellite launched, the American Telstar. Forry was quite excited about the space age, as it served as a real life proof that the marvels he and his friends had dreamed would some day come to pass were becoming as real and as current as the morning news! It was also gratifying to him to know that teenaged Judy Jetson on the popular Hanna-Barbera television cartoon series of the time, *The Jetsons*, mentioned in one episode that she had to finish her Modern Esperanto homework!

A wonderful opportunity to be with his heroes of childhood afforded itself when *Amazing Stories* celebrated its 35th anniversary in 1961, and Forry traveled to Newark, New Jersey, to attend this event. He found himself seated between Hugo Gernsback and Frank R. Paul, and was among those invited to come up to the podium to speak.[1]

Forry's talk consisted of reading the letter he had written in 1929 to *Science Wonder Stories*, which was partially reproduced in Chapter One.

In the spring of 1961 Forry began editing *Spacemen*. There were eight regular issues of *Spacemen* and a Yearbook.[2] In the premiere issue, July, Forry and James Warren introduced readers to the new periodical: "If you're interested in Space—and frankly we can't understand how any red-blooded American or green-blooded Martian (and we expect to have readers in both classes) couldn't be—this is the indispensable magazine for you."[3]

"Collision Course: There Is Nowhere to Hide ... When Worlds Collide!" was one feature in issue one. "Space Monsterama" was an attempt to lure *FM* readers. Advertisements in the back of the magazine offered a star-finder and home planetarium, a $2-satellite space balloon that was actual Air Force surplus, and a wireless telephone powered by solar energy. "Don't Miss the Space Boat," Forry admonished the readers, urging them to subscribe. "For 35 years Editor Forrest J Ackerman has been interested in the fantasy of space.... With every 35¢ you invest in SPACEMEN you are in effect picking 35 years' worth of FJA's brains (both of them)."[4]

The editing brought in twice as much as the agenting work. Forry also edited *Monster World* which was a companion magazine for *Famous Monsters*. Wendy was making a good living as a professor of foreign languages at the local East Los Angeles Junior College. Through his writing, agenting work and interviewing industry folk for *Famous Monsters*, Forry befriended practically everyone in the field of horror and science fiction film. He met George Pal, Curtis Harrington, and many other notables as he made his rounds in Hollywood. Thus, he was now doing a form of public relations work, the thing he had wanted to do for a favorite star. The difference was that he was being paid by Central (now Warren) Publishing Company to do the public relations work for motion pictures and television programs.

Forry was now aware that the majority of his *Famous Monsters of Filmland* readers were pre-teen children. He gave himself the nickname "Uncle Forry" for the young readers to use to refer to him. He wanted to be thought of as the kind host who would take their imaginations on wondrous journeys through unknown worlds of fear and wonderment, and in the process, learn that the Fearsome Green Head that made them hide their eyes in the movie theater was actually, behind the curtain, genial, harmless "humbugs" called the "makeup men," the "special effects providers," the "actors," the

5. The 1960s

"sound technicians," the "prop men," and the "Foley artists." *In Famous Monsters'* pages, they would learn that monsters were made, not by mad scientists, but by movie makers.

Some of the children then decided that they would be monster makers themselves when they grew up. Many of them followed through on their plans and began making amateur movies with the help of their relatives and friends.

It was in 1963 that Forry and Wendy embarked on a journey of 8,700 miles cross-country, of their own volition, to meet readers of *Famous Monsters of Filmland* on their own home turfs. Forrest and Wendy were planning to attend the World Science Fiction convention in New York City and instead of flying to New York, they thought they would stop at various readers' homes on their way east, burning up a great deal of time on the journey. *Famous Monsters of Filmland* ran an advertisement with a cheery 47-year-old Forry's face with a cartoon body, driving a cartoon jalopy. It read: "How Would You Like Mister Monster in Your Own Home?"[5]

This is an unusual thing for the editor of a magazine for children to do. If anyone reading this biography knows of the editors of *Jack and Jill*, *Highlights for Children*, *Ranger Rick*, *Tiger Beat* or any other magazine for young people going out at their own expense to make a journey by automobile across the continent, to Pennsylvania and to New York, to cities and remote ranches of Kansas to meet their readers, please feel free to contact me through the publisher. I seriously have my doubts that any other children's magazine editor has ever taken the time to do this; however I could be mistaken.

Forry received requests from 1,200 readers of the magazine but could only visit about 80 or so, and no more. One lad who sent him a letter was Daniel C. Kirk of Columbus, Ohio. He would try to have 20 to 50 local fans at his home to meet Forry and his wife, Wendy, and he would throw a party with lunch included. Wendy was the navigator for the trip. She planned the route and arranged for hotels and motels for them en route. Forry did stop by the home of Daniel Kirk and was crowned "King for a Day" by the enthusiastic young boys and girls who entertained him. A look at Daniel's collection in his bedroom showed that he was quite the collector of movie-related lobby cards and press book photos even as a boy. Many years later the grown-up Daniel was reunited with Forry Ackerman at a convention and will never forget both encounters.

Forry met hundreds of eager young boys and girls on that trip. Some gatherings were not as productive, however, as that visit with Daniel Kirk. One young fan promised Forry in a letter, "If you can come to my home, I will have fifty for you!" Well, when Wendy and Forry arrived at the little farm they found 50 all right — one boy and 49 sheep.

While on this trip, Forry recalled that the author of "The Thought Monster" lived in Pennsylvania. Wendy and Forry looked her up. Amelia Reynolds Long had written a 1930 *Weird Tales* story that the Ackerman Agency brokered for her, securing motion picture rights. The film was released as *Fiend Without a Face*. The story was one of only ten she had published during her lifetime.

Famous Monsters was becoming a solid fixture on the magazine stands and had, by 1963, outlasted most of its competitors. "Dean of the Horror Directors: Tod Browning"

```
                                            Daniel C. Kirk
                                            1255 Marble Drive
                                            Columbus 27, Ohio

   Dear Furry, (Oops! I mean Forry)
        If you came through Columbus, Ohio, I could have about 20 of
   my friends here. We could accommodate another 50 of your Columbus
   fans. My age is 11 and my guests would be from 8 to 12. We live
   7 miles east of the center of town. When you arrive in Columbus
   call Don Kirk at BE 5-4568 and he'll give you directions to get to
   our house.
        We don't have home movies, but wall of ads from press books. I
   have all the plastic monster models (gorgeously gruesome thanks to
   my magnificent choice of colors and exellent painting job. I have
   $52.00 worth of monster books and magazines, a mummy in a hand made
   case (the mummy is hand made too), two beasts from the planet
   Cambridge, an old man's head, and six masks. I was on television
   last year with my monster collection. My room is so scary that
   my mother won't come in to clean it. Oh Well! The cob webs from
   my pet spiders add to the effect.
        My family and I have had a spook room at my school canival for
   the past two years. We charged 10¢ admission and made over a hundred
   dollars each year. All this in a period of four hours.
        We will serve you a lovely meal when you come.

            Here is the menu for Forry's Feast

                    warm blood soup (98.6°)
                    moulded salad
                    Hungarian Ghoulash
                    Sppok-etti
                    Garlic bread (to keep vampires away. If you eat
                                  enough you'll keep everyone away.)
                    Devil's Food Cake and I scream (translation- ice cream)

   A feast fit for the KING- of all monster and other magazine editors.

   I hope I'll be seeing you soon.
                            Your greatest fan,
```

Daniel Kirk of Columbus, Ohio, was just a young boy bitten by the monster bug when he wrote his letter to Forry in 1963 (Daniel Kirk).

was a typical article that educated readers about the history of film. "Monster Kicks on Route 66" was an interesting feature on the *Route 66* television episode in which Boris Karloff, Peter Lorre and Lon Chaney, Jr. appear as themselves, trying out horror makeups and techniques on the attendees of a secretaries' convention to see if the old monsters indeed never grow stale. "Headlines from Horrorsville" was one of the regular columns. In the March 1965 issue, number 32, the "Master Model Maker Winners" showcased the winners of a customized monster model contest. The grand prize winner was Greg Gellman. He won a free trip to Hollywood, California. State winners included Pam Michals of Phoenix, Arizona, Michael Leonard of Lancaster, Pennsylvania, Robert Dunton of Cambridge, Massachusetts, and Judson M. Terrell, III of Laurens, South Carolina.

One little reader did something that really touched Forry. He sent off a request for a photo of Forry and a note which read, "I send you this penny out of my love."[6]

A young man who would become a dear friend of Forry moved from Oregon to Hollywood in the mid–1960s. Bill Warren decided to look up Forry when he and his fiancée, Beverly, moved there. He had become familiar with the name Forrest J Ackerman from a magazine he purchased from the newsstand in his small town back in the 1950s. The magazine was not *Famous Monsters*, but the short-lived science fiction magazine *Imaginative Tales*. Bill was working for an insurance company

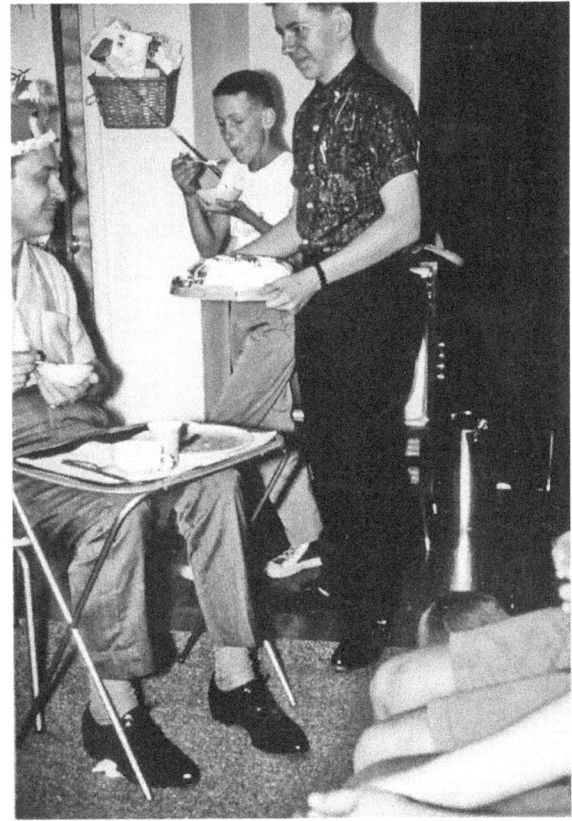

Top: Wendy and Forry Ackerman flank Daniel Kirk as his friend and some other children look on (Daniel Kirk). *Right:* Daniel Kirk serves cake to the King for a Day as his friend gobbles ice cream (Daniel Kirk).

Daniel Kirk shows Forry around his collection of lobby cards (Daniel Kirk).

5. The 1960s

when he first moved to Los Angeles, and he joined the Los Angeles Science Fantasy Society in 1966. Later, Bill went to work for Forry, doing secretarial work and anything else he needed to help keep his boss's increasingly busy personal appearance schedule in order.

When Forry met the soon to be famous Donald A. Reed for the first time in 1963 Donald was just a man of 28, knocking on Forry's door and telling him that he was to receive the very first Ann Radcliffe Award from the Count Dracula Society, his own society that he had founded. Forry joined the Count Dracula Society and became a vocal supporter. (Ann Radcliffe was a 19th century author of gothic horror novels. Boris Karloff was likewise awarded an Ann Radcliffe Award from Donald.[7]) Donald had been born in New Orleans in 1935 and had moved to Los Angeles during the 1940s. He earned his doctorate in the 1960s and was a college professor at Valley College, Woodbury University, and Columbia College, where he taught library science. He also served as a substitute librarian. His passion was film, and he decided to do all that was humanly possible to promote it. Reed was a friend of the van Vogts, who attended his college commencement exercises in 1968. Once, in 1975, the Count Dracula Society's awards ceremony was nationally televised.

By now, Walt Daugherty was doing almost all of the special photography for *Famous Monsters of Filmland*, covering film festivals and various promotional shoots sponsored by the studios. Forry routinely interviewed producers and special effects artists at the studios, and before long was invited to be in several motion pictures as an extra. One was *The Time Travelers*, directed by Ib Melchior for American-International Pictures.

The Time Travelers concerned a team of scientists at a university experi-

Dr. Donald A. Reed was the founder of the Count Dracula Society and the Academy of Science Fiction, Fantasy and Horror Films (Mary Ellen Daugherty [Mrs. Walter J. Daugherty]).

Walter J. Daugherty photographed Boris Karloff (left) and Forry together in the late 1960s (Jerald K. Smith).

menting with a viewer which shows scenes from the future. In the course of their experiments, one of the scientists, Steve (Phillip Carey), pushes a lever all the way to see what it will do, much to the dismay of fellow scientist Carol White (Merry Anders). The result is the opening of what looks like a dimensional screen to a future barren landscape. A curious janitor in the room (Steve Franken) walks right through it and thus it is dis-

To add a human touch Forry had Walt Daugherty photograph him vacuuming his collection at his original Ackermansion (Mary Ellen Daugherty [Mrs. Walter J. Daugherty]).

The caption, written by Forry Ackerman, reads, "For my pal Walto — World's Greatest Forry-tographer! On my 50th birthday" (Mary Ellen Daugherty [Mrs. Walter J. Daugherty]).

covered that the viewer is not a viewer at all. It is the actual campus landscape outside the walls of the laboratory, and they are in the future! The impulsive Danny hurries off to explore and the scientists go after him, only to find that the dimensional doorway is collapsing. They are stuck in the future time.

There had been a terrible war and all that was left of humanity are now deformed, mentally-deficient mutants and a small colony of "normals." The latter live underground, where they are building a starship which will, they hope, take them to a habitable planet in another star system they have discovered using their telescopes and spectroscopes. Our 20th century scientists are invited to join them.

Forry plays a robotics technician who has a few lines about "keeping our spacemen happy, keeping everything squared away," and at one point he grabs a gun when it is discovered that a security breach has taken place in the stronghold and some mutants have invaded.

Another notable role for Forry in the 1960s was that of a biology technician in *Queen of Blood*, directed by Curtis Harrington and released by American-International Pictures. Charles Nuetzel had written the original novel on which *Queen of Blood* was based. Forry was able to have several good non-dialogue scenes with Basil Rathbone at a scientific research center in the distant year of 1990, launching a ship to one of Mars's moons where it is discovered that a seemingly benevolent alien race has landed. Dennis Hopper and John Saxon go to the moon to find the aliens and see that only one has survived a terrible crash — a strange, silent, pale blue-green female (Florence Marly) who gets very upset if they attempt to do any scientific tests that involve a needle. She is more than just enigmatic, she is the queen of blood! Does science prevail, or will scientific curiosity be the undoing of us all, including Forry's character in the film?

Forry became fast friends with Florence Marly and she was a frequent guest at the Ackermansion. One evening, he decided to help make a connection between her and Fritz Lang, who was at that time unattached and complaining that the only women he seemed to attract were brainless gold diggers. Forry assured him that Florence was far from a gold digger and was, in fact, very cultured and intelligent. He introduced the two during a double date with himself and Wendy at a good restaurant. Lang seemed impatient with Marly, and at one point she began to venture an observation on some piece of artwork she had seen. His hand flew across her mouth in a gesture that made it clear that he did not want her to talk. "Woman! We don't want to hear from you!"

Florence told Forry she was hurt and perplexed by the behavior of the famed director. She kept quiet for the rest of her date and was eager for it to be over. At the end of the evening, Lang took her hand and Forry thought, at least, we can end this evening on a better note, as Lang is going to give her a continental kiss on the hand. Instead he bit it!

The monster craze continued on, with monster comic books, monster games, monster toys, monster television programs (*The Outer Limits*, *The Munsters* and *The Addams Family*) and the still-popular *Shock Theatre* syndication package. Forry covered the new

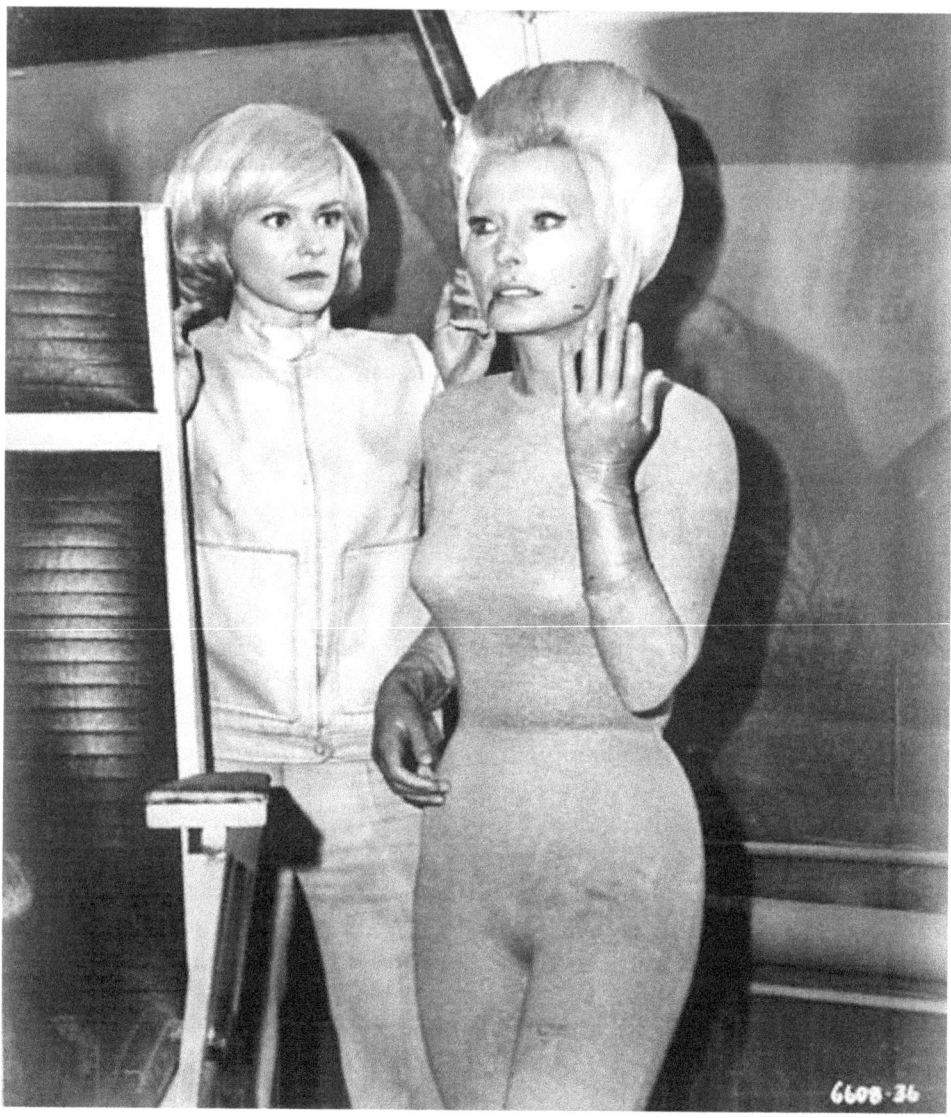

Judi Meredith (left), a scientist on a spaceship in American International's *Queen of Blood*, looks aghast at the hungry expression on the mysterious, silent female alien's (Florence Marly's) face. Forry had a small role as a scientist in the film (American International Pictures).

Munsters television series for the magazine and met Fred Gwynne and the rest of the cast. It was a good time for Forry's and James Warren's magazine.

Perry Rhodan was becoming a name that would be important to Forry and Wendy when a German film produced in Italy titled *S.O.S. aus dem Weltraum*, was released in 1965 in its English version of *Mission Stardust*. Perry Rhodan is an American astronaut and the first man on the moon.

5. The 1960s

Walter Ernsting, the man who helped Forry bring *Perry Rhodan* to the English-speaking world, was finding huge success. Since 1961 the *Rhodan* series was available in Germany as a digest-sized pulp magazine. The series had been heavily influenced by Doc Smith's the Lensman series and by motion pictures of the 1950s. *Perry Rhodan* is to Germany what *Doctor Who* is to Britain, an amazingly durable science-fiction phenomenon. The original corps of four writers is no longer contributing.

Forry, who had helped Walter Ernsting strengthen German science-fiction fandom, met him for the first time in 1965, staying at his home during a European trip. During their visit, according to Forry, Ernsting gave him and Wendy a complete set of the series he had created in 1961 with assistance from K.H. Scheer. Ernsting volunteered Wendy for the task of translating the series into English and said he would ask Donald A. Wollheim, then an editor at Ace Books, if he thought the series might work for English-speaking audiences. It took several years for this idea to come to fruition.[8]

Forry began to show up in the oddest popular culture references. David McDaniel's *The Man from U.N.C.L.E.: The Vampire Affair* was a novel in Ace's series based on the popular television spy drama. Forry meets U.N.C.L.E. agents Napoleon Solo and Ilya Kuryakin in Brasov, Romania, in a public library where they are all coincidentally poring over books on vampire lore. It seems that Forry has decided that since the Trieste Film Festival he is attending is relatively close to Transylvania, he made a side trip to the legendary land of Vlad Dracul to research him. The agents are doing the same thing because of reports of strange people that turn into wolves. Forry may be of some help to Ilya and Napoleon and so they take him with him. They have been trying to track down a vicious murderer with the aid of a Romanian count, a descendant of Vlad Tepes, whom they have befriended.

"Forry Ackerman of America," Napoleon says to him, "Meet Count Zoltan Dracula of Pokul."

"Really?" Forry holds out his hand. "*Well, How about that!*"[9]

Lee Harris recalls that Forry and Wendy were in a group that sang Christmas carols at Pickfair on the grounds and Mary Pickford came to the window and told them how great they were. Thus, Forry met Mary Pickford, America's Sweetheart, although from a distance.

Forry's good friend, singer, composer and pianist Verne Langdon wrote a script that he hoped Boris Karloff might be interested in recording when he was in Los Angeles for a project. Many of the famed actor's recent films, such as *Comedy of Terrors*, were hilarious and there was often a droll humor displayed when Karloff introduced episodes of Boris Karloff's *Thriller* for television. Verne Langdon has provided this biographical work with the true story of *An Evening with Boris Karloff and His Friends*. "Of the very small number of friends I consider 'close' Forry was indeed counted among them," he told this author.

> From the day I met him I liked him, and the feeling was mutual.
> We first met in 1963 — before most of you reading this were even born — and our friendship continued until he breathed some of his final breaths, with Jim Warren and I

by his side. He'd sent for both of us—Joe Moe phoned to inform me Forry had decided not to fight any longer and was ready to meet Prince Sirki. I dropped everything and drove down to L.A. and Russell Avenue, and Jim caught the next plane out from Philadelphia. Half-a-day later we sat with Forry, reminiscing, singing Jolson songs, laughing, crying, and running through all the emotions you feel when someone you love is about to catch the bus to Foreverafter.

One of Forry's favorite stories was how he came to write the script for "An Evening with Boris Karloff and His Friends," the album Milt Larsen and I created in April of 1966 and later leased to Decca Records. Forry always began the story with how he'd just returned from a long flight and been awake for 48 hours straight and how exhausted he already was and how he'd never written a script before in his life. According to his version of what happened, I called him and read a script Milt and I had written for the album, then FJA would always add dramatically, "that night at 11, Verne called and he said, 'Oh dear, Mr. Karloff was very gentle but he let me down." I commiserated with him and Verne then said, "I'll be right over." Well, the crying towel was soaking wet and I replied, "At 11 o'clock, what can I do for you?"

"Karloff says if I show him a new script by nine o'clock tomorrow, one he likes, he'll stay an extra day and do it." And on it goes. In fact, there was no crying towel, nor did I sob as Forry often embellished the story when I "pled" with him to write the script, nor is "Oh dear" now—nor has it ever been—a part of my vocabulary, which is more-frequently laced with four-letter words, none of which is "dear." I did rather dramatically "order" him to write it that very night, and made a bee-line to 915 South Sherbourne Drive (the first Ackermansion—I remember the address still) to make sure he had all the facts—he told me he needed "mood music" to work so I attacked his vintage grand pianner with relish (and just a dash of Worcestershire sauce) and made with the requested dark mood-inspiring threnodies and miserares. They must have worked, because the inexperienced ("I never wrote a script in my life. I don't know anything about the format, the language...") neophyte scribe Forrest J Ackerman turned out one of the finest damned scripts I've ever read, and for that matter, Boris ever read!

The rest, of course, is history, and it pleases me to tell you that in October of 2009 Electric Lemon Record Company released the brand new—ORIGINAL—"An Evening with Boris Karloff and His Friends" album/CD, which no one has ever heard ("Hear it again for the first time!") with a theatre organ horror score composed and performed by Yours Truly.

So now you know the story, the way it really happened, the way Forry came to be the writer of one of Horror's all-time classics. He and I spoke of "An Evening with Boris Karloff and His Friends" hundreds of times, and the newly released Original album is dedicated to Forry along with a number of other Very Important People who were "there" when it happened and most instrumental in its creation."[10]

Forry remarked in various talks at conventions, "I've been in Boris's company nine times in my life, but I never really had him sort of all to myself." One night in 1968 Forry had a most memorable evening with Boris because of a mutual friend, Robert Bloch. Forry was invited to Bloch's for dinner. Wendy, who was a good friend and admirer of Bloch, could not make it that evening, and Karloff was to be there. Robert asked for suggestions for another person to come. Forry suggested Fritz Lang—they were about the same age. Robert Bloch made the arrangements and what an evening it was. Robert, like Forry, usually loved to talk and chat up everyone, but that time, he

5. The 1960s

and Forry both just listened to Lang and Karloff talking about their lives, about *Metropolis*, about everything. Forry wished he had a tape recorder to record their observations. "Here we are, two old dinosaurs who have survived," Fritz Lang said to the English actor.

Boris Karloff passed on February 2, 1969. Forry and James Warren devoted an issue of *Famous Monsters* to him, issue number 56, the July 1969 issue.

Forry invented the character "Vampirella," a glamorous girl from the planet Draculon, where the rivers flow with blood instead of water. Vampirella had her beginnings in the first part of 1969. Forry recalled in one of his oft-told tales, which this author has committed (like so many of his stories) to memory, that it was just after Boris Karloff had died because Boris was slated to be the guest of honor at an international science fiction convention in Rio de Janeiro, Brazil, at the invitation of superfan Norbert Novotny of South America. Forry was to introduce him at the convention. Jim Warren approached him before the trip with the idea of creating a new comic line with the character of a "mod witch" and asked for some names.

"How about Miss Terry, for mystery?" Forry asked. No, that would not do, Jim Warren advised him. Meanwhile, James wanted him to keep thinking. Forry contem-

Vampirella original comic art from the late 1960s adorned the walls of the Ackerminimansion (Michael Ramsey).

plated the mod witch angle while heading down to Rio over the Amazon in a plane containing George Pal, the producer of *The Time Machine*, Yvette Mimieux, the blonde star of the film, Roman Polanski, screenwriter for *Rosemary's Baby*, authors Poul Anderson and A.E. van Vogt, and author Harlan Ellison. Forry's mind wandered as he saw the river snaking along under the wing and thought of the piranha looking longingly up at the plane, hoping it would crash so they would have a hot meal. "If this plane crashes," he mused, "and we survive, we will have the entire cast of a picture. We have George Pal to produce it, Roman Polanski to write it, and we have Yvette Mimieux to star in it and amaze the natives. We have Harlan Ellison to use his machete or his sharp tongue to get us through the jungle and finally, bedraggled, we will emerge from the jungle to be at the convention."

He didn't think anything more about the character of the mod witch until the convention was over and he was in the offices of Warren Publishing Company in New York City. He had gone there on business and, before he left, started pounding on a vacant typewriter in the busy office. Jim Warren walked in and peered over Forry's shoulder, expecting to see the words Peter Cushing, Lon Chaney or Boris Karloff being typed. Instead, he saw Vampirella, Draculon and many other odd names.

"What's this?" Warren asked.

"Well," Forry answered, "you asked me to come up with a character for the new comic book, and I'm writing it."

"*You're* writing...? Quiet, quiet, everybody. I didn't know we had a genius here!"

Forry was puzzled. "What are you talking about?"

"Well, it's one thing to write a monster magazine and another to write a comic book."

"Aw come on, I'm a grown man. I can't draw, but if I couldn't come up with enough 'biffs' and 'baffs' and 'zowies' to fill eight pages, I'd hang my head in shame, climb to the top of the highest building in New York and jump off!" Forry said.

"Well, I don't know. We'll have to see about this," James Warren replied, and Forry thought, "Gosh, the way he talks, one has to climb a mountain and study under the great masters to be worthy of writing a comic." Anyway, in several hours, Forry had written the first Vampirella comic and her origin. She was from Draculon, another planet, and was a blood drinker. The blood did not come from any creature, but flowed in the oceans and streams of her home planet. They were having privations on Draculon with a terrible drought and some of her people journeyed through space to find a planet where they could obtain some blood. Earth was her eventual destination. She generally got blood from blood banks when she landed on Earth or from a villain when circumstances permitted. James asked visitors to the office to look at some names for the character and he mixed Vampirella with some other names. If they had 50 cents to spend on a comic magazine, he asked the visitors, which title would they buy? Everyone chose Vampirella.[11]

Vampirella had a twin sister, Draculina, with blonde hair. Vampirella was perceived as a crime fighter who battled monsters.

5. The 1960s

Forry wrote three comic books for the new *Vampirella* series and also wrote "Vampirella's Feary Tales," a short comic in each issue which retold a familiar and famous story from a film. A pun taken from the title *Run for Your Life* was entitled "Run for Your Wife." Men were taken, along with their spouses, to an island and found to their dismay that it was run by a sinister big game hunter much like the one in the film *The Most Dangerous Game*. He forced them to leap obstacles, run down slopes and ford rivers swarming with crocodiles to save their wives.

As time went on Forry, with input from his wife, Wendy, came up with some more ideas. One of her more unusual contributions was that Vampirella had the ability to see a person's true character in her mind's eye. If a man was a lady-killer, she would see him as a wolf. If he was evil, he would look like a weasel to her. By now, others had taken over the writing of the comic and Forry was paid for the original story. He received $25.

Later, it occurred to him that Vampirella might be a good character for motion pictures. Perhaps, as he put it, it could be "a perfectly rotten movie and James Warren and I would cringe all the way to the bank." He approached Jim Warren one day with this idea and the idea that they could market a Vampirella doll with interchangeable wigs. Take the brunette wig off and put on the blonde one and the child has Vampirella's younger sister, Draculina.

"Well, the movie is inevitable, and I've already been talking to some toymakers about the dolls, but there's just one thing I don't understand, Forry," said Warren. "You talk as if you own Vampirella."

"Well, if she didn't spring from my typewriter and my brain, I don't know where she came from. I really do think she is my brainchild."

"But you didn't come to me, Forry, with the idea to launch a comic based on a character named Vampirella. I mentioned to you that I was thinking of a comic on a mod witch. The publisher takes all the risks in something of this type."

"You mean," said Forry, "that two words, 'mod witch,' mean that when I came up with this idea you and the company own everything and that my 25 bucks is all I get?"

"Well, yes."

"OK. Well, don't look now, but you just drove a stake through Vampirella's heart," said Forry. "I'm not going to go on creating ideas for her."

Later, James did relent and he approached Forry when a producer came to him with an idea for a picture. Forry was asked to polish the dialogue in the screenplay which had to do with her work as a sexy crime fighter. Forry felt that the film was rather silly in spots but he hoped that, if nothing else, he would make some money from it and even if the movie received rotten reviews, the critics would say "but the dialogue sparkled."[12] Unfortunately, the movie was not made. Many years later, Showtime aired *Vampirella*, starring Talisa Soto and Roger Daltrey, and Forry had a cameo in the film, dancing at a club. Regrettably, Forry's scene ended up on the cutting-room floor. (I was privileged to see the deleted cameo at Forry's 80th birthday party in Beverly Hills.)

While Kurt Bernhardt was the editor of the German language editions of *Perry*

An Academy of Science Fiction, Fantasy and Horror Films Golden Scroll Award of Merit is given to a beaming George Pal (center). He is flanked to the left by Ann Robinson, star of *War of the Worlds*, and her young son, and to the right by Dr. Donald A. Reed. Forry stands behind Ann Robinson (Mary Ellen Daugherty [Mrs. Walter J. Daugherty]).

Rhodan, Forry took on the job of being the series' English language representative and the managing editor during the years 1969–1978. For ten years one could buy the paperback in the United States and it had a circulation of 50,000 there. The page count was smaller than what Americans were used to, but after a few issues Forry suggested calling it a "magabook," so they would not have to print two novels in each book. Forry saw this as a chance to acquaint readers with the history of science fiction, just as he had seen his opportunity to teach a new generation about the classics of the horror genre with *Famous Monsters*. He felt that exposure to the great works of the past was essential so that they would not be forgotten. So he included in the magazine instalments of Garrett P. Serviss' *Pursuit to Mars* (a sequel to the better-known *War of the Worlds* by H.G. Wells), and reprinted a round robin serial entitled *Cosmos* which had originally debuted in an old fanzine but had been contributed to by A. Merritt, Edmund Hamilton and John Campbell, Jr. Forry also created editorials about Hugo Gernsback and added a letter column, making it resemble a magazine. Forry and Wendy assumed that the readership was young boys between the ages of 10 and 15, but when the letters started to come in they realized that the actual age of the readers ranged anywhere from 10 to 25 years — and sometimes even higher.

5. The 1960s

The sixties were also a very rewarding time for Donald A. Reed. He remained a friend of Wendy and Forry and was frequently discussed in the pages of *Famous Monsters*. Another project for the busy Donald had been the founding of the Academy of Science Fiction, Fantasy and Horror Films in 1972. Finding sponsorship throughout the motion picture industry, Dr. Reed was able to forge a mighty organization that made its way to televised status. Modeled after the Academy of Motion Picture Arts and Sciences' Oscars, the Saturn Awards recognize achievements in the categories of Best Horror Film, Best Science Fiction Film, Best Actor, Best Actress, Best Supporting Actor, Best Single Television Presentation, Service Award, and many others.

Forry spent many an evening going to the movies with Donald and talking about motion pictures with him. He learned that Donald was a man with eclectic tastes. Even though his favorite genre of film was horror, his favorite film of all time was Charles Chaplin's *City Lights*. Donald wrote a book on the career of Robert Redford and had a huge collection of photographs and newspaper clippings pertaining to Redford. Dr. Reed was a close friend of many prominent film stars and professionals, including Ray Bradbury and Vincent Price. Forry met Price, who visited the Son of Ackermansion. Forry was to be appointed Ambassador-at-Large for the Academy.

Two hundred friends threw a marvelous party for Forry the year he turned 50. Unfortunately, Forry had a series of mild heart attacks that same year and James Warren flew out to Los Angeles to visit him in the hospital. Forry said in one of his favorite convention stories that Jim seemed unusually solicitous and he wondered if he was worried that he had given him the heart attacks since he had put him under such strain, editing not only *Famous Monsters of Filmland* but also *Monster World*, which was the title that filled in the months when *Famous Monsters* was not being published.

In the mid–1960s Forry ran an editorial condemning *Blood Feast* by Hershel Gordon Lewis. He did not feel that such graphic "gore fests" were entertaining. Forry felt that he also had an obligation to the young minds reading *Famous Monsters of Filmland*. They were there for the fun monster movie coverages and the scary pictures and puns. If, when they were reading a magazine that was fun and scary, he could influence them to not take drugs, smoke, drink, or kill animals for sport; he could actually make an even more positive difference in their lives.

Forry wanted the young people reading his magazine to be interested in the older films that were seldom seen as well as those which were more commonly seen. Lon Chaney, Sr., films were notable examples. Chaney seemed among the most vulnerable to being forgotten because his films, mostly silent, were not often shown on television. *Famous Monsters'* editor was concerned that this talented and prolific star was not discussed in print or on the screen very often anymore, and many persons who saw his films when they were new in theaters were older now and their memories of his remarkable performances were fading. If his films were forgotten because few persons knew they existed, then the remaining copies would not be considered important and might not even make their way to a film archive for preservation. The only way to keep this from happening, Forry felt, was to tell the young readers how great Lon Chaney's films were and to create an appetite for them. If he used his usual superlatives, the youngsters would think, "These movies sound really scary and I will make an effort to see them." "Lon Chaney Shall Not Die!" was a favorite expression in *Famous Monsters*. Another one was "Lugosi Lives Eternal" and a third one was "Karloff Reigns Supreme!"

Forry did not mind expressing honest opinions on films, something that James Warren sometimes did not approve of because he wanted to keep on having good relations with all the film producers and did not want any relations to go sour. Forry, for example, wrote that he did not care for the film *Conquest of Space*, or *2001: A Space Odyssey*, feeling that, in the case of the latter, the storyline would have been much better had the astronauts journeyed through the solar system seeking something that would help mankind. He also did not care for the new *Night of the Living Dead*, just released in 1968.

Forry had his very first book published by Ace in 1966, *The Frankenscience Monster*, a biographical work on Boris Karloff with comments from many notables, including Ray Bradbury. He was very pleased to be able to contribute in this way to the history of horror.

Forry's friend, author Phillip Jose Farmer, wrote an X-rated science fiction novel in 1969 entitled *The Image of the Beast*, and its companion novel, *Blown*. Sex, drugs, thievery and forest fires combined to paint a very strange picture of Los Angeles in the last year of the sixties. Farmer placed the real Forrest J Ackerman and Wendayne into the novel, neither one participating in any of the debauchery. Farmer was careful to portray them as solid citizens and good guys. Forry facetiously made expressions of disappointment to Phillip Farmer when he read the books and realized that he was not allowed to participate in the sexy goings-on indulged in by the randy alien characters.

The author may have revealed a fact in his otherwise very outlandish novel *Image of the Beast*. A couple lives rent-free in the Sherbourne Drive Ackermansion in exchange for being caretakers; in the novel the husband is unemployed and bone-idle. Forry and Wendy rent an apartment elsewhere, as the Sherbourne Drive address is now filled with Forry's growing science fiction and horror collection. An eccentric (and fictional) rival of Forry's steals a prized (and just as fictional) Dracula painting located within the foyer of the home, and does so from under the caretakers' very noses. Did the Ackermans actually experience a similar incident? We may never know, as Mr. Farmer passed in 2009.

The landing of the Apollo 11 astronauts on the moon took place on July 20, 1969, and Forry was there in front of his television set at Sherbourne Drive that warm Los Angeles day, talking into a tape recorder to record his spontaneous comments. It was a moment he and his scientifiction-loving fellow fans had talked about wanting to see for decades. In the 1940s Forry was laughed at by many for expecting that, in his lifetime, men would walk on the moon. Now, one of the most fantastic of fantastic concepts in the 1940s was real, it had taken place much sooner than even H.G. Wells and many other authors had predicted.

5. The 1960s

Buzz Aldrin and Neil Armstrong left huge astronaut-suited footprints on Earth's satellite, planted a flag and spoke to the "folks back home" via a televised hook up. Michael Collins was in the orbiter around the moon that would take the three back to Earth. Forry shouted "Vindication!" into his tape recorder.

6
The 1970s — Colleges, Conventions and Creatures

Forry befriended Shel Dorf, who, by early 1970, was organizing conventions devoted to comic books. The very first Comic-Con for San Diego was born in March of 1970 as the Golden State Comic Mini-con. It was small then. These conventions have grown steadily since then and their attendance is now topping 100,000. The San Diego Comic-Con International is the largest comic book convention in the world.

During the early 1970s, Forry and Wendy were staying in an apartment because the house at Sherbourne was becoming filled with Forry's collection. The windows were covered in art. Many persons have asked Forry when visiting his Ackermansions, just how had he come to acquire some of these objects? How, for instance, did Forry acquire the Creature from the Black Lagoon's head and claws used in the classic Universal film of 1954? Forry explained that a janitor at the studio was sweeping up after the last day of shooting and saw the Creature's claws and head on the floor. They looked abandoned and unwanted, so he took them home with him, thinking his child would like to have them to play with. For several years, the boy played with this prop which cost thousands of dollars to build and then he sold them to another child for the princely sum of five dollars. Forry learned of this and asked the boy, "Hey, kid, care to double your investment?"

The youth said that when he was ready to part with the Creature, he would be glad to give it to Forry because he knew that Forry was a literary agent with a nice collection and he would keep it. But when the time came for him to visit Forry with the Creature, Forry was not home and the young man did not want to just leave it on Forry's doorstep. He left it in his rental car. Unfortunately he was in a hurry to return the car and forgot that the Black Lagoon creature was in the trunk. When he remembered, he hurried back to the rental car company and retrieved "Blackie" before he was lost for all time.

Something similar happened in the case of the *King Kong* Pteranodon. The brother of Rod Serling came into possession of the tattered remnants of the stop-motion model and telephoned Forry. Mr. Serling was going to mail it to him. It arrived in the mail in a shoe box. Forry, excited, brought it to the home of a fan to show it to him. His wife saw the small model and exclaimed, "Good heavens, what is that, a dead crow?"

6. The 1970s

Forry was so amused by this comment that for years he had a small yellow sign next to the Pteranodon which read: "No, Ondine Degas, this is not a dead crow ... it is the *King Kong* Pteranodon created by Marcel Delgado and animated by Willis O'Brien."

Forry, meanwhile, was a guest on *To Tell the Truth*, a program popular throughout the 1950s, 1960s and 1970s. For those unfamiliar with the format of this series, Garry Moore hosted the show. A panel of celebrities (Kitty Carlisle, Tom Poston, Orson Bean and others) were challenged in each episode with trying to deduce from a selection of three persons, all claiming to be the same person, which one was the real subject. The impostors would give answers that might or might not reveal that they were not the real individual. At that time, Forry was not yet as recognizable by the general public as he would be in the 1980s or 1990s, so the audience and the panelists did not recognize him as being the real Forrest J Ackerman instantly.

Several young men from the University of Kansas approached Forry about doing an educational documentary about science fiction films, and naturally, he rose to the occasion. The professionally done *Science Fiction Films: a Lecture* has a 53-year-old Forry talking about his favorite subject and using props, posters and lobby cards from the Sherbourne Drive Ackermansion to illustrate his points. Forry covered the main subgenres of science fiction films to date: the mad scientist, the giant creatures, tales about alien life on other planets or aliens coming to this planet, interstellar travel, future

"No, Ondine Degas, this is not a dead crow."

utopian or dystopian cities, and the Frankenstein-type story of a being created by science.

He drove home the idea that while many, many worthwhile novels and short stories had been published over the past several decades, the vast majority had never been made into motion pictures. An example Forry gave was A.E. van Vogt's *Slan*. Other authors whose work had been neglected were Robert A. Heinlein, Stanley Weinbaum, Ray Cummings and Jack Williamson. Meanwhile, he noted, the industry continued to crank out unimaginative and derivative horror and science fiction films. Forry expressed a fervent hope that the young people studying this film in class might make science fiction films their own business: "The theme from *Metropolis* was that the mediator between the head and the hands is the heart. If you have it in your hearts to do so, use your head and your hands to create better films." He hoped that the young people who were going to produce the next generation of films would have one eye on the past, one on the present and one on the future.

One statement Forry made in the film was that he had seen every film and television series of a science fictional or fantasy nature since he began seeing films back in 1922 and he intended to continue doing so.[1]

As the 1970s arrived, the sheer number of periodicals available on the subject of science fiction and the industry became so great that Forry could no longer read them all, so he mostly read *Locus* and *SF Chronicle* and seven or eight magazines. He was no longer purchasing every book that was available, simply because there were too many.

Al Adamson directed *Dracula Vs. Frankenstein* for Independent International Pictures in 1971 and it received much publicity in *Famous Monsters of Filmland*. Though it was a low budget film, Adamson had persuaded some famous names to appear in it. The amazing cast included J. Carrol Naish, Anthony Eisley, Angelo Rossito, Lon Chaney, Jr., Adamson's wife Regina Carroll, Forrest J Ackerman and Russ Tamblyn. Forry invented the name Zandor Vorkov, used by Roger Engel, the actor who played Count Dracula.[2] (With a name like Zandor Vorkov, how could he go wrong?) The press book for the film emphasized Kenneth Strickfaden's laboratory equipment as much as the stars of the film. The laboratory devices had been used in the 1931 Universal classic *Frankenstein*.

Forry loved to tell visitors to the Ackermansion an amusing story about his scene as the unscrupulous Dr. Beaumont. As a bit of backstory, Dr. Beaumont had been a rival scientist of J. Carrol Naish's character Dr. Duryea (secretly Dr. Frankenstein) at the university long ago, and the strange Duryea, working out of his hideout at a carnival, sends his Frankensteinesque creature and Dracula after Beaumont. Beaumont is driving in his sedan that night and realizes that someone is in the back seat — Count Dracula!

Dracula tells him that he is after the beautiful Judith Fontaine (Regina Carroll) and has plans for other conquests, wants an ally and tells Beaumont he has work for him, a special task for him to perform. "Oh, certainly! Whatever it is, I'll help," the cowardly Beaumont says, interested in saving his own skin. He parks the car as

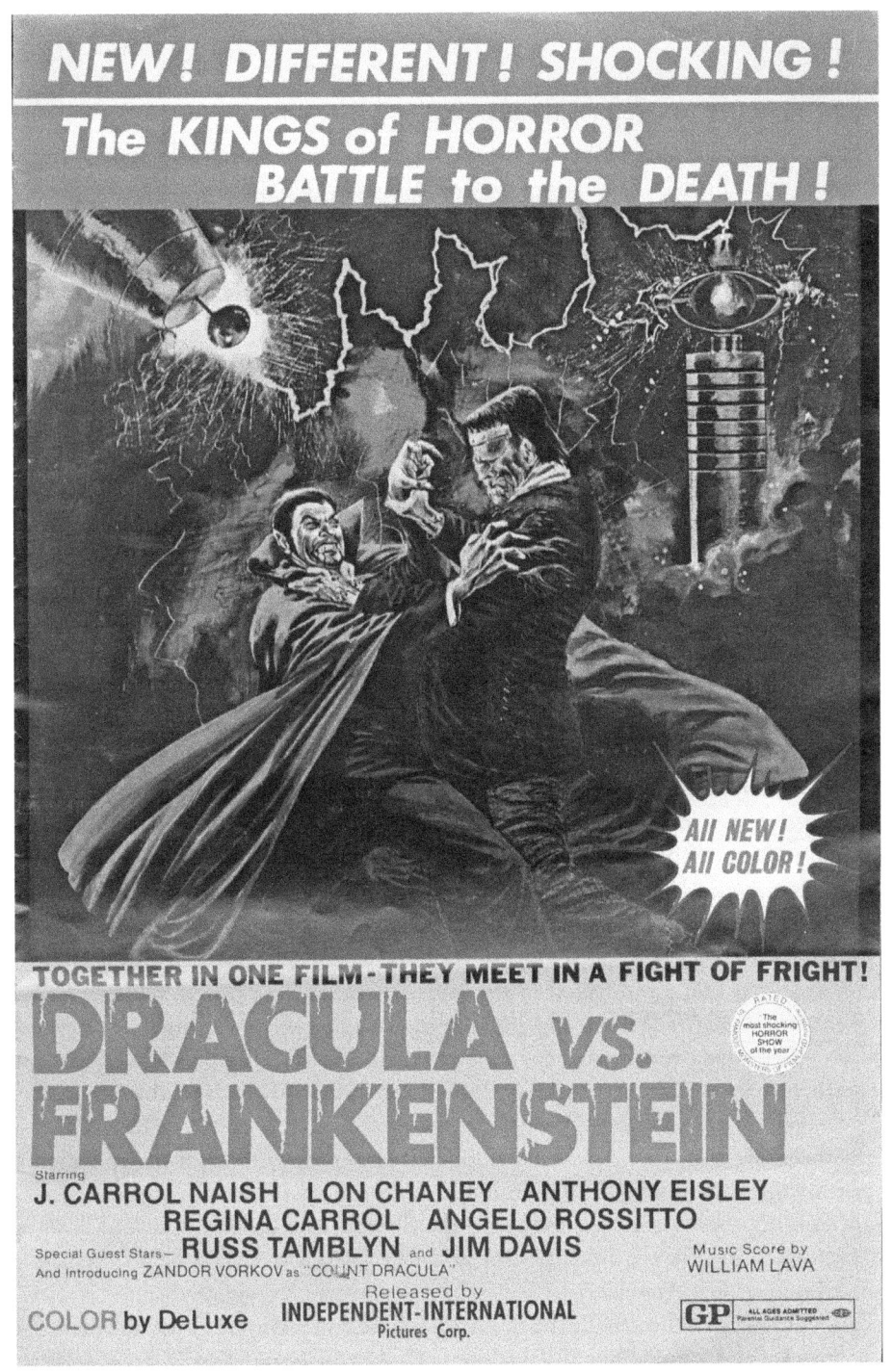

Forry portrayed Dr. Beaumont in this low-budget homage to the Universal horror classics of the 1940s. Other members of the cast included J. Carrol Naish and Lon Chaney, Jr. (Independent International Pictures).

instructed, but when he gets out the Monster (John Bloom) is waiting for him, lifts him from the pavement and strangles him to death.

Now, Forry had seen plenty of films over the years in which someone is supposed to be dead, but a little blink or a twitch would always give them away as merely acting. He felt that he would like to try to do as well as he could at conveying the idea that he was a corpse, so he didn't move, didn't blink, didn't even breathe! As time went by he noticed things had gotten very quiet around him. Furthermore, he had to breathe! So, Forry finally looked around, then got up. He was alone. The director had sent everyone off to lunch break and had forgotten to yell "cut!" So his brilliant scene as a dead man was wasted!

Bjo and John Trimble decided that on the occasion of Forry's 56th birthday they would rent floor space at the Ambassador Hotel in Hollywood and have a Fantastic Film Festival. A staggering 100 films were screened for the many attendees in a marathon which was covered in the pages of *Famous Monsters of Filmland*. Among the films the lucky fans saw were rare ones like Florence Marly's *Space Boy* and the classic from the late thirties, *Lost Horizon*. Other films that warmed the cockles of Forry's heart were *King Kong*, *Mission: Stardust* and *House of Frankenstein*. The only one he did not care for was *Son of Blob*.[3]

In 1973 Forry learned that Lon Chaney, Jr., star of *Of Mice and Men*, *Son of Dracula*, *Strange Confession*, *The Wolf Man*, and many timeless classics, was very ill. Forry asked readers to send letters to Mr. Chaney in care of him and he would see to it that he would get them. At first his grandson Ron Chaney recalled that Chaney was angry because he did not want to let the public know how ill he was. But when he saw the outpouring of affection and appreciation contained in the cards and letters, he changed his mind. It was good to know just how many people remembered him and his work.[4]

Ace published Forry's second paperback book, *Best Science Fiction for 1973*. Forry was most pleased and looked forward to more. However, he did not care for the "new wave" sf that was being published in the later seventies.

By the mid–1970s Wendy and Forry were able to take some time and money and go off on some trips overseas just for themselves as a second honeymoon. They saw the Cinémathèque Française, the Moulin Rouge, the Eiffel Tower, and the island of Bled in Yugoslavia.

In the mid–1970s the Ackermans decided that they could not go on indefinitely living in an apartment and having an entire house filled to the brim with Forry's collection. Pooling their resources, they sold the Sherbourne Drive home and bought the most famous home they would live in: at 2495 Glendower Avenue in the Los Feliz neighborhood of Los Angeles.

They almost didn't move to the home on Glendower Avenue. They decided, finally, to buy a house and were about 11 days into a 12-day option period when Wendy called Forry to see an 18-room home which had been the mansion of actor Jon Hall. It seemed very appropriate to Forry as Jon Hall had been in a science fiction film from Universal, *The Invisible Agent*, with a screenplay by Curt Siodmak. He and Wendy found it ideal.

6. The 1970s

Forry and Wendy moved to Glendower Avenue in the early 1970s (Michael Ramsey).

The move required 2,000 boxes of material, a large truck and the help of some fans to get everything moved. The Son of Ackermansion was born.

(The Sherbourne Drive address existed for many years after the Ackermans moved from it. The house is gone now and the site is occupied by an apartment building.)

In the 1970s Forry and Wendy were members of a nudist camp they visited on some weekends. By making mention of this in print Forry hoped to banish the idea from people's minds that nudist camps were bad or that anything wrong was taking place in them. They were, Wendy and Forry felt, places where people could shed their clothes and enjoy the sunshine and swimming. By the latter part of the decade they had ceased to go to the nudist camp regularly.

In 1975 Forry was a guest at the last minute for *The Mike Douglas Show*. Other guests included Lillian Lugosi and Arthur Lennig who were at that time promoting Lennig's book, *The Count*. Forry was seen to visibly cringe when the artifacts he had brought from his personal collection were practically tossed from one guest to another. He decided never to appear on the show again.

Forry's aunt Beezee came to live with his wife, his mother and himself. Beezee lived to be 91 years old. As they had rooms upstairs, the electric lift stair chair at the Glendower Avenue home was installed for Beezee's benefit and remained there for Wendy's later use.

It was during the 1970s that Harlan Ellison began to state his opinion on the (to him) odious term "sci-fi," and lambasted Forry for having invented the term. For decades he continued to berate "sci-fi" as insulting to the genre. He did not apparently mind, however, appearing in his own regular mid-1990s series to express his opinions on writing and on his career, on (egads!) something known as the *Sci-Fi Channel*!

Famous Monsters of Filmland was still being published in the early 1970s, and doing well. Regular contributors included Marc Anthony Russell and Peter J. Jarman. Foreign correspondents were Luigi Cozzi of Italy, Kristina Hallind of the Netherlands and Norbert Novotny of Brazil.

When Forry was editing the Wendayne translations of the Perry Rhodan series and adding stories by new authors, previously unpublished, the series' popularity and readership increased to the point that the magabook was now coming out monthly. Pat LoBrutto was the editor at Ace for the series' run with that publisher. Gray Morrow was the artist of the cover paintings and these doubtless enhanced the sales. Perry Rhodan number 13 introduced "The Immortal Unknown" by K.H. Scheer, the number wherein an alien gave Rhodan eternal life. In this magabook, astronaut Perry Rhodan meets the Immortal Unknown, which is taken with him because of his sense of humor. "He" respects him more than most humans and confers immortality upon him. In addition, "He" cures his co-astronaut which had been bitten by a poisonous creature on the last planet they had visited. There is only one catch to the immortality offer. Perry must come back to the Immortal One in 65 years for a renewal of his immortality. If not, he is reduced to dust immediately at the conclusion of the 65 years.

Perry Rhodan Clubs began to come into being in the United States and Forry actively encouraged and promoted them. Australian fans also grew in number. One of them was Alex Paige, who as of 2010 has been involved closely in Perry Rhodan fandom for 16 years. The first Perry Rhodan convention in the U.S. was held in Washington, D.C., in 1975. The guests were series authors Walter Ernsting, William Voltz and Kurt Mahr, whose real name was Klaus Mahn. A.E. van Vogt, Gordon Dickson and Ben Bova, prominent science fiction authors attended and, of course, Forry was a guest speaker. As the series continued, explorer Rhodan entered politics and became a democratically elected leader of the Terran World Government. There was some misinterpretation of the series because it seemed to some readers that the government was fascist when indeed it was not.

Wendayne was running the English-language subscription service from her own home and readers were being invited to come to visit the Ackermans in sunny Hollywood, California.

In 1978, Tom Doherty was the new president at Ace. He declared that the Perry Rhodan series was too "old fashioned" for modern tastes and discontinued the series after 118 novels. In their final two issues, Ace announced that Wendayne would be continuing with the series and it would be available via subscription. Stuart J. Byrne, a prominent science fiction author, believed in the series and continued to translate it for Wendy, and Wendy self published the books for another 19 issues. Because the series was no longer available except via subscription, sales fell off to about 5,000 total. Eventually, the German copyright holders advised the Ackermans to cancel the series. Wendy had brought the number of English language issues of the series to 137.

Meanwhile, by 1980 the storylines being published in Germany were becoming more sophisticated and less aimed at younger readers. The American fan clubs had, unfortunately, long since disbanded and Perry Rhodan's space adventures were being forgotten there.

John Foyt, an American, decided to bring Perry Rhodan back to English-speaking readers and, at the 1997 World Science Fiction Convention, he announced the new series, with an introduction by Forrest J Ackerman and a dedication to Wendy Ackerman. The series was now in a magazine format. It lasted for only a few issues because the old fan base was no longer present in the English-speaking market and new readers were not being attracted to the series due to lack of familiarity.

Alex Paige writes,

> As someone who has been involved in Perry Rhodan fandom for over 15 years, the only criticism of Mrs. Ackerman's translations I've ever come across has been from English-speaking fans who can't read German and like to hold on to the (erroneous) idea that the series is better written in its original language than the English translations would suggest. In contrast, I have spoken to quite a few German fans who have read Mrs. Ackerman's translations and they were all of the impression that they were fine. I was also a key member of an editing team responsible for translating *Perry Rhodan* #2200 from German to English as a special fan-based venture in 2006 (with the approval of the German publishers). As someone who has a reasonable grasp of German and who had to wade thru a raw translation of the text of #2200 from German to English (as well as having read copies of the Ackerman-translated issues in their original German) I can assure you the German originals are pretty raw pulp fiction and even #2200, written more than 40 years after the issues Mrs. Ackerman translated, is stylistically dreadful. I had to make numerous edits and deletions in the text for the simple reason that a "straight" translation from German was almost laughable.
>
> If anything Mrs. Ackerman's translations along with Forry's extensive editing IMPROVED UPON the German originals.
>
> The esteem the Ackermans' work on Rhodan was held in by German fans of the series is evidenced by the fact that Forry was invited to be special guest at the Perry Rhodan Millennial Worldcon in 1999, decades after the American series had been discontinued. If it is true that German fans in general were disparaging of the American translations, it is extremely unlikely this would have happened.[5]

Work continued at a frenzied pace for Forry in the motion picture realm, and he was to soon meet someone important in his life.

With the help of an uncle, a young filmmaker named John Landis secured the funding to produce and direct his first feature film, *Schlock!* (The alternate title was *The Banana Monster.*)

A friend called Forry on the phone one evening and told him there was to be the premiere of the film that night and he would love for him to attend. Forry was hesitant, because he had to catch a plane the next morning, but agreed when he thought of his vow to see as many science fiction and fantastic films as humanly possible. After the film Landis and some others congregated in the lobby. John Landis approached Forry and said, "Mr. Ackerman, there are three persons whose opinions I most respect: Orson Welles, Alfred Hitchcock, and yourself. What did you think of my little movie?"

"You're responsible for the film I just saw?"

"Yes, sir..."

"Well, you'll hear from my lawyer on Monday," Forry insisted, sternly.

The young filmmaker was shocked. "Wha—what do you mean?"

"Isn't it obvious? My suit. Look at it! Down on the floor, laughing! Who's going to pay for this?"

Landis then realized that Forry was kidding, as he found that he would often do. He asked Forry, whom he admired, if he would possibly appear in a non-speaking role in the farce about a Schlockthropus, a hominid you won't find in any of the paleontology texts. The creature runs amok in a town and befriends a pretty girl, only to be killed at the conclusion of the picture.

In one scene, the Schlockthropus is making merry in a movie theater. Seated in front of him is Forry Ackerman. The banana monster whoops, jumps up and down and tries his best to disturb Forry, who is totally absorbed in the film. He continues to eat his popcorn unimpeded by the furry creature.

Sammy Davis, Jr., once met Forry in an unplanned encounter. Forry rushed up to the entertainer at the same time that Davis was rushing up to him, each about to tell one another how glad he was to finally meet him. Both of them said, "Wow, I am one of your biggest fans!" almost simultaneously. Forry was surprised when he heard Sammy Davis, Jr., tell him he was so thrilled to meet him! Davis read *Famous Monsters of Filmland* and loved it.

In 1970 the sales of *Famous Monsters of Filmland*, and other Warren titles, were down, but that was in part due to a recession. The sales picked up again and James Warren began planning the first-ever *Famous Monsters of Filmland* convention for the year 1974. This was the first such convention in the world and it attracted hundreds of eager readers of *Famous Monsters* and their parents. Warren Publishing had a second convention in New York City in 1975. Peter Cushing was a guest and he was hugely popular. James Warren arranged for Peter Cushing, Leonard Wolf and Forry to guest on *The Tomorrow Show* hosted by Tom Snyder. The subject was horror films. Peter Cushing explained that his aim was to give people a good scare. It was therapeutic, like the scare one gets after riding a roller coaster. He didn't want to wink or nod to the audience during his portrayals because they would then lose that all-important emotional release.

Snyder asked Forry what Boris Karloff had thought of the Frankenstein monster. He replied that Karloff was most gratified that the ideas he wished to portray in his role as the Monster was that he was like a child, trying to learn how to get along. Children responded and he received letters from them saying they were not so much afraid of the Monster as that they had sympathy for him.

6. The 1970s

This *Famous Monsters* convention — the first of its kind — was held in 1974.

Snyder had more questions for Wolf and for Forry: "There have been all kinds of 'brain' films over the years, and 'daughter of,' 'son of,' and so on. How do you separate the good stuff from the bad stuff?"

Forry explained that, to him, it seemed that at that present time (the 1970s) we were most fortunate if several times per year we get something of the quality of *Rosemary's Baby*. In one 13-year period (between 1923 and 1936) we had what is called the Golden Age of Horror, with Lon Chaney in *The Phantom of the Opera*, Fredric March in *Dr. Jekyll and Mr. Hyde*, Boris Karloff in *The Mummy*, *Frankenstein* and *Bride of Frankenstein*, Claude Rains in *The Invisible Man*, and many others, one after another.[6]

In 1976 Forry was able to publish, partly with the financial help of James Warren, a magazine-sized soft-cover autobiographical book entitled *Amazing Forries*. He filled its few pages with tidbits about his life and accomplishments, and photos of persons important to him in his life.

In 1977 his mother Carroll Wyman Ackerman passed away at the age of 94 with what he described as a "beatific" smile on her lips. Said Al Paige in a recent interview for this biography: "I did find in a box at the Minimansion a copy of the eulogy Forry gave at his mom's memorial service! Didn't keep a copy of it but it was a nice speech. In it he recalled that when he was a boy playing out in the street his mom would call out to him 'Forryboy, come and take your nap!' to his great embarrassment. 'Forryboy' was her nickname for him and I think the other kids used to make fun of him. In the eulogy he said that when his time eventually came, he imagined he would hear her voice again calling out those same words to him. It was such a heartfelt piece I actually started crying reading it."[7]

Forry was invited to be in one of his ever-popular cameos. This time he was invited to be an extra in the New York street scene for the new *King Kong*, looking at the corpse of the giant ape as it lay in the street beneath the World Trade Center. Forry did not like the 1976 remake and gave it a negative review in his magazine.

Some of the artifacts Forrest J had in his personal museum by now were the Pteranodon that attempted to fly off with Fay Wray in *King Kong* (RKO, 1933), a publicity poster for a 1920s film that never saw the light of day (Raymond Griffith's fantasy film *Get Off the Earth*), a bicycle seen in an unidentified Georges Méliès "trick" film from the early 1900s, the monocle worn by famed director Fritz Lang, the beaver hat and the false vampire teeth Lon Chaney, Sr., wore in MGM's 1927 film *London After Midnight*, the ring worn by Bela Lugosi in *Dracula* (Universal, 1931) and the ring worn by Boris Karloff in *The Mummy* (Universal, 1932).

In the later 1970s *Famous Monsters of Filmland* continued with relatively strong sales. Ron Waite, Dennis Billows, Eric Ashton, Jeff Rovin and Randy Palmer were among the regular contributors to the magazine. Juan Camacho was the Mexican correspondent and Norbert Novotny handled the news from South America. Special services were provided by Gray Daniels, Phillip J. Riley, Larry and Paul Brooks, and others. "Fiend Clubs" listed fan clubs of specialized interest around the world. Robert Quarry, star of the Count Yorga films, had a club, as did Peter Cushing. Advertisements in the back of the magazine offered readers many items, and among them were a "Frankenstein Plaster Casting Hobby Kit," *Planet of the Apes* poster puzzles, and LP record albums of Boris Karloff in *Arsenic and Old Lace* and Bela Lugosi in *The Doctor Prescribes Death*.

Jeff Rovin edited his own short-lived monster magazine from Seaboard periodicals, *Movie Monsters*, during this time. The publisher was Charles Goodman. Rovin by now had written a number of well-received books such as *The Fabulous Fantasy Films*.

In 1975 the mayor of Los Angeles decreed that the week of November 20 through 26 was to be Science Fiction Week in Los Angeles. Can it be a mere coincidence that Forry Ackerman's birthday fell in that one week period? I don't think so.

6. The 1970s

Carroll Ackerman (seated), Forry and his wife Wendy celebrate Forry's 60th birthday, in 1976 (Mary Ellen Daugherty [Mrs. Walter J. Daugherty]).

By 1976, Forry began to realize that he should contact various universities to ask if they would archive his papers and manuscripts for books and magazine articles. California State at Fullerton, the George Arents Library of Syracuse University, the Golden Library of Eastern New Mexico University at Portales, Georgia Institute of Technology in Atlanta, the University of Wyoming at Laramie and the University of Kansas at Lawrence are the locations where Forrest J Ackerman's manuscripts and papers can be studied.[8]

In the mid–1970s the lives of Forrest J and this author intersected. Our contact was, at first, strictly on a professional level. I was perusing Suburban News, a newsstand at the corner of Little Creek Road and Granby Street in Norfolk, Virginia, when I saw the cover of issue number 125 with the Dino de Laurentiis King Kong, snarling his hate to jet planes attacking him as he straddled both towers of the World Trade Center. To paraphrase Forry's famous story about how he found his first copy of *Amazing Stories*, that issue of *Famous Monsters of Filmland* jumped off the newsstand and said, "Take me home, young lady, you will love the editor who brings me to the world nine times per year!"

I did not fall in love with the editor at that very moment. The minute I got the magazine home I began to wonder how I had ever missed out on so many issues. I owe my nephew Ed a great deal of gratitude for even making me aware of Warren magazines in those days. I had in the past made the mistake of assuming that because it had monsters on the cover and was placed on the shelf with *Creepy* and *Eerie*, this magazine was another horror comic like the aforementioned Warren periodical that young Ed had been recently reading enthusiastically and I had read less than enthusiastically. When I saw the *King Kong* cover I realized that this magazine was about monsters in motion pictures! Well, that was a different matter. I craved information about the technical aspects of moviemaking and biographies of stars such as Vincent Price, and had already read every such book available in my college library.

I did hear the "voice" of the *Famous Monsters* editor, this fellow who called himself "Forry." I knew he must be a charming fellow for his carefree style and personality to come through so loud and clear on the printed page. I liked the accessible nature of the editor and how he invited people to come to his Hollywood home and see his collection of stills and lobby cards. The intriguing magazine educated me about filmmakers like George Pal, actors like Vincent Price and special effects artists like Willis O'Brien and Marcel Delgado. The editor knew, or had known, most of them and could furnish the living film stars and filmmakers with our birthday or get well wishes if the occasion called for it! I was an enthusiastic participant, sending get well cards to Carroll Borland and Marcel Delgado, among others, by sending them to Forry Ackerman. He would then forward them to the stars.

Interestingly, when one reads the letter columns for various issues of the magazine during the late 1970s, one sees quite a number of young people complaining that the magazine has too much coverage of old films from the 1930s and 1940s! "I want more coverage of good new films like *Alien* and less on Chaney Senior" was one reader's

6. The 1970s

request. Forry and James Warren received many letters of complaint. Many of them are quite amusing to read. "I want to read good books, like *Cracked*!" one young person declared. "I dare you to print this letter!" was a taunt many a young man or woman would write in their letters. Forry usually did print the letter, deciding to take the child up on their dare, and knowing that the kid probably wanted to see his or her name in print. The child would then probably buy the issue and tell friends to buy it as well! The most disturbing letter he received in that decade was from a parent named Ron Leeds. *Famous Monsters* printed the letter in its entirety in the magazine. The letter made the cover as "The Most Horrifying Letter We've Ever Printed!"

Mr. Leeds informed Forry that he was very concerned that his son's interest in monster movies was bad for his emotional and intellectual development and he wanted to encourage him to read the classics of literature instead. His way of doing so was to destroy his son's entire collection of *Famous Monsters* magazines. "The world doesn't need your junk," Leeds wrote. "It's bad enough to start with." In issue number 129 Forry ran the letter. The response from readers of all ages was huge. Many parents wrote open letters to him in the magazine to explain that it was precisely classic horror that might well encourage his son's interest in literature. After all, Robert Louis Stevenson, Mary Shelley, and Jules Verne all wrote literary works that have survived the centuries. The subjects of their novels were frequently of a horrific nature. Stevenson wrote *The Strange Case of Dr. Jekyll and Mr. Hyde*. Shelley wrote *Frankenstein; or, The Modern Prometheus*. Verne wrote *A Journey to the Center of the Earth*. Their novels are classics read in schools. Seeing filmed versions might interest young people in reading the originals.

It is not known if Ron Leeds ever read these responses. If he had, he would have known he owed the editor $500 since he challenged him to print the letter; if he did, he would pay him that amount. Forry advised the author that he was not paid the money.

Forry always wanted to encourage creative expression among young readers. He seldom discussed his own views on anything in the newspaper headlines, but in his 1976 book *Amazing Forries*, he did discuss adult topics. He disapproved of bullfights, hunting and fishing for sport, big settlements for undeserving divorcees, New Wave Films, astrology, churches and religion, censorship, capital punishment, drugs, smoking, alcohol consumption, TV commercials insulting the products of other companies, persons who hassle homophiles, testing any more atom bombs, and the military mind. He did approve of cats and dogs, tennis, swimming, miniature golf, women's liberation, homophilial freedom, the exploration of space, atomic power development, abortion, euthenasia, and legalizing prostitution. Forry was undecided about the following subjects: The Future (would it really be better than the present?), telepathy and Scientology.[9]

Every person of my acquaintance that was a fan of the original *Famous Monsters of Filmland* has told me which issue was the first one they ever read. Usually, it was issue number 23 or number 59 or some other early one. That issue is forever burned into their memory. This author was late to arrive on the *Famous Monsters* scene and was not a stereotypical *FM* reader. Conventional wisdom dictates that *Famous Monsters* readers were all young males between the ages of 8 and 20 and they all wanted to be filmmakers when they grew up. I was 21, certainly not a male, and studying geology and the ecological sciences in college.

I wrote a number of letters to the editor, praising Forry's accurate assessments of the Dino de Laurentiis *King Kong* and Fritz Lang's *Metropolis*, and being cranky about the use of bat wings in pterodactyls in Harryhausen films. My first professional piece, an article on Tyrannosaurs in the movies and television, was submitted in the summer of 1979 to *Famous Monsters of Filmland* after I had carefully studied the magazine and its format. I sent the manuscript to Forry in care of James Warren in New York City. Forry accepted it in the spring of the year and wrote in a postcard to me that "if U can think of anything else offbeat & photogenic I will consider it."

October 31, 1979, was the best Halloween night of my young life. I got home from teaching an undergraduate school class that day, ready to go with my sister Pam to a screening of the silent *The Phantom of the Opera* at the Naro Expanded Cinema in Norfolk. My father told me that my newest issue of *Famous Monsters of Filmland* (the January 1980 issue) had arrived and it had my article in it! The excitement was enormous, but I had too much to do that day to do more than glance at the article, look at the photos and artwork that Forry had used from his collection, and then get over to a friend's house where I had agreed to baby-sit for an hour. My sister and I donned our Halloween costumes to go to the theater for the big event with live piano accompaniment. Later I was able to sit down and see the clever puns that Forry had used as section headings.

After that first article in the January 1980 issue I became a more or less regular contributor. Next was *The Alienvasion of Television*, the two-parter *Winged Things* (*Things with Wings* being its printed title) and a filmbook I wrote on *The Cabinet of Dr. Caligari* that did not actually see the light of day until 1985. But that is another story, one which shows how unusual an editor Forry really was.

7
The 1980s — The Best of Times, the Worst of Times

James Warren was expecting Forry to write everything in *Famous Monsters of Filmland* Forry advised me in 1980. If he chose to enlist others to write for the magazine, he was going to have to pay them out of his own salary. Forry was kind enough to do so. A few years later when I began writing for a variety of periodicals, I confirmed to myself that that is not the usual procedure. In most magazine offices the accounting department of a magazine pays independent contractors, including freelancers.

It was interesting to learn decades later, upon reading the Dennis Daniel book *Famous Monsters Chronicles* that Forry had so few female contributors to the magazine that he would ask the male contributors to assume female pen names like Taryn Arlington.[1] In the early 1980s when I was writing more or less regularly for *FM*, I thought I was one of four women who were writing for it, only to learn that at least one of them was, in fact, a male writer using a female pseudonym to give the impression to readers that there were many women who wrote about classic and modern horror films. At least Deborah Falen and I were real.

I was unaware of problems between Forry and James Warren and he did not share them with readers. What he did share with readers were his adventures with Jim Warren, photos of himself, Walt Daugherty and Warren, various stars, his wife, Wendy, and his telephone number and home address, which we fans were welcome to use to contact him if we wanted to waste his time chatting about monsters. I always felt he was too busy a man to bother and so I refrained from calling him.

Forry called me long distance, however, to chat several times between 1980 and 1983, and he even invited me to his 65th birthday party at the Crystal Ballroom of the Biltmore Hotel in downtown Los Angeles. The paper invitation, which arrived in September 1981, had a red-brown *Metropolis* robotrix and a menu. The menu included Breast of Capon and Braised Brisket of Beef. Sold-out items on the menu included Martian Canal Cantaloupes and Venus Seafood on the half shell. It was certainly a fabulous idea, to fly to a Hollywood birthday party, but my meager salary as a part-time teacher would not be adequate. I wrote Forry and told him that one day I would attend one of his sumptuous-sounding parties!

That party was indeed a fun event for Forry and all his friends. Brian Forbes was responsible for the logistics. Longtime friend Walter Daugherty shared emcee duties with Robert Bloch and screened a little amateur film he and Forry had made together just for the fun of it, in which Forry was the Frankenstein monster and Walt was the blind hermit in a scene spoofing *The Bride of Frankenstein*. During the party there was even a clothed dancer bursting out of a cake. Forry, at 65, was spry enough to jump down from the platform at one point to hurry over to acknowledge someone. He gave $20 bills to two children who came to the party. At the end of the announcements, Forry announced that in a couple of weeks it would be Walt's birthday and the entire party was for *him*! It came as a complete surprise for Daugherty.

Forry helped bring about the restoration of a "lost" fantasy film of the 1930s, *Deluge*. While visiting a cinema archive in Rome, Italy, in 1981 he spied a dubbed Italian print and brought it to the attention of Wade Williams, who paid for a translation for English language distribution.

Forry teamed with A.J. Strickland to write the thorough *A Reference Guide to American Science Fiction Films*, 1900–1929. This well-illustrated volume, the first of three planned volumes, is in effect a larger scale version of Forry's list he had made of films for *The Time Traveler* fanzine in the early 1930s. Volumes one and two cover dozens of serials, shorts and feature films of a science fictional nature, including many long lost. It is a valuable reference work, using contemporary reviews extensively. Unfortunately, after two volumes, the second covering the years 1929 to 1945, the series ceased.

Famous Monsters of Filmland was now covering many films of a science fiction nature, as the publisher insisted. *Star Wars* had been released a few years previously, and made so much money at the box office that many production companies rushed to emulate and imitate it. *Raiders of the Lost Ark* was also a smash-hit film. The cover of *Famous Monsters* #178, the October 1981 issue, featured Indiana Jones, Christopher Reeve as Superman, and the villains from *Superman II*. The only classic monster depicted was a tiny photo in the upper right corner from *An American Werewolf in London*. Opening the magazine one found some classic horror in the form of a film book of the 1931 *Dracula* and a film book of *Frankenstein* star-

Ultima Futura Automaton, a centerpiece of Forry's living room, was a re-creation of the robotrix used in *Metropolis*. The original was burned during the making of the film (Michael Ramsey).

ring Boris Karloff, as well as an interview with Terence Stamp, who had played General Zod in *Superman II*. Advertisements in the back of the magazine offered a "headlite skull glow kit," "full color *Star Trek* star maps," a *The Empire Strikes Back* turret and "probot" play set, and a number of other science fiction film tie in items.[2] Classic horror was still being covered, but the magazine cover would lead one to believe otherwise.

Forry met Joe Moe, a theme park ride designer who had recently moved to Los Angeles from Hawaii in the 1980s. Joe had enthusiastically read *Famous Monsters of Filmland* when he was a boy and finally, as a grown man, was able to see the Son of Ackermansion. Joe went to work part time for him doing cataloging tasks and being a general assistant.

Famous Monsters of Filmland folded in March 1983 after a bitter parting with James Warren. By this time, most of the Warren Publications had already suspended publication. *Eerie* and *Creepy* both ceased publication with the February 1983 issue; *Vampirella* went out of print in March of 1983; and James Warren, Forry told the author, felt that something drastic was needed with the format and slant of *Famous Monsters of Filmland*. Forry recounted to this author in a missive that the publisher felt that Forry was too old and his tastes too firmly cemented in classic horror. For years Forry had reluctantly written, or accepted contributions of, articles on *Motel Hell* and *Friday the 13th* when he did not want to cover such violently gory films in a magazine aimed at children and teenagers. But James Warren insisted. They had several discussions on this subject and the result was, "You may be the editor, but I am the boss." Warren would make trips to Los Angeles and not look Forry up during his stay in the area. Forry believed that he was going to be fired and so he resigned in early 1983 to avoid being let go. This happened as the magazine was celebrating its 25th year of publication. I received a missive to that effect, and was sad to learn this news. I told Forry I had no intention of writing for *Famous Monsters* if he was not editing it. Such would not have transpired in any event, since the entire Warren Publishing Company was soon to fold. The March issue carried an editorial which indicated that Randy Palmer was the new editor. That issue promised many issues of *Famous Monsters* to come. In fact, before the end of the summer Warren Publishing Company ceased publication of its entire product line. I thought, well that is all, no more monster magazines for Forry, especially with Randy Palmer's article in the final issue saying essentially that Forry was moving on to other interests.

The bankruptcy sale of all holdings of Warren Publishing Company was held in August 1983 and received little attention in the media or in fan circles.[3] Forry submitted his account of the falling out with James Warren in a 1983 *Fangoria* interview. He used one of his pseudonyms, Paul Linden, as the interviewer.[4]

James Warren was suffering from an illness that he did not divulge to Forry. This was one reason why he did not look him up in visits to Los Angeles in the later part of the 1970s.[5]

I met Forry Ackerman very soon afterward during the Labor Day weekend at the

"Constellation," the 41st World Science Fiction Convention in Baltimore, Maryland. Naturally, Forry was planning to be there, as he announced in his many missives to me that he had attended almost every World Science Fiction Convention since that first one in 1939. The schedule booklet for Constellation was full of events. One of them was a talk by the editor of *Isaac Asimov's Science Fiction* magazine, one was a panel with author Frederik Pohl, and the third was a panel in which Forrest J Ackerman would participate.

I attended the panel that Forry and Ben Bova ran with assistance from filmmaker Rick Newman and a young fan named Larry Wood. The subject was "Science Fiction in the Movies." The notes I took on the panel discussion are reprinted, in part, below.

Forry started off the discussion: "When I was a boy I wanted most to let all my friends see the latest Lon Chaney picture back in the 1920s. I've seen *Fantastic Voyage* on my 51st birthday with all the kids on the block and my wife. Some of the kids were Robert Bloch."

Rick Newman stated, "I was vacationing in Ohio to see my parents in the summer. I had a film in the can ... was almost ready to release it, and took it to a convention called Tri-Con. I called Ben Johnson, chairman. I walked into the convention with tickets for the entire con to see *Fantastic Voyage*. I was deluged with people. I had brought Italian color stills. I didn't know how to sell the picture. The artist for the film made a comment. He illustrated key art for *Fantastic Voyage*. They used a key line for a Ford commercial: 'Take a Fantastic Voyage in a Ford.'"

"Why the lack of plot in science fiction films today?" queried Larry Wood.

Newman answered, "*Star Wars*. Everyone feels you can do a *Star Wars*. Like a top car. Everyone flocks to the latest, and studios copycat. SF is a secondary type of film to the studios. Theater owners are scared of SF films. They give 90 cents of every dollar to the studios for *Revenge* [sic] *of the Jedi*. Most SF films lose money. On December 7, 1984, *Dune* is to be released and MGM releases *2010*. Paramount releases *Star Trek III: the Search for Spock*. Columbia releases another film. Too many to choose from!"

Ben Bova quipped, "A good day for bombing!"

"Which ones to play?" asked Newman. "That was the theater owner's dilemma."

"*Dune* is terrific, Frank Herbert says," Bova remarked. "There were ten different scripts to *Dune*. That's where I am going December seventh."

Wood continued. "Do you think *Star Wars* was actually good?"

Said Bova, "Not by calling a duck a duck does it become a duck, lay eggs, et cetera. I had to be the defender of sci-fi for *Analog*. Sci-fi is a marketing category. It could be *Conan the Kumquat* or Asimov solving binomial equations. Movies have adventure fantasies called sci-fi films. It is a marketing category."

The audience asked the panelists why there was no decent sci-fi on television.

Bova opined, "TV is heavily influenced by movies. TV did a two-part series of *V* last season. The feeling on TV is that sf is very expensive."

Forry Ackerman said, "I would defend *Star Wars* as a sci-fi film. Noise in a vacuum is one detractor. The audience would object."

7. The 1980s

An audience member queried him: "Then you don't believe in realism in film?"

"Music doesn't go on in the background in real life, does it?" Forry said with a smile.

The audience asked what the best definition of a sf film is. *Close Encounters of the Third Kind* was more sf than *Star Wars* in the opinion of one person. "How do we as the audience know if we are being ripped off?"

Said Wood, *"Close Encounters* was dull."

Bova responded to the remark: "A good sf story was just beginning when *CE3K* ended. What would happen to real life if aliens visited us? What changes in society occur at the end of *The Day the Earth Stood Still*? Is it done deliberately so that the audience does not get upset?"

An audience member said, "It hurts the box office, that's why."

Forry said, "As we sit here a company is being capitalized to produce nothing but space opera. Dressed as Superman I went to studios back in the 1930s and laid on the producers' desks a variety of space stories. 'But kid, this will cost five thousand dollars to make! We'd have to make all new costumes!' Now it is different, of course."

Wood noted, "You see hope for the future, then."

Forry opined, "Calm down to make plots now, not special effects."

Forry went on to name some films that were not good. One was *2001: A Space Odyssey*. "To me, it was a big buildup then a deflation, it falls down. I saw *Forbidden Planet* with A.E. van Vogt and did not feel it was science fiction."[6]

After the panel ended and everyone was leaving the room, I introduced myself to Forry and told him who I was. He gave me a big hug. Forry was wearing his favorite beige leisure suit with a red patterned shirt underneath, and his Science Fiction League pin along with a Stegosaurus pin. He had to run, but I managed to ask him a question. At the request of a science fiction fan club, I invited Forry to be the guest of honor at a convention named Atlanticon II that would be held in Virginia Beach, Virginia. Forry sounded interested. I saw him one more time that weekend on an outdoor patio of the huge convention center on the Baltimore Inner Harbor. "You know, Forry," I said, "the reason I went to this convention was to become acquainted with various fiction magazine editors I would like to write for, and to meet you for the first time."

"Well, there will be the boat cruise with famous science fiction artists. I understand there will be some famous folk there." Forry replied. I said that I was planning to take the cruise. He advised that he had a conflicting engagement and couldn't go on the boat ride, but hoped to see me again before the convention was over. When I got home I sent him a note, telling him that I would have loved to have spent more time chatting with him. I was ever so grateful to him for everything he had done for me, giving me my first big break. I wrote "Confucius says, 'A bit of fragrance always clings to the hand that gives you roses.'"

"Oh, yes. I remember when Confucius said that very thing to me!" he replied humorously in another note.

Two years after the 1983 World Science Fiction Convention, the Atlanticon II convention was held in Virginia Beach, Virginia, and Forry was indeed the guest of honor. The other celebrity guest was *Star Trek III: The Search for Spock* actress Robin Curtis. The focus of the convention was *Star Trek*, but general science fiction had its place as well. I assisted the local Star Trek club that ran the convention and had the "brilliant" idea of creating and sponsoring a raffle for the attendees; Have Breakfast with Forrest J Ackerman, only to discover that he did not eat breakfast! However, he made an exception and had cereal and coffee with an adoring fan.

Forry gave a most interesting slide show about his life and career. He included some photos of famous persons he knew, such as George Pal, Donald Reed and Fritz Lang. He was asked to be on a panel for which he had been given no advance notice or preparation. I thought he handled the "Sex in Science Fiction" panel well, considering he had had no idea what he was supposed to be discussing until minutes before the panel.

In the 1980s it seemed that science fiction conventions were as abundant as the fruit on the trees and there would be several each year even in eastern Virginia, never a major hub of fan activity. I assumed wrongly that Forry would return to the area one day. I regret now that I did not introduce him to my father, an archaeologist, and thus witness a meeting of two of the four most influential people in my life. I assumed that there would be more opportunities. Unfortunately, Forry never appeared as a guest at any other Tidewater Virginia convention. He did come to several Roanoke, Virginia, area conventions where I got together with him, first in 1990. Sadly, by then, my father was too ill to do much traveling. He passed early in 1994.

Forry Ackerman visited the Soviet Union in a rather harrowing two-week-long trip in 1982. Forry recalled that some well-known science fiction author friends of Wendy's and his, including Tom and Terri Pinckard, author Joe Haldeman and his wife, Gay, and Octavia Butler, had arrived with him and Wendy at the border patrol, and Forry had spent about $100 to purchase copies of his latest book, *Mr. Monster's Movie Gold* from Donning Company Publishers as gifts. The officers asked him what this was when they saw the green covers and the mutants from Metaluna with their clawed hands. Forry attempted to explain and when he said "monsters" and "science fiction" they said to him, excitedly, "Monsters! Nyet! Nyet!" And $100 worth of gifts to science fiction aficionados stayed behind at the gate.

The rest of the trip was not so terrible, however, and he was entertained warmly in the homes of several Soviet fans. Dimitri Victorov Chekhovich, a pen pal of his back in the thirties, met him in person in Kiev. Some artists gave him more artwork to display in the Son of Ackermansion. He learned that Ray Bradbury, Clifford D. Simak and Arthur C. Clarke were incredibly popular authors in Russia.

I kept up with Forry's various publishing ventures such as his new *Lon of 1000 Faces* book on Lon Chaney, his *Mr. Monster's Movie Gold* book, and his travels to conventions and film festivals all around the world. He also did columns for various magazines and was interviewed extensively. There were no monster magazines in his life at that time and so I was beginning to think that there would never be another. Yet just

7. The 1980s

two short years later he was approached by Hal Schuster and James van Hise who had begun a publishing venture called New Media Publishing.

New Media Publishing, out of Canoga Park, California, published *Enterprise Incidents*, a *Star Trek* fan magazine, and approached Forry about editing a new monster movie magazine. At first Hal Schuster, the publisher, stated that Forry would be compensated well and be paid better than he had been by Warren Company Publishing. His salary had not been adjusted for inflation since the early to mid–1970s. Forry was told he would be given complete editorial freedom with the new monster magazine.

Unfortunately, he received far less pay than he had been receiving at Warren Publishing Company to edit and to write columns for *Forrest J Ackerman's Monsterland*. In addition, instead of allowing Forry to edit the magazine as he saw fit, major decisions were being made by committee.

Hal Schuster objected to Forry's term "imagi-movies" and said that readers would not understand the term. Forry said in an interview with Shel Dorf that he was amazed that Mr. Schuster would object to something so obvious. Anyone reading a magazine like this already knew that they were reading a film magazine about imaginative scripts or storylines in which imagination or highly fanciful characters and situations figured prominently. Forry won this argument by a hairs-breadth.[7]

Something that Forry thought he had made clear to Schuster and the rest of the staff from the beginning was that smoking, drinking and drug use were always to be condemned in the magazine; there was to be no use of curse words in the magazine; and there would be no "slasher" film coverage in the magazine. Forry soon began to be aware that when he would leave the country for a week or so to a film festival overseas, the publishers would place coverage of a film in the slasher genre in the magazine after he had sent them the galleys for the issue prior to his trip. The issue would contain the article. He would find out about the "stealth editing" upon his return from the convention or film festival.

Some of the writers for the magazine included Ron Magid, James van Hise and Nancy Mills, as well as this author. An article I originally wrote for *Famous Monsters of Filmland*, a "filmbook" of *The Cabinet of Dr. Caligari*, was published in the new magazine. Forry had held onto the manuscript for three years and then transferred it to the new magazine and new publishing company. I wrote three more articles that were printed in *Forrest J Ackerman's Monsterland*, but alas (to use a Forryism), he parted ways with the publishers in early 1986 and my last two articles appeared in print in a *Monsterland* without Forry's editorship. After about a year with *Forrest J Ackerman's Monsterland*, Forry lost all interest and left the magazine. James van Hise became the editor. The magazine folded only a year after Forry left, and the entire company ceased to publish its titles at roughly the same time.

Forry was to repeat this action of holding onto something I had written for a project of his published many years later. I wrote "filmbookettes" of lost and all-but-lost fantasy and horror films of the 1920s and 1930s for a book he was planning in the mid–1980s. *Stark Mad, Seven Footprints to Satan, The Return of Dr. X, House of Horror,*

Supernatural and *The Terror* were some of the titles of films I researched. All but *Supernatural* were missing and presumed lost at that time. The book project did not come to pass, but when *Famous Monsters of Filmland* was relaunched in 1993, three of these pieces appeared in the new magazine. A whopping nine years had elapsed since Forry had assigned me these filmbookettes and the time they saw print. No other editors in my experience have to date emulated this action in quite this way. If an editor leaves a magazine they leave the unpublished manuscripts and photos with the new editor to do with as he or she sees fit. The vast majority of newly arrived replacement magazine editors keeps manuscripts and may contact the authors. If a magazine has folded, the editors will return the manuscripts to their authors and leave it to them to market them elsewhere, whether assigned or unassigned. Forry felt that if he assigned an article he was responsible for it and he wanted to be sure that the author had a place to see unpublished material in print, so he held onto them, placing them in his files. He got my work published in another of his monster movie magazines again in the 1990s. He also did this for many of the heirs of various writers' estates. When he was the editor of Dynacomm's *Famous Monsters of Filmland* he often reprinted old horror tales from *Weird Tales*, illustrated the stories with stills from various films, and arranged to send payment to the heirs of the long-gone authors.

John Landis, the young director who had directed *Schlock!* many years previously, approached Forry in 1985 with a request that he appear in *Michael Jackson's Thriller*. The scene in which he does appear is when Michael and his girlfriend are in a movie theater. Forry is seated behind them, oblivious to everything, still wearing the same leisure suit he wore in *Schlock!* still engrossed in the film, and still munching his popcorn.

Forry was the host of *Lugosi: The Forgotten King*, a very insightful 1985 documentary on Bela Lugosi which aired on Public Broadcasting. Produced by Operator 13 Productions and directed and written by Mark S. Gilman, Jr., it featured interviews with Ralph Bellamy, Lugosi's co-star in *The Ghost of Frankenstein*, Carroll Borland, his co-star in *Mark of the Vampire*, Alex Gordon, one of Lugosi's producers for the British production of *Old Mother Riley Meets the Vampire*, and John Carradine, who had worked with Lugosi in *Return of the Ape Man*.

One of Forry's many thoughtful activities was demonstrated to me personally when I was just beginning to know him better back in the mid–1980s. Forry invited me to come out to Hollywood anytime to see the Son of Ackermansion. To add icing to the already-delicious cake, I could be a houseguest of his and Wendy's. The summer of 1986 provided this opportunity. Just an hour or so after I stepped off the jetliner and secured my rental car to drive to 2495 Glendower Avenue in Los Feliz I found myself deep in the middle of a typical Saturday at the House of Ackerman. I met his charming silver-haired wife, Wendy, and their little Chihuahua, Bonnie Barker. "She is a little deaf and so you will have to be careful when you approach her because she may not be able to hear you," Wendy advised me.

I will never forget what Wendy said then when I made friends with the dog: "You must be a good person, Debbie, because Bonnie doesn't usually like strangers."

7. The 1980s

"Wow," I thought to myself, "I think I must be good because a good man like Forry thinks highly of me. And animals like me too, I suppose!"

A friend of Forry's stopped at the Ackermansion. She had just gotten off work from her job portraying Rainbow Brite© and she still wore her costume and had her black woolly monkey which she used in her act. Well, I thought, this visit is already incredibly interesting and I have only been in town for two hours!

Forry had obtained tickets for the three of us to attend a celebrity roast of Harlan Ellison at the Los Angeles Press Club auditorium. Robin Williams would be roasting him. Forry's friend Kenneth Anger came by with a copy of a new film he had directed and he was excited. Forry introduced me to the author of *Hollywood Babylon*.

At the entrance to the small auditorium stood none other than Ray Bradbury, Robert Bloch and Robert Silverberg! Naturally, Forry knew them all and he introduced them to me. "Ray, I want you to meet a fan from back East, Debbie Reynolds — I mean, Debbie Painter." Bradbury shook my hand and I felt the same energy that had passed from "Mr. Electrico," the carnival worker who touched the very young Ray back in Waukegan, Illinois, with an electrified sword, pass into my hand. It was the energy of creativity.

Robin Williams was one of the many who roasted Ellison, and after some hilarious ad-libbing, admitted that he never met the man before that night, and was simply being paid to roast him! However, Ray Bradbury and Robert Silverberg said that they were happy to do it for free.

Williams must have been wearing track shoes because I never saw a celebrity speed away so fast after his roast was concluded.

When the roast was over and the celebrities flocked to a small courtyard under the moon, I looked about for Forry and Wendy. Kenneth Anger told me to tell them that he was going to walk home and he gestured with a wave of his hand a street nearby, saying that it was ok, tell them not to worry, he lived only a few blocks away. When Wendy and Forry did come out, they asked where Kenneth had gone. "He told me he was going to walk home, as he lives only a short distance away," I told them. Forry said that his home was a good mile from there and he would have to cross a bad neighborhood. We drove up and down several streets looking for Mr. Anger and did not find him. He later called them to let them know he got home safely.

The next morning Forry hollered up to me from the bottom of the steps, "Oh, Miss Reynolds! Curtain call, five minutes!"

We also visited Universal Studios and had grand fun. That Sunday, Forry had some time to spend with me and after a delicious brunch at a hotel in the Burbank area, we drove to a science fiction convention at Manhattan Beach, as I had indicated that I had never seen the Pacific Ocean before and I wanted to collect some of the sand. Forry and Wendy were uninterested in the beach and so they parked in a nearby neighborhood and waited until I collected my sand. From that point we went to the science fiction convention. The convention was winding down and the only area still open was the dealer's room. As Forry and Wendy entered, people greeted them. Everyone seemed to know them. I met James van Hise as he stood by his dealers table, and he immediately knew my name from my work for *Forrest J Ackerman's Monsterland* magazine. After that little excursion we visited Bel Air and he and Wendy showed me that neighborhood. Wendy said wistfully that she wished she and Forry could purchase or rent some rooms on the *Queen Mary* and move in, and I wondered just how Forry could fit any significant portion of his collection on board. I had never actually seen the *Queen Mary*, thus I had no idea of how spacious the accommodations were.

As we rode along in the car, Wendy pointed out to me various species of ornamental plantings along the street. She was so knowledgeable about them that I was confused. I thought she had said she was a professor of German and French. She knew her plants as well as an instructor in botany would know them.

Forry told me a story on that trip I have remembered all my life since then, the story of Karl Gustav Chindberg.

"Years ago," Forry began, "I received a call from a stranger. Said he, 'My name is Karl Gustav Chindberg. I yoost flew in from Schwaeden. I vonder if I could meet yoo?'

"'Where are you?' I asked.

"'New York,' the man answered.

"We were fast friends the moment Wendy and I picked him up at the Los Angeles airport a day later. He stayed for several days and on the last night we were driving very late down a street filled with coffee shops. 'I vonder, vood you like a midnight snake?' Chindberg asked us.

"We were perplexed.

"'You know, something to eat — a midnight snake.'

"We said ok, and the next day we were wrapping gifts of some duplicate books from my collection for him to mail to himself when he noticed my return address of the time, 915 South Sherbourne Dr. He asked me, 'Who vas Doctor Sherbourne?'

"I realized he was confusing the abbreviation for drive with the title of a doctor and so I explained, 'He is the man who drove all the midnight snakes out of this area!'

"Many years later Wendy and I visited Karl at his manor in Sweden. He had a huge place with a forest, a lake and a private cemetery for hundreds of years of servants. After we ate with him, I was waiting in the rental car when Wendy came out to me and said, 'Come over here and see this!' Chindberg had had a wall painted as a mural with a knight on a horse chasing midnight snakes."

Forry and I went to Hollywood Boulevard for a while during my visit in Hollywood and he directed me to the famed Grauman's Chinese Theatre forecourt with the hand and footprints of the stars. The forecourt was filled with tourists, as is usual for this landmark. One Japanese tourist asked Forry to pose in front of the theatre. He did not know who Forry was; he merely wanted a picture of a "typical American." "Forry isn't at all typical," I thought, amused.

Forry and Wendy later showed me the Los Angeles River aqueduct near the Union Station and told me that this was where the giant ants had made their nest in the climax of Universal's 1952 science fiction picture *Them!* We stopped at Ships, an odd looking little restaurant, and we had lunch. The owner of the restaurant stopped by our table to chat with the Ackermans. They must have been regulars at Ships. It was a day in the life of Forry and Wendy.

Forry and Wendy took a trip to Australia and New Zealand in 1985 to attend the World Science Fiction Convention with friend Nola Frame-Gray, a member of the Los Angeles Science Fantasy Society. Nola recalled for the author that Forry was very solicitous toward Wendy all during the trip.

By the mid–1980s I had become a very busy magazine freelancer and changed careers from teaching science to field work in environmental science. I wrote about horses, geology and travel, then as today. I was not aware of any classic horror magazines from the time period of 1987 to 1993 other than *Filmfax*, which I read often, and I wrote nothing for *Filmfax* or for any film magazines or book publishers until Forry became active once again as an editor in the American magazine publishing field in late 1993. I did not pursue any other genre film magazine markets because I felt such loyalty to Forry that I was waiting for Forry to edit another monster magazine. I was sure he would get back in the saddle sometime soon. And he did!

Forry was rightfully concerned with what would become of the huge collection he owned and so he contracted with L.A. mayor Tom Bradley back in the 1980s to have a museum funded by the city for the bulk of his collection. This did not come to pass, even though he received a letter from the city assuring that the museum would be built. FJA auctioned off some of the excess overflow in a New York Guernsey's auction in the late 1980s. One hundred and five boxes overflowing with books, props and paintings failed to bring him any appreciable sum. He was unable to see many of the hoped-for bids materialize, even though Guernsey's advertised the auction and printed a striking silver cover for its catalog. As he recalled to me, "The auction cleared some pocket change for me, but not much more." Priceless collector's items were going for, in some cases, only five percent of the estimated bids. Some items were going for ridiculously low sums. An original autographed photo of Lon Chaney, Sr., remarkable in itself for being one of a small handful of such autographed stills known to exist, had been expected to sell for $5,000, sold for $50, of which Forry received $40. Several years previously Forry had sold one of his least favorite Margaret Brundage paintings for $25,000, but at the Guernsey's auction, one of his Brundage paintings (that was notable for being her first for *Weird Tales*) went for less than half of that amount. He had hoped to retire on the sales of these items and was sorely disappointed.

In 1989 Forry escorted Patsy Ruth Miller, the female lead in Universal's 1923 *The Hunchback of Notre Dame*, around the Universal Studios lot. She was in her seventies at that time. It was a truly memorable day for Forry.[8]

Forry found himself in more and more demand for film roles. He was particularly pleased with his role as the curator of the last museum on Earth in the film *Aftermath* in 1988. It was a poignant aspect of a generally low-budget film about a post-apocalyptic America. Forry is encountered by the young hero of the film, Newman (Steve Barkett) who is wandering the countryside. He enters a darkened museum, in which he is the only visitor. Forry shows up along with a little boy of about nine (Christopher Barkett). Forry gives a soliloquy on how he has been maintaining the museum for years, hoping that man would bring civilization back one day. He found the boy after the child's parents had been killed. Now, it is his time, and time for the boy to take over. He retires to his bedroom, presumably to die, and Newman takes the boy under his wing and leaves the museum. Forry's performance lends dignity and subtlety to a film in need of it.

In John Landis's *Amazon Women on the Moon* in 1987, Forry was president of the United States, appearing on television to wish Godspeed to the astronauts on that historic day when they blast off for the Moon. His next low-budget opus, *Turkeys in Outer Space*, was considerably bigger. He was president of the World. As Forry liked to tell this story, I will let him conclude it: "But after two terms I was out of a job, and all I could get was to be a judge in *Nudist Colony of the Dead*." His film résumé certainly included some colorful titles! One of them from the late 1980s was *The Wizard of Speed and Time*, a fast-paced and fun musical satirizing Hollywood studio moguls, the idiotic decisions made in board meetings, and an overly idealistic, struggling special effects artist, Mike Jittlov, the "Wizard" of the title. Mike has no union membership and cannot apply for one until he has had some experience with a film done under the auspices of a union. His dilemma forces him to seek work with a shady producer and his less-shady co-producer. The young man and his friend Brian are tasked with creating all the special effects for an entire TV special about Hollywood effects without being paid a dime up front. Mike has to sell his lifetime collection of comic books at a garage sale to finance the project. Forry had two roles in this picture. One was as a man at the garage sale and the other was of a man holding a sign. The film is undeservedly obscure.

Wendy Ackerman was seldom asked to be in any films, though she was the woman behind the successful man. She tolerated many a fan. She even tolerated Forry's posing for photos with nubile starlets. There was never any reason for this author to believe that he was unfaithful to Wendy just because he posed with women for publicity photos.

Forry and Wendy were friends with George Pal, Curtis Harrington, Jim Danforth, Willis O'Brien's widow, Darlyne, John Landis, David A. Kyle, Ray Harryhausen, Mike Jittlov, Ray Bradbury, Carroll Borland, Bob Burns, Kenneth Anger, Boris Karloff, Curt Siodmak, Catherine Moore, Bela Lugosi, Ron Chaney, Carla Laemmle, Robert Bloch, Julius Schwartz, Joe Dante, Brother Theodore, Jim Nicholson of American-International Pictures Corporation, Angus Scrimm, Fritz Leiber, Bjo Trimble, Ib Melchior, Fritz Lang, David Allen, Celia Lovsky, Anton LeVey, Vincent Price, and hundreds of other notables who have distinguished themselves in some way in the horror, film, music, television or literary fields. Many of them attended the last birthday party of Forry's that Wendy attended, the 1989 one in which she announced at the podium, "I grew up reading about utopias and I found my utopia here in America."

One Naples, Italy, convention in 1989 that the two of them attended would proveto

7. The 1980s

Wendayne Ackerman stands alongside Forry near the entrance to a hotel at Manhattan Beach, California where a science fiction convention was being held one July weekend in 1986.

be a heartbreaking trip and the worst thing that ever happened to either one of them. While they were in their rental car in a parking garage, a mugger broke the side window glass and struck Wendy in the head. He robbed Forry of a million lire. He then fled, and Forry immediately called an ambulance. Wendy was treated in a Naples hospital and flown back to Los Angeles for further treatment. The blow to her head brought on a stroke.

While she was recovering at home from the stroke, complications developed and Wendy's kidneys failed. Forry put aside most of his public appearances and speaking engagements to take care of her around the clock. Her health continued to deteriorate and, after many months, she decided that she did not want any further treatments to prolong her life. The last few weeks were especially difficult.

On March 5, 1990, Wendy passed.

Forry and I talked on the telephone about her passing a few days after the funeral. I had not attended the funeral but sent flowers to him when I heard the terrible news and one night he called me and we both cried together. He said he felt that he did not do enough for her and I corrected him: "You did all that you could do, caring for her 'round the clock."

Producer George Pal (far left) laughs as Forry clowns around with an Egyptian pharaoh's crown behind Walt Daugherty. (Walt was known for his keen interest in Egyptian history.) Looking on is author Fritz Leiber (Mary Ellen Daugherty [Mrs. Walter J. Daugherty]).

The next few months were difficult indeed, as Forry was devastated by Wendy's passing. He was the guest of honor at several conventions later that year as he tried to resume a normal life. He seemed depressed to me when I saw him at the Rising Star science fiction convention in the Salem, Virginia, convention center that October. My then-husband and I gave him a lift to a party and he was not his usual punning self. Forry seemed not to be enjoying the convention at all. I wrote to him a week or so later and told him I should have been a better companion to him, apologizing to him for not showing enough understanding of the terrible feelings he was experiencing. I had been going through some problems of my own, as my father had not been well. Both of us were having bad experiences and struggles in the early 1990s.

Forry never stopped missing or loving Wendy and even though he kidded around with various females about marriage over the years and took out a few, he never proposed to anyone seriously and never remarried. Forry flirted mercilessly with pretty women but we all knew he was not really serious. He would tell a naughty joke or two occa-

7. The 1980s

Mark Layne (left), and David Hawk (right) flank Forry at the 1995 Rising Star science-fiction convention in Salem, Virginia.

sionally. Forry enjoyed some dates, but his adult activities after his wife's passing were sporadic. He told me that it was because most of the girlfriends he had gone out with in the years just after Wendy's passing all decided to stop dating him when things began to get a little more serious. Apparently the age difference made a difference to them. In only one case did he date someone who fell in love with him and really wanted to marry him. The lady, who shall remain nameless, was mad for him and he really liked and admired her. She had a solid career in a solid profession and in almost all areas they were a perfect match, but Forry had to tell her the truth, he was not in love with her, and thus he did not want to marry her. I got the impression from him over the years that no one could ever really begin to replace his one and only spouse. For several years his missives would have the heading "World Without Wendy" and the number of years that had elapsed since 1990.

8

The 1990s — Pinnacles of Achievement

One of Forry's most difficult-to-find films was lensed in 1990. *My Lovely Monster* was directed by Michael Bergmann and starred Silvio Francesco-Valente as "Maximillian," Bobbie Bresee as a Hollywood actress, Desi Arnaz Hines as a policeman, and Sara Karloff and Forrest J Ackerman as themselves. Its unusual plot revolves around a silent film vampire forced from his own film when it ignites due to the highly combustible silver nitrate content. He spends the rest of the movie trying to get out of the movie theater and into the movie. (This author has regrettably not seen this film and information about it is scarce.)

Forry was an inductee of the Horror Hall of Fame for lifetime achievement in 1990 and his award was telecast on national television. In 1992 Forry was honored at the Academy of Science Fiction, Fantasy and Horror Films Saturn Awards, sponsored by the Count Dracula Society.

In 1991 Forry met a young man who seemed to be a good friend, brimming over with enthusiasm for classic horror and science fiction, and collaborated with him on several video projects and a new magazine. Ray Ferry, originally a fashion portrait photographer for a small agency turned video project entrepreneur, appears to have met Forry very soon after Wendayne passed. The author had never heard his name mentioned by Forry prior to 1990. Before I knew it, Forry was collaborating with Ferry and his friend Gene Reynolds on two video projects, *Hooray for Horrorwood!* and *Forrest J Ackerman's Amazing Worlds of Science Fiction and Fantasy*. These were documentaries on the history and appeal of classic horror and science fiction.

The documentaries included movie trailers as well as interviews with Ray Harryhausen and Gene Roddenberry. The former featured a little tour of Forry's amazing collection at Glendower Avenue and the latter featured Forry visiting his friend Ray Harryhausen at his London home as well as visiting the home of H.G. Wells where he wrote *The Time Machine*. The latter film recreated Forry's first encounter with science fiction literature back in 1926 at that little pharmacy at the corner of Western and Santa Monica Boulevard, with a cute little blond boy portraying young Forry. This was probably the first time anyone had portrayed Forrest J Ackerman in a film.

All systems appeared "go" with Forry's newfound collaborator. By 1993, Forry was

A longtime Forry friend, Bobbie Bresee (left), meets Jim Morrow (Jim Morrow).

announcing the upcoming rebirth of *Famous Monsters of Filmland* in some of the missives he sent me. It seemed that Dynacomm, of which Ray Ferry was president, would be bringing big things, not the least of which was the third *Famous Monsters of Filmland* convention in history, to be held in Crystal City, Virginia, with a guest list that included Robert Bloch, Sara Karloff, Gloria Stuart, Dwight Frye, Jr., Noel Neill, William Schallert and Ray Bradbury. At this convention would be unveiled *Famous Monsters of Filmland* issue number 200, the issue that was never published by Warren Publishing.

The convention, held from May 23 to May 30, 1993, was a lavish affair that attracted 7,000 aficionados of classic horror. Forry told me that he had a grand time at the convention with hundreds — perhaps thousands — of fans coming up to him to tell him how he "made my childhood, kept me off cigarettes and dope." The event was like a family reunion for him in many respects. Thus, it was one of the greatest conventions he had ever attended, and he had attended hundreds. Forry mentioned that Ray Bradbury had enjoyed the convention immensely. (I did not personally attend, but wanted to do so and I heard much about it secondhand from friends like Mark Layne and William King who did attend and had an enjoyable time.)

The relaunch of *Famous Monsters of Filmland* was seen by Forry as a chance to do

8. The 1990s

Forry won this "Grimmy" in 1990 (Michael Ramsey).

even more good, this time, to reprint stories in the magazine by the greats of the past who had once seen their works in *Weird Tales* and *Thrilling Wonder Stories*. David Keller, Raymond A. Palmer, Eando Binder, Cyril Mand, Julius Long, Ralph Milne Farley, and Otis Adelbert Kline were among the authors whose works Forry republished here and in other venues, using appropriate stills from mystery and horror films as illustrations. He would then arrange for small checks to be sent to their estates.

However, working with Dynacomm had its share of ups and downs — mostly downs — as he was soon to discover. "More fun than a barrel of mummies" was the masthead for the magazine but it was proving more expensive than fun for the editor.

A fourth *Famous Monsters of Filmland* convention, the second run by Dynacomm, was held in Burbank, California, in 1995. It was substantially smaller than the second one in Crystal City.

For the first year, Forry told me, Ray Ferry and Dynacomm sliced $1000 per year off Forry's already-small paycheck for editing the magazine and for the year 1994 to 1995 paid him nothing. Late in 1995 Ferry was informing the public that he had to edit the editor's work so that *FM* could survive. Forry wondered why, if that were true, Ray Ferry never edited a word of any of the articles he wrote that did see publication. Furthermore, Forry Ackerman edited before publication all materials which I had sent him for the new *Famous Monsters*. Forry complimented me at one point in 1995 by saying that he appreciated the fact that my work needed few or no editorial touch ups. I did not see one single editorial change made by Ray Ferry. The articles appeared in print as I had written them. For *Famous Monsters of Filmland* Forry wrote eight articles on how he had first met Boris Karloff, Fritz Lang, Christopher Lee and many other notables, and Ray Ferry sat on these articles for over a year and never ran them because they were, as Ferry put it, "dull."[1] At one point the publisher told Forry that he was lucky to have him and James Warren in his life or he would, as Ferry put it, "be selling newspapers."[2] This seems unlikely since during World War II Forrest J Ackerman edited the second most popular of 2000 military publications, the *Fort MacArthur Bulletin/ Alert*, having brought it up from obscurity. In addition, he had written books galore and had even received an honorary doctorate in literature from St. Andrews University.

In the autumn of 1995 I had the great pleasure of seeing Forry again after five long years. I had learned that he was to be a guest at the Rising Star science fiction convention at Glenvar High School in Salem, a small city nestled between two mountains in Virginia. Forry stood by himself at the entrance to the high school. Without a word I ran up to him and gave him a huge hug and he saw my customized Forry brooch I had created. "Mr. Science Fiction" smiled his smile and called me "my protégée." "Forry, I understand that Frederik Pohl, one of my favorite science fiction authors, is going to be a guest," I said. "I can't wait to see him again, as it has been years." He introduced me to Mr. Pohl. I had just gotten a photograph of myself run in *Famous Monsters of Filmland* again for the second time, the first being sometime in the late 1970s, and Forry dedicated that issue, number 209, to me. I told him how nice that was, to see the issue dedicated to me, a contributor from the old days. I asked him how things were going at Dynacomm and with Ray Ferry and he said "so-so." He did not elaborate, preferring to talk about the big news events of the day, like the notorious O.J. Simpson case playing itself out in California. I also recounted his Vampirella origin story to him so he would not have to tell it to me.

As it happened, that was one of the last times that Forry would dedicate any issue of *Famous Monsters of Filmland* to anyone, since the next, issue number 210, was the last one he would edit.

Forry resigned from editing *Famous Monsters of Filmland* in late 1995. He sent me a missive to let me know, and he also invited me to his 80th birthday party, to be held in December 1996 at the Friars Club in Beverly Hills.

Just days after receiving this missive, I received a letter from Ray Ferry and Dynacomm informing me that even though Forry Ackerman was no longer editing the magazine, he liked my writing and wanted me to continue with the magazine. He wrote that he would pay me for my contributions. I found that interesting since he had never paid me for the three I had already had published in the Dynacomm *Famous Monsters*. I had no intention of continuing with the magazine. Of all the editors I had worked with up to that time, none had ever been a true friend, and relationships had always been strictly business. This circumstance was different. My response was a professional

8. The 1990s

letter advising him that I would not be writing any more articles for *Famous Monsters of Filmland* since I only wrote my classic horror material for magazines or books Forry edited and that I was withdrawing from consideration several articles I submitted to Forry that year.

Famous Monsters of Filmland did continue for years afterward. It ran articles on all the old monsters and their makers, like Lionel Atwill, but also ran articles on television's *Batman*.

In 1996 Showtime aired the movie *Vampirella*, produced by Concorde–New Horizons and starring Talisa Soto. Forry even acted in the film as a dancer in a club and a teen-aged boy named "Forry Ackerman" (David B. Katz) meets Vampirella soon after she arrives on Earth to fight the evil Vlad (Roger Daltrey) who has fled justice on Draculon to hide out here. David B. Katz did not resemble Forry at that age or at any age.

These hats were given to attendees at Forry's 80th birthday party in Beverly Hills (David Hawk).

An excerpt from this film was shown at Forry's 80th birthday party which was held, right on schedule, at the Friars Club on Santa Monica Boulevard in Beverly Hills.

I arrived in "sunny" California on a cold, rainy night to attend his party. Trips West had been unfortunately suspended for many years due to financial woes incurred by my marriage, which had recently ended. My sister Pam had sponsored my trip in part. I met Walt Daugherty for the first time at Forry's home that weekend as they were planning the party and I helped them with a few tasks. Walt couldn't have been sweeter or friendlier. I asked him what I could do to help and I checked off some names on lists. At the soirée that evening I met Lee Harris, voice actor for many films including *Horror Show* and *Pair of Aces* and producer of *Flying Saucers Over Hollywood: The Plan Nine Companion*. The party was lavish and the food extremely fancy and choice — caviar and brie. It was there that I met Brian Forbes, Forry's assistant, as well as Hajime Ishida, who had been the translator of the Japanese version of *Famous Monsters of Filmland*. Everyone was having a grand time. John Landis spoke of how many terrible movies Forry had sat through so that he could say he had seen as many horror and fantasy films as humanly possible. Ray Bradbury was in tears as he told how Forry helped him when he was broke and struggling and how he owed so much to him. I met many other people at that party, including someone who would be a close friend for many years — movie maven and radio announcer Don Stewart.

Even after his association with *Famous Monsters of Filmland* and Dynacomm ended in 1995, there were plenty of other magazines around the globe that were clamoring for Forrest J's special reporting style and huge connection with everyone of interest in the field. He edited *Spacemen and Spacewomen* for editor Buddy Barnett for a few brief years, and did a regular column for the magazine. *Cult Movies* was mostly devoted to The Three Stooges, Buster Keaton, Bela Lugosi, Terrytoons, B-movies and a few X-rated films and whatever else Mr. Barnett and publisher Michael Copner enjoyed publishing. *Cult Movies* was a moderately popular magazine which ran from the early 1990s to around 1999 and Forry was a regular columnist with his "The Whollyweird Reporter" column. For about two years *Spacemen and Spacewomen* shared the same magazine. If one turned a copy of *Cult Movies* over one would find the back cover to be the front cover of *Spacemen and Spacewomen*. Forry assigned me a film book on the Soviet science fiction film *Aelita, Queen of Mars*, and it felt very good to be back in the pages of a Forry-edited magazine once more.

The magnificent coffee table book *Forrest J Ackerman's World of Science Fiction* debuted in 1997. It is a history and criticism of science fiction written as only the Master Popularizer of Science Fiction could write it and included special chapters on the Frankenstein novel and the films that it inspired it, as well as chapters on lost lands, future societies and dystopias. Forry repeated his plea which he made in *Science Fiction Films: a Lecture*: read the works of the early greats like Verne, Wells and Shelley. Then read Bradbury, Asimov, Heinlein, Stapledon, Pohl, and Kuttner. Have them form a basis for your understanding of science fiction.

Ciak! was an Italian magazine to which Forry contributed in the 1990s. The editor, according to Lee Harris, was a man by the name of Andrea Ferrari. Forry took items from the American tabloids and rewrote them. They would appear under the name *Hollywood Babylon*. Forry would send Kenneth Anger, the author of *Hollywood Babylon*, a small check each time for the use of the name.[3]

Bjo Trimble, a member of the LASFS since the 1950s, and the person who organized a massive fan letter writing campaign to keep *Star Trek* on the air when it was about to be canceled in 1968, published *Bjo Trimble's Space Time Continuum* in the early 1990s. Later, she changed its name to *Bjo Trimble's Sci-Fi Spotlite*. Both Forry and I had our own separate columns in this bimonthly science fiction television and film news publication which remained in print until 1997. Forry also had a regular column in *Scarlet Street* from its very beginning. Richard Valley and Jessie Lilley were the original publishers of *Scarlet Street*, a magazine devoted to science fiction, fantasy, horror and mystery and detective films, published out of Glen Rock, New Jersey. Its title is taken from an Edward G. Robinson noir drama of the 1940s. The death of Mr. Valley in 2007 did not close the magazine; it continues under the capable editorship of Kevin Shinnick, Harry Long and Ken Hanke. Arlene Domkowski is the associate publisher.

Catherine Moore, Forry's and Wendy's dear friend, contracted Alzheimer's Disease at an early age. Forry visited her frequently before her death and read to her. It was heartbreaking for him to hear her say to him, after he had read her some passages from stories she had herself written, "I think I read that somewhere, sometime."

8. The 1990s

Forry continued his film career. Robert Tinnell directed *Frankenstein and Me* which appeared on the Disney Channel and is available on videocassette. This charming film covers the travails of 12-year-old Earl Williams (Jamieson Boulanger) and his struggles for creative self expression via animating a "Frankenstein's Monster" that has fallen off the back of a carnival truck. The film stars Burt Reynolds as Earl's father. Louise Fletcher is his teacher who is convinced he is a problem child because of his interest in the "horrible" monster magazines and the fact that he likes to draw the Frankenstein Monster and the Wolfman. The elder Williams dies of a heart attack and Forrest J Ackerman plays the pastor presiding at the interment.

Forry also made a cameo appearance as a man on the street in a film produced and written by his friend Donald F. Glut, *Dinosaur Valley Girls*. It is a fun romp through prehistoric times. William Marshall is a Natural History Museum of Los Angeles County paleontologist who shows visiting action movie star Tony Markham (Jeff Rector) a strange stone painted with images of comely women and dinosaurs. It is in the Museum's collection of "paleontological embarrassments." Another paleontologist on the Museum staff jokes that the rock may

Top: Forry (left) is getting ready to kiss science-fiction author Catherine Moore, who collaborated with him on a short story and who remained friends with him and Wendy for decades (LASFS Archives). *Bottom:* Robert Tinnell directed Forry in the delightful film *Frankenstein and Me.*

have special powers. Maybe if someone wishes on it they will be transported back in time. Tony does wish on the stone and he is indeed transported to a very strange place. Here, California women in fur bikinis who say "fer shure" live in an interesting place called Dinosaur Valley where creatures from many ages are living in one spot. Tony has to use his brawn and his wits to show the cave guys who have been annoying the women that he is their equal.

That Little Monster was written and directed by Paul Bunnell, originally as an episode for the television series *Monsters*. Bunnell expanded it into a feature-length film. A foreign-exchange student (Melissa Baum) works as a babysitter for the Willock family. Reggie Bannister, as the spooky butler, warns her that all is not well but she does not believe him. It's a baby, and that is all ... right?

Forry introduces the film as "Edward van Groan," in a spoof of the introduction Edward van Sloan gives at the beginning of the 1931 *Frankenstein*.

In 1996, Forry's collection was nearing the very peak of its size, with approximately 300,000 items. There was the entranceway with its huge dark paneled doors on the second floor, opening into the foyer. In the foyer, art covered the walls. One of Forry's proudest possessions was a painting that Frank R. Paul himself had painted for him, a very personal painting. This was a takeoff of the art done by Paul for the first issue of *Amazing Stories* in 1926. This one was a little different. Its title was *Amazing Forries*. Instead of the bearded polar explorer greeting the huge sapient crustacean at the pole, Forry himself, clad in a tuxedo and cape, was greeting it, just having embarked from a 1940s style spaceship with the name "4SJ" painted on its hull. In the foyer, to the left as one entered, was a small table with a guest book where guests could sign in and record their comments, and a little tray for donations to the upkeep of this expensive collection so that it could continue to exist for the enjoyment of the public. Most visitors commented with accolades like "Magnificent," "Can I live here?" and similar statements. I never read a critical comment!

The stairwell was to the right of the table. Off to the immediate right was the kitchenette. Forry had a small office here by one of the front stained-glass windows where he kept stamps and envelopes for mailing off his many "missives" and his correspondence for the Ackerman Agency. The walls of the kitchen were filled with art, much of it original paintings from older science fiction magazines that were given to Forry by the artists. A huge poster of Wendy was on display here. As one passed by the kitchen one noticed a small room off to one side. This was the broom closet for the servants. Wendy at one time employed a maid and her husband. Daisy and her husband were from San Salvador. I met them in the 1980s and by the late 1990s they were no longer in Forry's employ.

As one exited the kitchen one entered the dining room. The dining room had a large wooden table where no one dined. Forry had each wall filled with art. Forry would point out the first piece he had ever collected. It was the frontispiece, "Midnight Mail Goes to Mars," from the first of only two issues of *Miracle Science and Fantasy Stories* back in 1931. He obtained it directly from the artist. In those early days a boy like Forry

8. The 1990s

4SJ of Karloffornia heralded the entrance to the Son of Ackermansion for many years (Michael Ramsey).

could write a fan letter to an artist telling him or her how much their work in a scientifiction magazine was admired, and the artist, being flattered by this unexpected attention, would very often give the original painting away to the fan.

Tony Brzezinski painted many of Forry's favorite Frank R. Paul covers for him, and Forry had these on display in the living room and the foyer.

The dining room also contained, on the wall facing the arroyo behind the house, a large wooden shelf with slanted brackets to contain huge binders. These were Forry's scrapbooks, filled with advertisements and film reviews from Los Angeles newspapers dating as far back as the 1930s. There were also letters to Forry, science fiction convention program booklets, published clips of his letters to editors of various science fiction magazines from the earliest days, and odds and ends such as a dream journal which he kept for several years to record his dreams. Facing left as you entered the dining room from the kitchen was a three-sectioned floor-mounted glass-enclosed bookshelf with Frankenstein books (Forry tried to obtain every volume of *Frankenstein* that he could, plus various oddities that were spinoffs like *Frankenstein's Aunt*). Atop the shelf were little sculptures and dolls with the image of the Monster.

On the walls above were paintings by Ken Kelly and Basil Gogos of their cover art for issues of *Famous Monsters of Filmland*. Vincent Price as Professor Jarrod from

Art, art, and more art adorned the walls of Forry's foyer (Michael Ramsey).

The House of Wax, Lon Chaney, Jr., as The Wolf Man, and Fredric March as Mr. Hyde all stared down at the visitor.

As one's eyes moved toward the small rooms to the north, one saw on a low table a weird sculpted clock done in the mode of a piece of abstract art Above this were copies of original pencil sketches Ray Harryhausen had done for *Valley of Gwangi* and Mario Larrinaga had done for *King Kong*. For a while, a three-foot-tall foam latex monster from the *Outer Limits* episode "Don't Open Till Doomsday" occupied some floor space. There was a doorway to the Lon Chaney Room and to the immediate right of that was another low table with a marble top, and there was the *Horror Hall of Fame* plaque presented to Forry. Next to the plaque was a small gong modeled after the one in *Metropolis* and the original costume worn by Talisa Soto in *Vampirella*.

On the opposite wall were original panels from the first *Vampirella* comics. More science fiction and fantasy book cover paintings adorned the higher portions of this wall, and on the opposite side of this wall from the kitchenette entrance was a wall-mounted glass case containing the cream of the crop, some of Forry's most celebrated collectibles. These were a first edition of *Dracula* by Bram Stoker with autographs of Carl Laemmle, Bela Lugosi and Christopher Lee, and an early edition of *Frankenstein* with Boris Karloff's and Elsa Lanchester's autographs (and a little sketch of the Bride done by her), plus a leaf from atop the tomb of Mary Shelley. Fritz Lang's monocle rested here.

8. The 1990s

Proceeding north and entering the Lon Chaney Room one could view on the right-hand side of the doorway a glass case containing the beaver hat and the pointed vampiric teeth worn by Chaney as the detective disguised as a vampire in *London After Midnight*, the legendary lost 1927 film. Also in the room was a full-page newspaper spread from the front page of a 1930 edition of *The Wisconsin News* newspaper announcing the death of Lon Chaney. A one-sheet of *West of Zanzibar* (MGM, 1928) vied for space with a black-and-white lobby card for *Where East Is East* (MGM, 1929).

A framed photograph of Mary Philbin was propped up in a chair where a *Sideshow* model of the Phantom of the Opera was placed.

An iron and ironing board were set up here for touch-ups, a reminder to all visitors that this was someone's home as well as a huge collection of fantasy and horror marvels.

The kitchenette was seldom used for cooking and most of the wall space was devoted to more oil paintings and sketches. A little plaque reading "Wendy's Kitchen" was placed on the east-facing wall. The stained-glass windows you saw in the little kitchenette, and the desk mentioned earlier with the containers for stamps, completed the kitchen.

Among Forry's many rare items was this original *Frankenstein* volume by Mary Shelley, autographed by Elsa Lanchester, the actress who portrayed Shelley (and the Bride) in *Bride of Frankenstein* (1935) (Michael Ramsey).

Custom-made paintings just for Forry were created by his fans (Michael Ramsey).

Proceeding to the immediate left of the foyer was the living room. On the side facing Glendower Avenue was a golden upholstered sofa flanked by two small end tables. One sported a replica California saber-tooth cat skull. The other had become the repository of some books. The walls were covered in more science fiction book and magazine art from the 1940s through the 1970s as well as a poster for Douglas Fairbanks, Sr.'s *Thief of Bagdad*. A huge picture window afforded a sweeping view of downtown Los Angeles and Forry even had a reflector telescope that one could use to view details.

On one's left as one sat upon the sofa was the Frank Frazetta wall for Frazetta paintings. There was a fine-looking white brick fireplace opposite the picture window, and awards all over the walls as well as trophies. A Saturn Award, Burroughs Bibliophile Awards, a Hugo, Count Dracula Society Awards, and many others filled this corner. A huge banner advertising *The Vanishing Body*, a re-release title of *The Black Cat*, starring Bela Lugosi and Boris Karloff, stretched across the top of the wall above the fireplace. A green shag carpet covered the floors here for many years. In the 1990s Forry gave me a piece of the carpeting affixed to a piece of paper listing the hundreds of names of famous and not-quite-famous persons that had trod the carpet. Only Forry, among my many friends, would think of doing something like that when carpeting needed to be replaced in their homes.

An arm prop from *The Thing from Another World* (RKO, 1951) reached for visitors

8. The 1990s

Forry filled this bookshelf in his living room with his scrapbooks. The chair that Abraham Lincoln sat in is to the right.

from atop a bookcase. Forry kept more books here in this room in one small book case but mostly the living room was devoted to the chair in which Thomas Cridland bade Abraham Lincoln to sit for his formal portrait, and the beautiful piano that Forry and Wendy could both play. It, like practically everything else in the Son of Ackermansion, had knick knacks, awards and memorabilia adorning it. One of the beautiful objects was a porcelain white and gold eagle statuette. Forry also kept a little plastic three dimensional photo I had given him of himself and Wendy. A frame containing Vincent Price's last autograph rested here. On a wall here in the living room Forry kept in a frame the automatic writing message his grandparents had received in the 1890s that told George Wyman to take the Bradbury Building assignment.

At the top of the stairs, when one turned left, one saw his bedroom which I seldom entered, giving him privacy. Off to the left of that was the Metropolis room with a huge poster of the city of Metropolis on the door, and inside, various small mockups of *Metropolis* memorabilia. To the left of that room was a bathroom and shower. A small bedroom with a charming little window with wooden white lattice work faced one as one exited the bathroom and turned right. More bookshelves dominated that room. The author vividly recalls seeing a hardcover copy of Frances Trego Montgomery's *The*

Top: "Mark Wyman Take the Bradbury Building and you will be successful" is the scrawl written allegedly via automatic writing by the spirit of a deceased brother of Forry's maternal grandfather (Michael Ramsey). *Bottom:* At the Ackerminimansion, this beautiful painting duplicating a *Metropolis* one-sheet of the 1920s held center stage.

8. The 1990s

Wonderful Electric Elephant on one of these shelves and wondering if this seminal juvenile science fiction book had been in Forry's personal library as a child, or if he had acquired it later. Forry sometimes rented this room to boarders.

To the right of that room and near the staircase was the Karloff-Lugosi Room. Here there were more bookshelves, as well as a marvelous collection of posters from films like Lugosi's *The Death Kiss*, Karloff's *Frankenstein* and *The Devil Commands*. Bela Lugosi's smoking jacket that he wore in *The Raven* was there. A small sofa was positioned along one wall and next to that was a "coffin table" that was a real coffin from a funeral home.

Proceeding back down the steps from the Karloff-Lugosi Room, one could then turn right again and re-enter the foyer to go downstairs to Forry's office.

The office was accessed via a small and narrow yellow handrail along the small staircase just off the foyer. A reproduction one-sheet from *The Ghost of Slumber Mountain* was tacked to the door. One of the indelible images that is burned into my mind forever is Forry standing at the bottom of the photo-lined steps, wearing his pastel Mexican style short sleeve shirt and blue slacks, saying in his spoofing way, "Dare you enter the lair of the ... Ackermonster? Well, you have been warned. I can't be responsible for anything that may happen."

The Karloff/Lugosi room (Michael Ramsey).

Downstairs one would turn right and see Forry's office corner. It was usually untidy and whenever I could I would try to help him straighten up a bit. It was usually in disarray again on my next visit.

On one entire wall of this wing of the house, facing as one entered, were rows and rows of metal filing cabinets. Atop them were Aurora monster models youngsters could build from model kits in the 1960s. Here, in these gray cabinets resided thousands of stills which formed the bulk of the illustrative material he used for his various books and the magazines he edited or wrote for over the years. Many a young person all over the world was educated about film and television by looking at these photographs. Forry had a bookshelf on the other side of this file cabinet row and in the shelf were his reference works, the ones he thumbed through most frequently. Philip J. Riley's works on Lon Chaney's *A Blind Bargain* and others were there, and not a few of Forry's.

Down there for many years he kept in a large glass case the *Metropolis* robotrix that Bill Malone had made for him. Wendy did not want these objects upstairs, Forry told me. After she died he moved the statue to a prominent place in the living room and moved a good many other props and materials to the living room as well.

In this wing, with its low ceiling, were the lobby cards Forry had spent decades collecting. Also, his huge book collection was here. It was, for a number of years, the largest collection of fantasy and science fiction in the United States. Forry had built wooden shelves of the ordinary kind for most of the books, and for the ones along the far wall, he had a shelf on a sliding runner. Behind this shelf was another entire shelf and this one was filled from floor to ceiling with books, just like the one in front of it.

Forry owned thousands of books downstairs in his office area — and I should know because I inventoried them. He had the majority of them categorized according to subject. On one shelf facing the backyard were all the books that he had collected that had been made into films. Here on this shelf behind you were the books on Atlantis. This section included, strangely enough, a book by Alfred Wegener, *The Origins of Continents and Oceans* that was a true science book and the beginning of plate tectonics study.

Next to the Atlantis novels were the books and novels on cavemen and prehistoric beasts. There was a section for the Tom Swift books, and so on. Modern science fiction novels (post–1979) were grouped on several wall-to-ceiling shelves.

Off to one side of the bookshelves on the side of the house facing the backyard was a tiny bathroom which Forry called the Odd John, after a huge-brained character in an Olaf Stapledon novel. A tiny illustration of Odd John adorned the top of the bathroom door. I cleaned this room out; it had a shower as well, and it had not been used as a bath for many years.

Forry had on display here a shadow box painted red, made for him by Mary Ellen Rabogliatti, now Mary Ellen Daugherty. It was called the "Ackerminimansion," and if you looked inside you saw a representation of the Ackermansion, complete with rolled up posters and little dinosaur stop-motion models in plastic display cases. In the center of this curio box was another small rectangular red box, another Ackerminimansion, implying that they just kept going on into infinity.

8. The 1990s

Lobby cards by the scores covered the walls in one wing of the Son of Ackermansion (Michael Ramsey).

Walter Daugherty and Mary Ellen Rabogliatti were married in 1987 and Forry was Walt's best man (Mary Ellen Daugherty [Mrs. Walter J. Daugherty]).

Forry kept many photos down here of Jean Harlow and other stars. He also kept a ray gun that someone had made for him many years before. He also had in this main library room archival sleeves by the hundreds, filled with *Amazing Stories*, *Science Wonder Stories* and *Weird Tales*. Being in this small room with this collection made the author feel surrounded by the essence of imagination itself.

In a small room off the large library was the Ray Harryhausen room where the stop-motion models were kept. The early dinosaur Ray used in his film *Evolution* was there, as were the Capitol Building, the destroyed Washington Monument, the Treasury building and a flying saucer from *Earth vs. the Flying Saucers*. The portion of the Golden Gate Bridge torn down by the six tentacled octopus in *It Came from Beneath the Sea*, and a portion of the ferry harbor entrance model was also there. Here were stop-motion models from *King Kong*. The pteranodon, the stegosaurus, the gas bomb used to fell him, and the mechanical brontosaurus that rose from the water to attack the sailors were arranged on a shelf with Jim Danforth's Chasmosaurus stop-motion model from *When Dinosaurs Ruled the Earth*. Forry also had the stop-motion brontosaurus that grabbed the sailor who had tried unsuccessfully to escape it by climbing a tree in *King Kong*. Also here were a backpack from *Ghostbusters*, a helmet from *The Rocketeer*, a mechanical man head from various Republic serials and the head from *The Wizard of Mars*.

Top: The author poses in the stop-motion animation room of Forry's Son of Ackermansion with Mr. Sci-Fi during a 1986 visit. *Bottom:* Flying saucer models crashed into this model of the Capitol Building. These were used in *Earth Vs. the Flying Saucers* and were on display in the Ackermuseum for years (Michael Ramsey).

***King Kong*'s** brontosaurus stop-motion model was one of Forry's better-known possessions (Michael Ramsey).

The Agathaumas, a horned dinosaur, was built by Marcel Delgado originally for RKO–Radio Pictures' *Creation*, an unfinished film that was the foundation of *King Kong*. It did, however, appear in a museum in the Cary Grant film *Once Upon a Time*. The model was in a small plastic cabinet above the cave bear and the Styracosaurus from *Son of Kong*.

He had the radiation suit used by the main character as he tried to communicate with the dead in the film *The Devil Commands*, starring Boris Karloff, and two little Martian war machine models which Forry said were used in the background shots in George Pal's *War of the Worlds*.

Forry said he owned a flying saucer used in Edward D. Wood, Jr.'s film *Plan Nine from Outer Space*, but what he had was actually just two pie plates someone had glued together and spray-painted silver. The film employed flying saucer model kits available in 1950s hobby shops, not pie plates. Forry also had the Washington Monument that was destroyed in *Earth Vs. the Flying Saucers*. The Harryhausen material was given by Forry back to Ray a few years before Forry passed.

Forry owned a painting of Ray Harryhausen animating Mighty Joe Young and displayed it in this little room. He also had hanging from the ceiling a reproduction of the *Nautilus* submarine in the Disney *20,000 Leagues Under the Sea*. In a little alcove

8. The 1990s

The Devil Commands starred Boris Karloff. This "protection suit" was worn by Karloff in the science fiction film (Michael Ramsey).

was a display of life masks made for Tor Johnson, Bela Lugosi, Vincent Price, Basil Rathbone, Lon Chaney, Jr., Charles Laughton, Peter Lorre and even himself. Masks from *Tourist Trap*, John Landis's mask from *Schlock!*, a mask from *Close Encounters of the Third Kind* and facial appliances from *Planet of the Apes* were displayed here. *The Albatross* from *Master of the World* was here. Forry sometimes displayed his Gremlin from the Joe Dante film here, and sometimes he displayed it in the lobby card area. The servant's quarters were in a tiny room off the lobby card room. Here, Joe Moe lived for years, having moved there when Daisy and her husband moved out.

This wing also housed a small display case on a table. Here one could see the original Mr. Spock ears and hand phaser used in early *Star Trek* episodes, and the golden idol that Indiana Jones stole from a pedestal deep in the Central American jungle in *Raiders of the Lost Ark*. A segment of the Death Star from *Star Wars* and an oversized wooden coin that was used in the scene in the original *Mighty Joe Young* wherein the gorilla plays an organ grinder's monkey in a stage show, also occupied the case.

The "Forrybidden Zone," a takeoff on the Forbidden Zone of *Planet of the Apes*, was a small storeroom off the lobby card room. I was Forrybidden to clear out this room. It was all in a jumble.

Off the lobby card room were the back porch and the laundry room. And to the right of the back porch was another room with a separate entrance. Forry called this the "Rainbow Room" or "The Garage Mahal" and it was formerly a garage, now with the front doors sealed off, and filled with two shelves carrying huge wooden racks. These racks were painted various colors and hinged in such a manner that they could be thumbed through and viewed one at a time. They contained his impressive collection of posters of foreign and domestic fantasy, science fiction and horror films as well as a few non-genre films from the 1940s through the 2000s. Posters from *Planeta Burg*, *2001: A Space Odyssey* and many, many more were stored here.

Director Joe Dante (*Gremlins*) (Jim Morrow).

8. The 1990s

To the left of the door to the Rainbow Room were shelves where he kept historically significant fanzines from the earliest days. Here also were extra copies of various books Forry had written or edited, to take to conventions with him to autograph and to sell. The lowest level of the home was at the bottom of a white concrete flight of steps. Here was the basement, entered from outdoors, the subterranean level which Forry had dubbed "Grislyland." It was where various props and other odds and ends that were not especially rare or collectible were kept in the dark. It could be a bit hazardous down there and one needed a flashlight to avoid tripping on anything.

If one stood on the front sidewalk of the home one could look eastward and see the home designed by renowned architect Frank Lloyd Wright, the Ennis-Brown House which was used as the exterior for the 1958 *The House on Haunted Hill*.

That was the Son of Ackermansion. The home is still there as of 2010 but has had its interior extensively remodeled by its current owners. It looks very much like the old

A *High Treason* duplicate poster and a painting by Robert Bloch adorned this wall of Son of Ackermansion in the early 2000s (Michael Ramsey).

Son of Ackermansion from the outside with the exception of a low wall added where Forry once parked his Lincoln Continental with the "Sci-Fi" plates.

In 1996 the late Wendayne Ackerman became a grandmother as her son Michael Porjes's daughter Wendy was born.

Forry tried to start another magazine in 1997. *Monster World* was to be re-launched under a new publisher, and Forry invited me to submit something. I wrote a filmbook of *The Valley of Gwangi*, a 1969 Columbia-Hammer-Seven Arts production with special effects by co-producer Ray Harryhausen. One of my treasured mementoes of Forry is a photocopy I kept of my filmbook manuscript for *Monster World* with Forry's notes and chapter titles in the margin, the original having been sent back to Forry.

Sadly, *Monster World* did not come back to the newsstands.

The late 1990s saw monster conventions coming back stronger than ever. Monster Bash in Pennsylvania was a new classic horror convention providing family friendly activities like "drive-in movies" on the lawn. Forry was a guest at almost all of the Bashes, including their Winterfest in winter 2000. Chiller conventions, founded and headed by Kevin Clement, were held in New Jersey and Forry guested at several of these, as well as the Monster Rally in Crystal City, Virginia, and book and paper shows in the Southern California area. Horror conventions have been eclipsing most *Star Trek* and many other genre conventions in overall attendance figures. Chiller is the largest and best attended of the classic horror conventions.

By the 1990s "Mr. Science Fiction" was no longer regularly reading all the new literary science fiction, and his original aspiration to see every film and television series of a fantastic nature was no longer practical. What was possible in 1970 was no longer. The volume of films and television series of a science fictional nature simply was so great that he was no longer watching everything. He did have favorite series, such as *The X Files* and *Battlestar Galactica*.

The year 1999 was a difficult one for the 83-year-old Forry, despite the fun of having his handprints in cement in front of the historic Vista Theatre at 4473 Sunset Drive alongside Ray Harryhausen's, attending conventions and having more books in print, including the hardcover book, *Forrest J Ackerman's Worlds of Science Fiction* (with a foreword by director John Landis). Astronaut "Buzz" Aldrin, who had left his footprints on the moon, surprised Forry with a visit to the Ackermansion. That was a major thrill for Forry. Still, it was a difficult time because he was having problems associated with the publisher of the new *Famous Monsters of Filmland*, and working even harder to make a living.

In 1999 Forry was beginning to face the unpleasant fact that he would have to probably take Ray Ferry to court over the defamatory statements he was making, and, among other factors, a breach of contract. Forry had paid out of pocket for several stars, among them Ray Harryhausen (I recall him saying), to be flown over from Europe to attend the *Famous Monsters of Filmland* Convention held in Southern California in 1995. In all, he had invested $20,000 for both *Famous Monsters* conventions. When he tried to be compensated, according to Forry, Ray Ferry and his business partners told

8. The 1990s

Forry and Ray Harryhausen speak at the 1998 Monster Bash. Forry beams as Ray Harryhausen gets his award.

Joe Moe (left), Forry (center) and Michael Ramsey enjoy the Monster Rally in 1999 (Michael Ramsey).

him that the convention made no profit and he would thus be unable to pay Forry. However, Forry heard from a number of people on the staff of the convention that the second convention had indeed made money. For years Ferry had not shared the profits he had made from sales of *Famous Monsters of Filmland* or such products as *Dr. Acula's Cardiac-Cards* and other collectible items. Ferry was using terms like "Horrorwood" and phrases like "You Axed for It" and signing his editorials "Dr. Acula." This is the very name that Forry had used when he was editing the magazine. Moreover, he had used that name for many years before he became involved with Dynacomm.

There had been no formal announcement in the pages of the magazine to indicate that Forry was no longer working on the magazine in any form. Ray Ferry told Forry that he was trademarking the terms "Horrorwood," "Dr. Acula" and a number of others, and Forry had no right to use them. Forry had been advised by his attorney, Jacqueline Appelbaum, to send facsimiles to Ray Ferry asking for payment. None of the facsimiles were answered to Forry's satisfaction. Forry told me that he was also accused by Ray Ferry of getting his octogenarian friend Walter Daugherty to stalk him.

Two months or so prior to the actual trial date, I called Forry to see how he was doing and asked him if there was anything I could do to help him. I would have done anything that I could. I would also bring a friend and fellow film buff from West Vir-

8. The 1990s

ginia, mechanical engineer Michael Ramsey, with me. "Well, honey," Forry replied, "I guess my lawyer, Jacie, might be glad to have a helping hand carrying things for her, legal briefs and so on. I could use a few more character witnesses, too, since several people are going to be testifying against me. Meanwhile, if you ever find anything that I had in print in the 1950s or 1960s in which I used the term 'Dr. Acula,' please send it to me." I asked him if there was any way he could avoid this trial, as it was doubtless going to be very expensive. "Must you go to court?" I inquired.

"It looks as though I have no choice. Ferry sued me first and I have to file a countersuit," Forry replied.

I promised we would be there.

A friend recently let me borrow *Life Is but a Scream!*, the book on *Famous Monsters of Filmland's* revival written that year by Ray Ferry, so that I would have some information on the problems he and Forry were having. Ray Ferry admitted in his own book that early in his association with Forry, when they were planning to bring back *Famous Monsters* magazine, he was not held in very high regard by a number of Forry's close associates. He sat in Forry's living room and asked an assistant of Forry's point blank why he so distrusted him. Brian Forbes called him an (expletive). Forry said nothing, but let Ferry walk out angrily, saying all the while, "I'm not going to sit here and take this kind of lip from this juvenile. If this is how you treat your guests, I'll be leaving." Forry did not ask him to come back in, even though he actually stood outside the house for a half hour hoping to be invited back in. The next day Ray Ferry resumed business talks with Forry. He asked Forry for $7,500 of seed money for some of the expenses for the upcoming *Famous Monsters of Filmland* convention they were planning, and Forry gave it to him.[4]

The original intent of Ray Ferry toward Forrest J Ackerman is, of course, known only by himself and any of his associates with whom he cares to share his true feelings. I have never spoken to him in person although I have crossed paths with him, and have only exchanged brief communications via mail when he was still the publisher at Dynacomm. Empirical evidence I have observed suggests that he had his eye on Forry's collection early on and was showing evidence of desiring to obtain it. I was to see this evidence at the 2000 trial.

In late April 2000, Michael Ramsey and I arrived in Los Angeles to assist Forry and his attorney and friend, Jacie Appelbaum, during his trial. The trial had already gone on for a week prior to our visit. We hauled "briefs" to the Van Nuys courthouse and sat in on the trial for the first day. Forry had to try to remember the content of every facsimile, every e-mail and every telephone call that had transpired between himself and Dynacomm during the late 1990s, and it was not an easy task. I could tell he was doing his best. For a man of 84, Forry was doing a remarkable job of withstanding the pressure of being on the witness stand.

During the civil trial by jury the lawyer for Forry Ackerman produced documents projected on the courtroom screen via overhead transparency projector. One of these was a paper that Mr. Ferry had asked Forry to sign in the early 1990s. At the time in question, Forry was suffering from gallstones and had to go to the hospital to have them removed. Ray Ferry asked for the signature the very night when Forry was in the hospital prior to his gallbladder surgery. The document stated that should he pass on, Ferry had the exclusive option to purchase from the estate $250,000 worth of collectibles for $250.

(If this author asked a friend to sign a paper such as this the night before her friend's surgery I posit that others would assume that she was interested primarily in the person's collection and was not as interested in the person getting well as she was interested in acquiring possessions. The timing is particularly telling. The night before this relatively minor surgery was a time when it seemed potentially possible that the person might not be able to make that decision, or any others, the following day, due to untimely death. This is a reasonable evaluation and the author certainly would not fault a person for assuming this, had she done such an action. A lawyer friend of mine has identified this as "exercising duress.")

Michael Ramsey and I were in Los Angeles for nearly the entire week, taking an afternoon to visit Bob Burns, a fortuitous meeting made possible by my friend Don Stewart, and to see Bob's own magnificent collection of movie props which he keeps in his home in the San Fernando Valley. On the fourth day of the week Forry learned that the lawyers were done with him and he would not have to provide any further testimony. He was quite relieved when we picked him up at the courthouse and we went to a restaurant and relaxed.

Forry was in a good mood for the first time that week. While Forry was concluding his testimony that day, Mike and I had spent part of the day at Topanga State Park, hiking and looking at the wildflowers in bloom. I mentioned that at the state park we had spied a sign warning about mountain lions that sometimes roamed in this scrub country.

The author looks worried about the 2000 court trial, but Forry is all smiles (Michael Ramsey).

8. The 1990s

Forry (left) poses with fan Don Stewart in Forry's living room in the late 1990s (Don Stewart).

"You shock me, Dee Bee," he said.

"I do? Why?"

"I always thought mountains told the truth. I never heard of a mountain lion."

Forry is starting to be in a better frame of mind, I concluded.

The trial went on for weeks after Mike Ramsey and I departed, and among the persons testifying on Forry's behalf were Gene Simmons of the rock band *KISS* and Ray Bradbury. Bradbury had had a stroke shortly before but still appeared to testify. Apparently Harlan Ellison testified as a character witness against Forry. Forry nevertheless prevailed and the jury dispensed its verdict, which was announced May 15, 2000. The $25 million lawsuit filed by Ray Ferry against Forry for stalking was dropped, and Dynacomm was to pay punitive damages of $750,000 for breach of contract and trademark infringement, reduced to $500,000. The paper that Ferry had had him sign that gave him the right to purchase $250,000 worth of valuables for $250 was rendered null and void. The trial was mentioned several times in the *Los Angeles Times* and some smaller Los Angeles newspapers.

Forry was not paid a penny of the judgment. Ray Ferry, meanwhile, did not pay the state of California for fees required and some years later he had to surrender the Dynacomm company. The magazine continued to be published for many years afterward despite a court order to cease and desist publishing the title *Famous Monsters of Filmland*, as the court had seized this title along with other assets and sold it. The periodical was published well into the late 2000s.

James Warren had his own issues with the way Dynacomm was reprinting entire articles from the 1960s issues of *Famous Monsters*. Dynacomm had purchased the title but not the entire magazine. Warren was reunited with Forry during the legal problems; they resumed their friendship and after that made many personal appearances together. James was still combatting some health problems but did travel to California to attend various functions and relive some of the fun of the *Famous Monsters* days with the fans. He joined the "Bat Pack," a pun of the term "Rat Pack," a group which, in the 1960s and 1970s had consisted of Frank Sinatra, Sammy Davis, Jr., Peter Lawford, Joey Bishop and Dean Martin. Forry, Joe Moe, Ray Bradbury, Kevin J. Burns, Tim Sullivan, John Skerchock, Dan Roebuck, Ron Borst and some other friends comprised the Bat Pack.

Forry visited China with an entourage of American astronauts. He joked, "I met a billion people, and I think only nine or ten didn't get my autograph." Forry got tired of Chinese food after a week or so and saw to his surprise a McDonald's restaurant in Beijing, where he promptly devoured a burger and some fries.

A long-time dream project came true in 2001 when James A. Rock & Company published *Thea von Harbou's Metropolis 75th Anniversary Edition*. Lavishly illustrated with graphics from Forry's own collection, as well as the collections of Peter Latta, Irving Klaw and Ron Borst, the coffee table-sized book is available in both hardbound and softbound editions.

On March 18, 2001, Dr. Donald Reed passed away at the age of 65, and in the

8. The 1990s

summer of that year the 27th Annual Saturn Awards paid homage to his memory. I was privileged to be present for a portion of this event, held at the Park Hyatt Hotel in Century City, California. Bruce Boxleitner was the host for the event and actor Jeff Rector was the event announcer. The George Pal Memorial Award was given to Sam Raimi, and Bob Burns received his Service Award. Actor Bill Paxton was one of the presenters. As the ceremony was drawing to a close, paparazzi and reporters crowded all around the entrance to the hotel, looking like a seething horde of locusts, wanting to enter the ballroom, shouting "Bill Paxton! We need to see Bill Paxton!" Guards would not let them enter through the doors until he was ready to make his appearance outside with his personal assistants close at hand. Even then, Paxton was not eager to stay for more than a minute or two to speak to them. However, only 30 or 40 minutes previously, I had strode directly to the doors of the banquet hall and up to the burly guards at their folding tables just outside the ballroom and, in a casual manner I would have used had I been back in Virginia, told them I was there to give a ride to Forrest J Ackerman. I pointed toward the ballroom. "There he is," I said.

The guards said "fine." They didn't even check my driver's license or other identification. It was one of the strangest things that has ever happened to me in Hollywood. On the terrace of the hotel I chatted with Jeff Rector, Forry, Bob and his wife, Kathy. Afterward, actor Bill Blair, Mike Ramsey, Forry, Jeff Roberts and I all visited the House of Pies, at Forry's request, for a typical late night pie repast. My own personal philosophy is that when one treats actors like people, not commodities, one has better responses.

As the months passed, the cost of the Dynacomm lawsuit was a huge financial loss for Forry and he was forced to cut back on his purchases and trips. Many of his friends contacted fan circles in the fantasy and horror field to spread the word that Forry, who had done so much for his fellow fans and for science fiction, could use some help now. There are hundreds of thousands of fans of science fiction and classic horror. If they all had donated even five dollars per person to him he could have paid the legal fees. It seemed for a while that he was optimistic that he would weather this storm. I asked him how he was doing with the legal

Left to right: **Bill Blair, Michael Ramsey, Jeff Roberts, Forry, and the author eat at the House of Pies following the 2001 Saturn Awards ceremony.**

bills and he replied that he believed that Ray Ferry was going to be paying what was owed him according to the judgment. Forry remained busy with many projects, including books for Rock Publishing in Rockville, Maryland, and more film appearances in such films as *The Vampire Hunters Club* with Bob Burns and other stars. An entire line of Forrest J Ackerman books was published by James Rock. One of them was *Expanded Science Fiction Worlds of Forrest J Ackerman & Friends PLUS*. In it, Forry shared stories which he had written in collaboration with famed authors. Catherine Moore, Christian Vallini, Marcial Souto, and Robert A.W. Loundes are some of Forry's writing partners in this anthology.

Another fascinating collection is *Rainbow Fantasia: 25 Spectrumatic Tales of Wonder*, with an introduction by Anne Hardin, college professor and friend. This collection was taken mostly from the old pulps, with the exception of a few new titles, such as *Yellow Imagicide* by Brad Linaweaver. When one reads pulp stories for the first time with the benefit of not having to worry about breaking the deteriorating and yellowing pages of 70-year-old magazines, or tearing the covers, one finds them to be utterly intriguing and well written. This, of course, was Forry's plan. This collection has stories representing every color of the rainbow. There was *Gray Ghouls by* Bassett Morgan, the tale of a doctor working in New Guinea, whose wife has a terrible accident and he preserves her the only way he knows how; the beautiful *The Man in the Green Coat* by Eli Coulter, about a love that survives everything, even death; and the ecological disaster caused by a pervasive mold in *The Black Harvest of Moraine* by Arthur J. Burks. Forry Ackerman included *Resume of Rays*, a poem about the spectrum which he wrote in his high school days.

Forry told me about his face-to-face meeting with Bassett Morgan in the 1970s and of finding out that someone he assumed was a man was actually a little old lady who was delighted that someone remembered the writing she had done nearly half a century before. He introduced her to his mother and they got on splendidly. He also told me of how he met Mary Philbin, the star of *The Phantom of the Opera* and *The Man Who Laughs*. For years he had posted notices in *Famous Monsters* requesting her to please contact him, and gave his home address in the magazine as always. He had heard that she was living somewhere in Los Angeles but knew nothing more. An assistant of Forry's went shopping for his own groceries one day, and while at the market saw an elderly lady struggling with a bag. He took her bag out to her small wagon and then offered to give her a lift home. When she was at her door with her groceries, she asked the kind young man what his name was and she offered her name: Mary Philbin! He arranged for her to not only meet Forry but to attend a public screening of *The Phantom of the Opera* with an appreciative Forry at her side.

In March 2002 my friend David Hawk and I were on our second half of a trip out to the southwest. We spent three days visiting friends Terril Shorb and his wife, Yvette Schnoeker-Shorb, in Prescott, Arizona. We were also due at the Son of Ackermansion, that week to conclude the trip and give Forry a helping hand with anything that needed to be done. When "Hawk" and I arrived that evening at the Ackermansion

8. The 1990s

Beautiful reproductions of pulp magazine artwork were displayed side by side with the originals in Forry's home in Los Feliz (Michael Ramsey).

Forry was not there but filmmaker Sean Fernald was. In addition, William Shatner's daughter was filming a scene in Forry's kitchen for her web site. Sean took us aside and told us Forry had gone to the Kaiser Permanente hospital on Sunset Boulevard. He had had what seemed to be a stroke and was not doing well. We were unable to see Forry that week, although Joe Moe was able to keep us informed on his progress. It seemed that his speech had become very halting a few days before while he, Joe, Sean and some friends were eating lunch and they rushed him to the hospital. David and I stayed in the Ackermansion and did some chores. We went with Joe and special effects artist John Deall for a little distraction trip to Universal Studios and Universal City Walk and the next day we had to head back to the East Coast. Forry could not receive more than a few visitors and was heavily sedated. David and I did not see him on that trip. We went to the hospital and even entered it, wanting to be near him but knowing he needed rest. Sean kept us updated via phone calls. Forry went in for brain surgery to relieve a clot before it could become life threatening. Many friends went to see him after his surgery, and a world was pulling for him to recover.

Forry did make a rapid recovery, although it was uncertain at one point if he would, in fact, pull through. He spent some time in a rehabilitation center and finally came home. Forry recalled some of the group activities and mental exercises that he had to participate in while in rehabilitation. At one group session several patients were asked where they would like to take a trip if they were able to go somewhere that very day. Everyone else said New York City and Disney World, but, with his sense of humor intact, Forry pronounced very carefully the name of the city he would like to visit: "Liechtenstein."

Forry remained frail for months afterward but slowly gained his strength and by the summer was feeling much stronger.

Sadly, he could no longer keep up the home at Glendower or pay for it or the upkeep of the collection. The mounting hospital expenses proved too great, even though he had received some assistance from friends and fans. Hugh Hefner had lent him money to help him out, and Forry repaid him. Forry announced a giant "yard sale" and sat in his folding chair in the yard, watching people come up to him to pay him one dollar for a poster or some other memento worth $50, and giving free autographs to buyers.

The most valuable and sentimentally cherished awards, paintings, fanzines and books in his collection went to storage units and the Son of Ackermansion was sold.

I felt helpless that I had not the financial resources to come to the rescue of someone who had come to my spiritual rescue several times in my life, frequently without even knowing he had done so. What money I could give was not enough.

Fortunately, the home at Glendower fetched a good price when it sold and Forry felt better knowing that he would be able to live comfortably for a good many years on the money from its sale.

The House on Haunted Hill, the Ennis-Brown House, would no longer look over toward the collection of the world's greatest super fan, as the Son of Ackermansion was no more.

9

The 2000s — Documentarian and Octogenarian

In 2002 Forry rented a small "bungalow" at 4511 Russell Avenue in the charming and artistically vital neighborhood of Los Feliz. The new home was approximately a mile and a half from his old home, and near three important places: the post office, the House of Pies restaurant and the Los Feliz Theater where the manager had given him free passes for life. The Russell Avenue home was just large enough for him to have a small sampling of his original collection on display. Much more was kept in storage units. Joe Moe deftly hung his artwork and the two settled in. Forry was still "Mr. Monster," regaling visitors with stories of Boris Karloff and James Warren and Isaac Asimov, and the Ackerminimansion was still a mecca. Just as he had done since the 1950s, Forry opened his home to the public on Saturday afternoons when he was home. His telephone number was the same, and all a person had to do was to call a week or two beforehand to make an appointment. He even kept his book rack from the Son of Ackermansion and sold books and magazines. The new "Ackerminimansion" even displayed the little "Ackerminimansion" built by Mary Ellen Daugherty, the young second wife of Walt. Here, we had an Ackerminimansion within an Ackerminimansion. Other treasures included the brontosaurus from *King Kong*, the vampire teeth and top hat from *London After Midnight*, one Metropolis robotrix, a beautiful painting inspired by a *Metropolis* poster of the 1920s, a lobby card from Will Rogers's *One Glorious Day*, *Vampirella* comic layout proofs and Al Jolson mementoes. Forry adopted a philosophical attitude about not having as much of a collection on display. "Well, there isn't much use in my having a collection that I can't look at from my chair," said he.

That fall we celebrated Forry's 86th birthday at the China Inn in Glendale, California. The guests formed a veritable who's who of stars. The packed banquet room of the Chinese buffet restaurant included Ray Bradbury, Bill Warren (author of *Keep Watching the Skies!*), Michael Copner (the publisher of *Cult Movies*) and his wife, Coco (who helped him publish the magazine and interviewed many celebrities for it), Verne Langdon (makeup wizard), George Clayton Johnson (screenwriter for *Logan's Run*, the original *Twilight Zone* and the original *Star Trek*), Shel Dorf (the originator of the largest science fiction convention in the United States, the San Diego Comic-Con), Ronald V. Borst (author of *Graven Images*, a movie poster book that has received much acclaim),

Forry moved to this bungalow in 2002 (Michael Ramsey).

Forry's good friend Ann Robinson (star of *War of the Worlds*), and John Landis (the director of such films as *Oscar* and *Beverly Hills Cop III*).

James Rock, the publisher of Sense of Wonder Press, took the time to chat with me and my friend Michael Ramsey. Science fiction author and First Fandom alumnus Arthur Jean Cox was also there. He looked like a man half his age. Physician Juan Camacho, who served as *Famous Monsters'* Mexican correspondent in its glory days, came up from San Diego. The director and star of *The Wizard of Speed and Time* and *The Hiking Viking*, Mike Jittlov, was the object of attention for many avid fans of his work. Carla Laemmle, looking very youthful at 92, kindly gave autographs to her many admirers. She was still active in dancing and in appearing in documentaries on the topic of Universal pictures.

Joe was one of the organizers of the event, along with Brad Linaweaver, a writer of science fiction and alternate history novels. Brad began the party with the following words: "It means more than we can put into words [to be able to be here today]. After going through innumerable travails, Forry made it through, and we all know it's not easy to get rid of the most 'Famous Monster' in the world." Brad went on to add, "Dragon*Con, which I am intimately involved in, will initiate a brand new award next year. The trophy will look like the Maria robotrix. It will be an award called the Futura award ... the Forry award for multimedia science fiction and fantasy, starting in 2003 and continuing as long as Dragon*Con exists."

9. The 2000s

The Russell Avenue bungalow held a condensed version of Forry's collection of film and science-fiction memorabilia, including this painting of Hugo Gernsback (Michael Ramsey).

Top: Carla Laemmle (right) relaxes with Forry at a friend's home in the 1990s (Rick Atkins).
Bottom: Forry stands with Rick Atkins near Carla Laemmle's home (Rick Atkins).

9. The 2000s

Verne Langdon told us that earlier that week he had received a call from Jim Warren in Philadelphia, reminding him of Forry's birthday party and asking Verne to tell Forry that he had shipped to him a vintage 1952 cherry special neon Cadillac — windshield ... wiper!"

Forry good-naturedly endured the roasting from his faithful friends. Lee Harris ribbed him mercilessly as he toasted him, and John Landis followed it with a toast to Wendayne. Lee added that John Landis had a new Disney film in the can, *Darn Those Pods!*, a remake of *The Invasion of the Body Snatchers*. He was spoofing us, although I didn't realize it at the time and kept my eyes open for that movie for about two years!

Forry announced the winners of the Forry Awards initiated at his 85th birthday in 2001. The winners in 2002 were Ron Borst, Ingrid and Joe Hirscher, Sean Fernald, Joe Blasco and Brian Anthony and company.

Pamela Keesey, who had collaborated on *Sci-Fi Womanthology* with him for Sense of Wonder Press, presented to him on behalf of the World Fantasy Society the "Gods and Monsters" Lifetime Achievement Award, a bust of H.P. Lovecraft.

Sean Fernald, production assistant for *Stan Lee: Mutants, Monsters and Marvels*, told everyone assembled of a personal trip down memory lane that he took when he

"The Sci-Fi Guy," Forrest J Ackerman, autographs an item for a fan while Joe Moe (right) looks on (David Hawk).

Verne Langdon pursues his lifelong passion at the Gordon Theatre (Frank Bresee).

and Joe Moe helped Forry move in 2002 from the Glendower Avenue home into his new home. Sean found among Forry's memorabilia a letter Sean had written to him when 11 years old. The letter read: "Dear Mr. Ackerman. I bought my first issue of *FM* in 1969. I have been a reader for at least two years. I visited my grandparents in Australia when I was a kid; you didn't send *FM* to Australia back then. When I got back home I remembered how good *FM* really is and I ordered all the back issues I could get. Right now I have almost all of them, including the sold out ones, and I have asked for the rest as Christmas gifts. If I don't get them all, I will use my Christmas money to buy the rest. I think you should get the word out about how good the Don Post masks really are (the thirty-nine dollar ones). My friend Joe Moe purchased one and he has won every contest he has entered with it."

George Clayton Johnson stood and told the assembled guests, "I know that this group knows how important FJA is. The media is less than 100 years old. It took off in Forry's childhood. All that we call 'media' today came from those early days. I think of Shel Dorf, Julius Schwartz as the ones who, in the early days, published fanzines, founded the conventions, country to country, year in and year out, established rules of order. They passed the Worldcon down from year to year. Media grew to be the dominant force in our society."

9. The 2000s

Left to right: Sid Kross, Tor Johnson, Verne Langdon, Foresst J Ackerman, and L. Strock Rupert, president of *Stunt Stars from Screenland* and creator of the Unimart Touring Don Post Monster Show. (Don Post Studios).

Johnson gave Forrest Ackerman 90 percent of the credit: "Sci-fi fandom as we know it is an astonishing phenomenon, bringing people from every country together. Many of the chairs at the Los Angeles Science Fantasy Society were bought by Forry when the building was being purchased."

He concluded his speech with a statement directed to Forry: "I am amazed, baffled, dazzled by your accomplishments, Forry. You are a superb individual. I think you will live in history as one of the great men of our era. God bless you!"

Forry invited everyone to come by his new home after the party and "carry on" over there. The next night, Forry's birthday was mentioned on *Entertainment Tonight*, made possible, no doubt, by Kevin J. Burns and other friends in the industry.

Forry continued to celebrate his birthday each year. The parties would usually be held at the Orchid Restaurant near Wilshire Boulevard and the downtown area, the China Inn in Glendale or the Thai Plaza on Hollywood Boulevard. Forry continued to

Top: Forry and the author spend a little time together at Monster Bash 2004 (David Hawk). *Bottom:* Forry (left) points to Ray Bradbury (Jim Morrow).

become stronger and resumed his convention appearances at the World Science Fiction Conventions, Dragon*Con and the Monster Bash conventions, among others. Just two years after the sale of the Glendower Avenue home, life was improving financially for him.

Martianthology, published in 2003 by Sense of Wonder Press, contained stories assembled by Forry from the grand old days of *Science Fiction Monthly*, *Planet Stories*, *Amazing Stories* and others. Entertaining stories in this volume include LASFS charter member Ross Rocklynne's *Water for Mars*, John Russell Fearn's *Martian Miniature*, *The Magic Ball from Mars* by Carl L. Biemiller, and *Mars Is— Hell!* by Forrest J Ackerman, a 1950 discussion of the film *Rocketship X-M*.

Forry, with the help of John Goss, had a web site for a number of years beginning in the late 1990s. *Forrest J Ackerman's Wide Webbed World* was a large site with a floor plan of his Son of Ackermansion, some scary monster masks made by friends, a very long list of famous people who had visited his home, a very long list of persons who had pleased him over the years, a short list of initials of persons who had had a falling out with him, a mail order opportunity to buy a few items, and a contest with prizes. It also had the amusing pages entitled "Forry's Brain," which took one into the unusual cerebral cortex, brain/blood barrier, cerebellum and other parts of the brain of the "Ackermonster."

Frank Bresee (left) smiles for the camera at one of Forry's parties (Jim Morrow).

The Los Angeles County Natural History Museum now has Forry's brontosaurus stop-motion animation model from *King Kong* and is taking care of it.

Forry never saw a public museum filled with his huge and important collection, but some of his important items are displayed in the Science Fiction Museum in Seattle, Washington. The Bill Malone *Metropolis* robotrix is there.

New Zealand's highly regarded director Peter Jackson purchased most of Forry's *King Kong* stop-motion model and prop collection for a good sum. This money went toward Forry's daily living expenses. Peter Jackson now has the gas bomb that felled the beast in the original *King Kong*, as well as the cave bear and Styracosaurus built for *King Kong* but cut from the film and used in its sequel, *Son of Kong*. One can now see the Styracosaurus in a documentary that Jackson created on the making of his version of what the lost spider pit sequence of the original film might have looked like. The foam rubber, latex and steel Styracosaurus was X-rayed at a local hospital so that they could study the materials and methods used in its creation and construct their own, using a tabletop jungle and glass paintings just as the technicians used in 1932 to make the original RKO film. This is a DVD extra in the most recent 1933 *King Kong* DVD release entitled "RKO Production 601: The Making of Kong, Eighth Wonder of the World."

Forry felt strong enough by 2004 to do without a live-in nurse, and he and Joe managed well on their own for many years. Joe assumed many of the day-to-day operations but Forry made all the important decisions that affected his own life. He and Joe Moe would often head over to Las Vegas and play the "Munsters" game, which Forry would frequently win. Forry continued to edit anthologies of classic horror fiction and science fiction for Sense of Wonder Press and Rock Publishing Company. They included *Rainbow Fantasia*, *Martianthology*, *Sci-Fi Womanthology*, and *Dr. Acula's Thrilling Tales of the Uncanny*. The latter is a most interesting assemblage of frightening tales from *Weird Tales* and other older magazines. Many of the authors such as Dr. David Keller, a psychologist and a master of knowing what scares us, were discovered by me in various reprinted collections in the early 1970s before I met Forry, but it was most gratifying to see a collection like this made available in 2005. Forry wrote a delightful book for Sense of Wonder Press, *Famous Forry Fotos*, which is a good companion piece for *Forrest J Ackerman's World of Science Fiction*. He was working on his autobiography, "Life in a Time Machine."

A typical day in the life of Forry Ackerman in 2004 would involve writing a column, having a nap in the afternoon, going to the House of Pies or Sizzler for dinner and then resting up for the next day's work of having Joe or Dennis Billows drive him to a film shoot.

Forry's birthday party in 2004 was a gala affair at the Thailand Plaza Restaurant on Hollywood Boulevard. Ray Bradbury could not attend because he was being honored by the president of the United States that week in Washington, D.C., Brad Linaweaver spoke on Forry's collaboration with him on a hardcover coffee table book, *Worlds of Tomorrow*, a book of science fiction art from the classic magazines and books of the 1920s through the 1960s. Forry announced his donation to the American Cinematheque which would make him able to endow the American Cinematheque on Hollywood Boulevard, the Grauman's Egyptian Theatre, with money toward its operation and named some of the seats in honor of Ray Bradbury, King Kong and George Clayton Johnson. Richard Valley, publisher of *Scarlet Street* magazine, was there at the party, and it was one of the last times David Hawk, Mike Ramsey and I would see him, for in 2007 he would be gone from our lives, a victim of cancer.

9. The 2000s

Forry's birthday party in 2005 was held at the Orchid Restaurant near Hollywood and his many close friends helped him celebrate. *The Sci-Fi Boys*, a Paul Davids project featuring Ray Bradbury, John Landis, Peter Jackson and Forrest J Ackerman was partially screened for our benefit.

Forry was a guest at the 2006 Monster Bash in Moon Township, Pennsylvania, and mesmerized the audience with his recollections of seeing Lon Chaney's *London After Midnight* in 1927. He had brought with him from Los Angeles his beaver hat used by Chaney and told the audience of his impressions while viewing the legendary lost film. He was in all likelihood the only person any of the attendees had met who had vivid, almost total recall memories of the movie from childhood viewings. "I saw it four times, and it remains my third favorite Lon Chaney film. I recall that the way Chaney walked as the false vampire was in a manner similar to the one used by Groucho Marx." He was a little concerned that if anyone actually finds the film they may be disappointed that he walks in this way that might be interpreted as imitative of Marx, although Chaney was the first to walk in this manner in a film.

Brad Linaweaver at one of Forry's birthday parties in the 21st century (Jim Morrow).

"To my mind," he said, "there was an unnecessary humorous scene, a woman being frightened," Forry explained. He shared some insights with the audience about why such scenes were included. In those days of film, supernatural terror themes were uncommon and it was believed by the producers that the audience needed comedy to keep the proceedings from being too intense.

Forry was still going strong. If someone asked him if he wanted to be in a movie, he said "Yes." If someone wanted to do a documentary, he was ready. Ian Johnston and Michael MacDonald directed and wrote *Famous Monster* for the Space Channel of Canada in 2007. *Famous Monster* told the story of Forry in a condensed form and was done with Forry's cooperation. Forry contributed to *Future by Design*, an architectural film from Open Edge, in 2006, discussing the Bradbury Building which his grandfather George Wyman had designed. Forry wrote his last foreword for *Forrest J Ackerman's Anthology of the Living Dead* in 2008.[1]

Forry appeared in his final cameo in *Red Velvet*, a horror film by Ulalume Films, co-produced by Sean Fernald and Joe Moe. Forry played a gentleman in a restaurant, flirting with a waitress. In other words, he played himself.

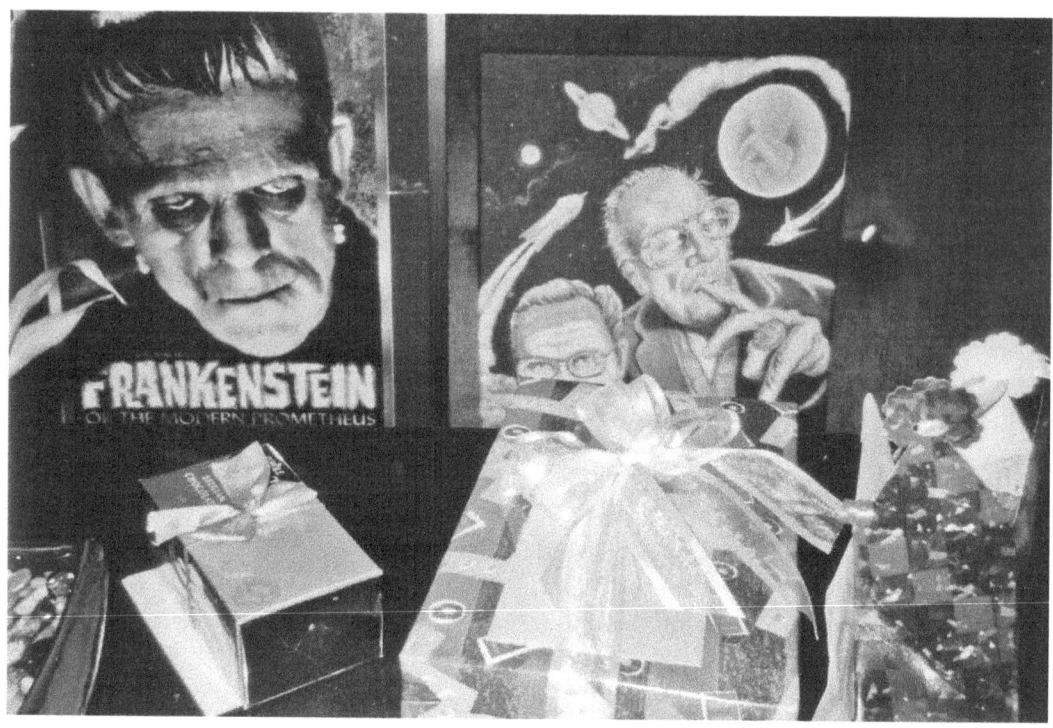

Forry had many gifts at his 89th birthday party at the Orchid Restaurant in Los Angeles.

Walter Ernsting, the gentleman with whom Forry had created the idea of an English-language Perry Rhodan series, died in 2006 at the age of 84. Forry's old friend Walter Daugherty died on June 14, 2007. Forry had to have hip-replacement surgery in 2007 and his recuperation was slow. He would never be able to attend any more out-of-town conventions as a result. His doctor forbade him to travel by air or train. This was a huge disappointment for the man who had tried to attend all the World Science Fiction conventions, and who had missed only a few such conventions in his 90-plus years.

Forry also seldom went out to eat anymore with fans and friends at the House of Pies because he could no longer taste food. His taste buds had ceased to function. Forry's 90th birthday party was a big event, attracting hundreds of his friends, and so was his 91st. By now, Forry had seen hand-held cell phones that allow the owner to log onto the Internet. He saw automobiles with GPS technology that assist the driver with navigating the highways. Women were now holding high offices around the world. Kidney transplants and cochlear ear implants were not only possible, they were commonplace. Forry had seen photos taken by spacecraft landing on Mars and a Hubble Telescope that, since it was outside the Earth's atmosphere, could photograph incredibly distant stars with amazing clarity. So many things were coming true that had been forecast in the pages of his beloved *Amazing Stories and Science Wonder Stories*.

9. The 2000s

At the 2006 Monster Bash, Forry entrances attendees with tales of seeing *London After Midnight* as a boy. Organizer Ron Adams (right) looks on.

On December 1, 2007, the Thailand Plaza restaurant was once more bustling with notables, the most important being Forrest J Ackerman, the man of the day. There to help him party were, among his faithful friends, Ray Bradbury, Ann Robinson, actor Curtis Armstrong (*Boston Legal* star), and Mike Jittlov. Eric Caidin also came to the party. A close friend of Forry, Eric was the owner of the Hollywood Book and Poster Company on Hollywood Boulevard. Walt Lee, author of *Reference Guide to Fantastic Films*, was a new face to me, but Paul Davids, screenwriter and director, and Arthur Jean Cox, a science fiction fan who befriended Forry back in the early days of the Los Angeles Science Fantasy Society, were both familiar. Also present was George Clayton Johnson. The lovely Lydia van Vogt, second wife and widow of science fiction author A.E. van Vogt, talked at length with me. Terry Pace, literature professor, was a welcome sight, and so was Ron Borst.

Looking very debonair, Forry wears his traditional lei garland for this 90th birthday portrait (Jim Morrow).

9. The 2000s

Forry (left) was still doing well on the occasion of his 90th birthday. Here, he poses with longtime friend Jim Morrow (Jim Morrow).

Musician Michael Gough played "Happy Birthday" to Forry on the theramin.

Casey Wong, special effects artist, did an accurate voice impersonation of Forry at his own party. Venice, California-based Olio, Incorporated, designer and Forry friend Troy Zimmerman, shared his observations of visiting Forry when he was ill several years previously: "I always admired and respected that he would open his collection to visitors. When I saw his home in the 1990s I felt he was a class act — and continues to be. In 2002 Forry became ill and was in the hospital, and I visited as soon as he was able to have people in his room. He looked bad. He was arranged painfully under the sheets, but he was smiling — greeting people! He insisted I take a complimentary magazine. A person in his situation could have been miserable but he was not.

"For the Son of Ackermansion (the big home on Glendower Avenue that Forry lived in before he moved to his current home), our company, which dreamed up the Atlantis Resort in the Bahamas, sent him an Atlantis set to place on display in his home."

Troy concluded, "Forry's brain is just so invaluable!"[2]

Author Brad Linaweaver could not attend but he made sure each celebrant got a complimentary copy of *Mondo Cult Magazine*, which he co-published with Jessie Lilley. Joe Moe and Sean Fernald were in the midst of producing a new horror feature, *Red Velvet*. The cast was to include Kelli Garner, Henry Thomas of *E.T.*, Carol Ann Susi of the cast of *The Night Stalker*, and of course, Forry Ackerman.

Forry was in fine form, chatting, telling jokes and enjoying the festivities. This was the first party I had attended in which he did not address the partygoers but just sat relatively quietly and signed autographs. He was deaf in one ear but otherwise seemed to be doing well. After the three-hour party was over, his nurse and Joe Moe took him home to Russell Avenue for a rest.

Forry's unusual turns of a phrase included these examples.

Many lustrums ago H.G. Wells penned *The Time Machine*. A lustrum is a period of five years. It is a real term once used by the Romans.

Eating places were where you went to dine. Everyone else I know calls these "restaurants."

For many de-CADES (not DEH-cades), he brought Halloween to the children of the world nine times per year with his *Famous Monsters of Filmland* magazine.

The firstime I saw the word "firstime" in *Famous Monsters* I thought it was a typographical error but realized that it was a shorthand way to spell. There may not be a lastime to see it spelled that way.

Twilight Zone writer George Clayton Johnson (Jim Morrow).

The project died a'borning (meaning that the creative project, be it novel, film or whatever, did not get far past its beginning stage.). In other words, it remained in the "Realm of Unwrought Things" (another Forry phrase).

If one wishes to take a Forrest J Ackerman tour of Los Angeles and the San Fernando Valley there are several sites where access is easy. The Warner Bros. Museum at the Warner Bros. lot in Burbank is a place where the visitor can find Forry's name. The Museum does not allow photography, but when you enter the first floor there is a large display of names of grateful acknowledgments. The first name on the large black board as you enter the door on your left, at the base of the flight of stairs, is Forrest J Ackerman's.

When one visits Hollywood, one

9. The 2000s

Jim Morrow greets the beautiful Lydia van Vogt, widow of science fiction author A.E. van Vogt (Jim Morrow).

can see Forry's handprints in cement alongside Ray Harryhausen's and Ryan and Tatum O'Neal's at the Vista Theater at the corner of Hollywood Boulevard and Sunset Drive, just east of the intersection of Hollywood Boulevard and Vermont Avenue. The interior has been restored to something approaching its original 1923 décor. If you wish to go to the same movie theater frequented by Forry, see a film at the Los Feliz Theater at 1822 North Vermont Avenue, just a few blocks to the north, and walk across the street from the Los Feliz to the House of Pies at 1869 North Vermont and order a milkshake and a plate of spaghetti in his honor.

Perry Rhodan is going strong in Germany; as of 2009 it was at issue 2492.

In 1926, according to Forry, he beheld the first issue of *Amazing Stories* at a pharmacy. "You may not realize it but in those days magazines spoke," he would say at conventions. "This one jumped off the newsstands, grabbed me and said, 'Take me home, little boy, you will love me!'"

Nowadays a visit to almost any grocery store will deluge one with talking coupon dispensers, talking stuffed toys that sing when one squeezes them, greeting cards that play music and soft fabric balls that screech when one bounces them. Among the few things in the supermarket that *don't* talk are the magazines!

Forry's public wish was that he might live to be 100 and become the George Burns of Science Fiction.

Michael Porjes, his estranged stepson, died in July 2008 at the age of 67, in Hawaii, where he had lived since the 1970s. He had been a computer artist and futurologist. Mr. Porjes' wife, Susan, and daughter, Wendy, still reside in Hawaii and his son Daniel is in Israel. His son Marc is in California. The Alcor Life Extension Foundation in Arizona has cryogenically preserved his body.[3] In this, Michael had much in common with Forry. Forry himself had toyed with this idea in the 1990s but decided instead that his earthly remains would be laid in the crypt next to his wife Wendy's at Forest Lawn in Glendale, California.

Recently I confided to my brother Floyd that I had never thought of Forry as an icon back in the 1970s, 1980s and the 1990s. I had regarded him as an extraordinary person, a wonderful friend, a fellow with his feet on the ground more firmly than most people I have known, the magnet of the science fiction universe who drew others to him like a piece of charged iron ore draws filings, a man of immense generosity and intelligence, and the best editor anyone ever had. Any writer whose first editor had been Forrest J Ackerman is blessed indeed. I knew that I was blessed. Forry would go out of his way to include us friends on his many grand adventures in Hollywoodland and elsewhere. I understood the ways in which his presence in my life had blessed me, and I was pleased as punch when I would read that Forry was the guest of honor at some convention. He most certainly qualified! But, I told my brother, I did not think of him as an icon until the beginning of the 2000s. Perhaps I became aware of his iconic status when I noted that the number of fans who clustered about him at conventions grew exponentially from the 1980s, when he would be surrounded at all times during conventions by at least 10 to 20 fans, to the early 2000s, when 30 or 40 fans would swarm about him. It was long overdue for Forry to have that many fans mobbing him at a convention, I felt. I thought that was most appropriate and had, in truth, always wondered why he had ever had small crowds surrounding him at a convention! Did the science fiction convention attendees not know who this man was and why he was so tremendously important in science fiction?

There were also his increasing appearances in everything from comic books (*The Flaming Carrot*) to documentaries (*Finding the Future*), which cemented his iconic status.

Forry's dear friend, college professor Terry Pace, named his and his wife Anita's child after him and Ray Bradbury in 2004. Forrest Phillips Bradbury Pace is six years old at the time of this writing and is a towheaded boy who rather resembles Forry when he was that age. The Paces also have a daughter, Alexandra, and both knew Forry and visited him many times in his bungalow. The children continue to visit with "Papa Ray," as they call Ray Bradbury.

Forry posted on Harry Knowles' *Aint It Cool News* web site in 2004 that he realized he would be passing sometime in the next ten years. He wrote, "My maternal grandfather died with a beatific smile on his face as though he were seeing angels or loved ones. Maybe I'll get lucky and imagine my mother calling, as she did when I was a child, 'Forry, boy, come and take your nap.'"[4]

Top: Forrest Ackerman and Forrest Phillips Bradbury Pace wear their matching Dracula capes in 2004 (Terry Pace). *Bottom:* Forry sings a Jolson song to his namesake, Forrest Pace, and Forrest's sister Alexandra at Forry's Russell Avenue home (Terry Pace).

Forry

Forry became very ill the day before Halloween 2008 and had to go to the hospital. Joe Moe called me Halloween night and gave me the shocking news that Forry might only have a few days left and that he had asked Joe to call me and other friends to let them know that he had pneumonia. I did call Forry at a prearranged time a few days later and he sounded very weak. I decided to ask for some vacation time from my understanding boss, Rosetta Billups, and catch the first plane I could catch out of Norfolk, Virginia, the following week. Forry had been showing some signs of improvement according to all emails I had received and posts on Internet forums devoted to classic horror films and television. I arrived to see Pamela Keesey and Earl Roesel staying with Forry. The pneumonia had cleared up but he still was weak. He had had congestive heart failure for quite some time (according to the doctors) and no one had known it until the day before Halloween when he could not stand. He had declined any heroic measures to prolong his life and opted to go home and be cared for by his friends and by his regular live-in nurse, Dolly Ynarez, and his physical therapist, José.

I spent several days in Los Angeles and spent as much of them as I could there. Forry was sleeping quite a lot, which was understandable. Pam Keesey had flown in from Seattle a week before and was telecommuting. She, Joe Moe and Earl Roesel, who lived there with Forry, attended to his every need. I brought some DVDs of films freelance photographer David Hawk had furnished that we thought might cheer him up. José came twice a week to give him some therapy so that, if he continued to show signs of improvement, he might walk again. Staying in bed would be very deleterious to his muscles. Forry was majestic in these days. He very seldom complained, even though he had been in pain earlier that week. I have never seen anyone who was aware that they were dying to be as dignified about it as he. "I don't want to be a burden or a bother," he said to his physical therapist. "You're not bothering nobody," José kindly replied. Forry would attempt to make a crack or joke occasionally. Joe Moe and Sean Fernald came by each day to stay for several hours with Forry and supervise progress. I could tell that they were deep down as discouraged as I.

The outpouring of cards, email wishes and gifts from fans all over the world made Forry feel that he might need to tough it out a little longer. Once again, his fans needed him, the world needed him and so he made a conscious choice to live a little longer. Some friends of his, including Nivek Ogre (Kevin Ogilvie) of the rock band Skinny Puppy and actress Candy Clark, came to see him during my visit. Said Lee Harris of those weeks in November, "The last Jolson song Forry heard was 'Rock a Bye Your Baby (with a Dixie Melody).' I brought over a ghetto blaster with some CDs, and in his bedroom played 'Here Lies Love' by Bing Crosby (he may have been dying but still loved 'em torchy), plus one other Bing, maybe 'Out of Nowhere.' It was one of the early '30s hits. Then I put on the Jolson. 4e did the same hand gestures he had done all his life with the song, including pounding both his fists in the air with the heavy 'bum, bum, bum, bum' notes preceding 'a million baby kisses I'll deliver, if you will only sing that 'Swanee River.' So he was always up for enjoying Jolson the same old way, but had tired of living.— bummer —."[5]

9. The 2000s

The night I said goodnight to Forrest J Ackerman at his little bungalow on Russell Avenue in Los Angeles had been a fairly good night for him because one of his favorite shows was on television, *Dancing with the Stars*. Joe Moe and Sean Fernald stopped by and we moved some furniture. Earlier that evening Lee Harris came over to deliver more of the rare DVDs he brought almost every day for Forry. Lee told Forry some truly dreadful puns and we all laughed, even Forry. I wished Lee did not have to go home because it was such a wonderful hour, one I will be comforted by for some time. I dared not say to Forry that I wanted him to get well because I knew better and he had made it clear to Joe that he really was tired and did not want to keep struggling indefinitely. I knew that he really felt it was time for him to move on soon. I respected that. For years I had tried to broach the topic of life after death and the scientific evidence for this. Over the years I had mentioned this subject a few times and named some of the pioneering scientists such as Ian Stevenson of the University of Virginia's School of Health Services, but never went into much detail because it seemed he did not want to believe in such things. That night of November 18 I did everything I could to stay calm, and it was hard to do. I acted toward him the same way I acted toward my father a decade and a half before when he was suffering from a disease of the nervous system and was growing weaker and more frail and harder to understand with each passing week. I acted positive toward Forry, almost nonchalant, as though, in smiling, laughing and telling stories to him, I was telling him nonverbally that everything was normal, everything was fine, and all would be all right. And it would.

I held his hand and made some promises. Then I bade him goodnight. I did not tell him goodbye because there will never be a time for me to say goodbye to that which is eternal about Forrest J Ackerman. Not goodbye, as you know, my friend.

Forry passed on December 4, 2008, near midnight, surrounded by his friends.

His mortal remains were interred in a crypt in the section known as Dawn of Tomorrow at Forest Lawn Cemetery in Glendale, California, next to Wendayne's crypt. A photograph of Wendy and one of Jacie Appelbaum was placed in the casket. The crypt faces the morning sun rising over the mountains.

Forry's friends Joe Moe, Earl Roesel, Kevin J. Burns and Sean Fernald teamed up with dozens of other friends and with the American Cinematheque and organized a tribute in March 2009 at the beautiful Grauman's Egyptian Theatre in Hollywood. The line outside the theater stretched down the block. If all the persons who had admired Forrest J Ackerman had been able to attend, the theater could not have held them all. David J. Skal, Carla Laemmle, Terry and Anita Pace, George Clayton Johnson, Ron and Jaclynn Chaney, Jeff Roberts, Ann Robinson, John C. Stoskopf, Angus Scrimm, Arlene Domkowski, Juan Camacho and many, many other friends were there. Many persons spoke on how important Forry was to them and how much they were inspired by him. Rick Baker, John Landis, Jovanka Vukovich, Bill Warren, Paul Davids, Guillermo del Toro, Ray Bradbury, Joe Dante and scores of others expressed their love for him. Joe Moe and some of his musician friends played "Forry Boy," to the tune of Al Jolson's "Sonny Boy" and showed a video recorded at Forry's home in which he said

Some items to be auctioned off in May 2009 were on display at the American Cinematheque tribute to Forrest J Ackerman in March of 2009 (David Hawk).

"farewell" to everyone and "sci-fi." The original sci-fi guy got his wish after all! The documentary *Famous Monster* was screened, as was the science fiction film *The Time Travelers*. Some who had never seen this picture were able to see a Forry in his forties. Michael Gough once again played the theramin at a Forry party.

Butler, Pennsylvania, is the traditional home of the Monster Bash International Film Conference, a fancy title for a huge family reunion of monster fans of all ages and from a half-dozen countries. In 2009 the convention hosted no less than three tributes to "Mr. Science Fiction," who had been a special guest at most of the Bashes since they began in 1997.

The Monsterpalooza in Burbank, California, took place in the late summer of 2009 and was a convention filled with aficionados of masks, models and movies. Phil Kim will be the new publisher of *FM*, and at the Monsterpalooza he announced that the magazine would return in some form. Forry and James Warren had approved his efforts and gave him their blessing in 2008. Indianapolis, Indiana, was the setting for the newest *FM* convention, set for July 9 through 11, 2010. *Famous Monsters* is apparently one very popular monster that will be coming back for sequels for quite a few years.

9. The 2000s

Forry wanted to promote quality science fiction; it was his life's work. What is the future of science fiction and fandom?

The Internet is making convention attendance something that can be done online. Flycon began at midnight, Friday the 13th in March of 2009 in Australia and continued across the globe as the sunlight made its path across the sphere. There were podcasts, discussions and a blogosphere. IRCs and a bulletin board were run and everything was coordinated through the Live Journal community with rss feeds.[6]

Would Forry be pleased to see the online sci-fi convention? He might! He believed in a future where there were choices galore for a person who was interested in science fiction.

Fans of Forrest J Ackerman talk to one another about which films and television series he loved, which ones he did not care for, and which ones he never took interest in viewing.

Top: David Hawk places carnations at Forry's crypt at Forest Lawn cemetery. *Bottom:* Friends, business associates and admirers of Forry Ackerman paid their respects at the American Cinematheque (the Grauman's Egyptian Theatre) in Hollywood in March 2009.

This is how influential Forry's tastes have been on several generations of film aficionados.

Forry won an Italian version of the Hugo Award, the Burroughs Bibliophile Award, the Count Dracula Society's Ann Radcliffe Award, three Hugos, and was the inspiration for three awards named after him, the Forry Awards. He also received Forrys. One was awarded at the annual Monster Bash in western Pennsylvania. A second Forry Award, the Futura, is handed out at the Dragon*Con, and a third Forry Award is given at the LosCon. Fred Patton won the 2009 LosCon Forry.

Forry's legacy is, I hope, to be fivefold.

Compassion

Forry spoke about some of his beliefs and feelings about life in *Amazing Forries*. "Can you believe," he wrote, "that I truly wish that there was some way to move about in this world *and not crush a single ant*? That I wish it wasn't necessary to swat flies? To pluck fruit from trees? In Dr. Schweitzer's famous 'Reverence for Life' I feel he apparently overlooked the fact that in treating diseases we are destroying millions of lives (of microbes). I don't know any solution but I regret it nonetheless. (But not to a fanatical extent, only on a philosophical level.)"[7]

Forry would feed the raccoons which came to his backyard and he would also feed fans who were in need. Every Thanksgiving he would treat fans who had no family with whom to share the holiday. When other celebrities sold autographed stills of themselves for $20, he sold his for $10 because he felt that fans were usually not wealthy. He would lend money to various fans and some never paid him back, but he continued to love the fans regardless. Compassion was something that motivated him throughout life.

Forry was a gentleman who rarely uttered a curse word. Only if he was extremely angry would he ever utter such a word, and I seldom saw him angry.

A Different Way to Regard the Aged

Many a person could learn a lesson or two from Forry's life on the subject of how to regard our aged. Too often in our Western society the elderly are pushed aside in the rush of modern news reporting and forgotten about. The media are interested in the shapely, the young, the athletic, the nubile. Young people frequently avoid the elderly. Old people remind the young of their own mortality—and death is something that is feared. When someone dies it is seen as a "tragedy," not the natural result of living. Old people. They are boring, are they not? Many individuals regard them as such. They don't go to film festivals, do they? Don't even ask them if they would want to be in a movie. They would never want to be in a horror or science fiction film, would they? Nor would young directors ask them to be in a film, would they?

9. The 2000s

Well, they would if they had the appeal of Forrest J Ackerman!

And what is that appeal?

Simply put, Forry could not sit still! Even though he loved the classic science fiction books and the classic science fiction films and classic horror films, and promoted them tirelessly, he also liked some new films and books and wanted to know more. Among his favored newer theatrical releases were *Run Lola Run* and *Midnight in the Garden of Good and Evil*. His craving for knowledge about the new world of entertainment was vast, and he had a young person's interest in life.

How would most of us know this if it weren't for his writing and his many documentary appearances and convention appearances?

Well, how many of our seniors are sitting in their chairs *right now*, with information and memories to impart, but we are not showing enough interest and encouragement?

Might older adults take a cue from Forry? Might those of us who are not yet 70 and over ourselves decide we might be a little more open-minded? Perhaps we might decide that when we are old in body we will not be old in mind. Perhaps we will watch our behavior and think of how our thoughts create our reality. Mayhaps we will joke a little more, and watch a comedy or be willing to try something new and socialize a little more with young people. Maybe we will not focus on our old bodies quite so much when we are aged, a temptation indeed when we are frail and even in pain from various maladies. If anyone asked Forry how he was, did he reply with, "Well, my bursitis has been acting up"? No, he replied, "Never better."

Almost no one thought Forry was too old. Perhaps it is because he himself did not believe it. He often said in interviews, "As long as I am alive and I am able to impart some valuable information, I am willing to give it. I am a science fiction sponge ... squeeze me." That request was especially meant for the ladies!

Hard Work

Forry enjoyed work. He worked whenever he was not entertaining guests from out of town, or attending a convention or a LASFS club function or going to the local Los Feliz Theater or the nearby Cinerama Dome. Sometimes he did a promotional appearance at one of the conventions he attended, giving talks or autographing books or stills, so he was actually working at these as well! He worked out of necessity. He was a freelancer throughout most of his life. The only times he punched a time clock or drew a salary were when he worked as a timekeeper, when he worked at his dad's place of employment for a month, when he operated the varitype machine, when he was in the Army, when he worked for the Academy of Motion Picture Arts and Sciences, and when he edited *Famous Monsters of Filmland* and several other publications for Warren Publishing Company. These steady engagements account for slightly less than half of his life. He spent 25 years editing the magazine and writing for other Warren Publications and did not receive any of the standard benefits such as sick leave, life insurance or health insurance. Those were only available through his wife's employment. James Warren bought him an orange Cadillac in the late 1970s, purchased a big-screen television and a new typewriter, and partly financed Forry's autobiographical magazine *Amazing Forries*, and those are some of the benefits over and above his pay for editing several magazines.

After he resigned in the early 1980s to avoid being fired from *Famous Monsters of Filmland*, Forry wrote many books and made many film appearances to bring in as much money as he could. He ceased agenting work long before he retired from editing and writing. In fact, Forry was still editing book anthologies and writing as late as 2008. The Ackermans' home on Glendower Avenue was a huge operating expense, and although the home at Russell was less so, it still remained an expense to maintain. Various persons and institutions would donate money to the Fantasy Foundation, as he called his collection. However, no wealthy benefactor supported him and no one other than he and his spouse paid for any home Forry lived in since the 1950s when his father bought his first home on Sherbourne Drive. No one except Forry himself paid the rent for the little bungalow on Russell Avenue.

An Attitude of Gratitude

We have all met people who do not even thank us for a favor done them or a gift given them. We are often left puzzled and somewhat hurt and wonder why the person does not thank us or acknowledge the gift or our time and care. Our minds stray to the idea that maybe the person feels himself superior to us and does not feel the need to thank us. This may or may not be true, but the fact remains that they did not take the time to thank us.

James Warren presented Forry with an orange Cadillac on his 60th birthday, in 1976 (Mary Ellen Daugherty [Mrs. Walter J. Daugherty]).

Forry was grateful for anything anyone ever did for him and told them so. He would repay a kindness whenever possible and tried to acknowledge favors, often most spectacularly in the form of bringing their names up at a big ceremony or thanking them on the printed page of a magazine or a book. When he was in his late eighties and early nineties he became too frail to write letters or send e-mail messages in any large quantity. But, for as long as he was able, Forry was crouched over his word processor, writing letters and sending postcards and emails. I think most of us could keep his example in mind and express gratitude. Far from being a chore, it actually encourages people to do more for us. Forry was not too busy to thank people and he learned when he was a young man in his forties to give people credit.

Forry has been criticized, even vilified, for wanting to surround himself with persons who would praise him and give him encouragement. I have heard people criticize him for not wanting to be around people who criticized him. It is very difficult for me to understand this particular assessment. Who among us prefer the company of churlish and critical persons if we can be in the company of those who encourage us and our creativity? Critics of Forrest Ackerman have often said that he had a massive ego that needed to be stroked constantly. Forry had an ego, but he was quite the egalitarian. Much of what uninformed persons thought was a massive ego was merely necessary self promotion. He had to sell his persona to be in films to earn money, and as a freelancer he had to sell books and CD-ROMs to pay his bills, and promotion was the way he accomplished this.

Some have noted that "he is just a boy" and "he never grew up." I have observed that he was wise enough to forgive people if they did not consciously do him harm. Not everyone is so wise. I noted also that he was wise enough to stop driving soon after he turned 83, knowing that his reaction times would be too slow for safety, something not every octogenarian will admit. Many was the time that I would struggle with other senior friends who wanted me to take them out shopping for another car when they had just totaled the one they had been driving, and I did not have any long-distance worries about Forry taking his car out on the road at 86.

I have heard people accuse him of having a massive ego that made him take credit for things he was not responsible for. I have seen egotism on the part of Forry, but I do not recall any instance when he deliberately took credit for something that he knew was done by another. Forry made it a point to promote other people's work, something that these individuals neglect to mention. He was very careful to give credit where due.

When we friends had Forry to ourselves for a while, away from the rush of a convention or an event, where he had to self promote to make his living, the quiet, humble and comical side of Forry was very evident. In situations where he did not feel he had to "work," but just relax among friends, run errands or just do his normal day-to-day tasks, Forry mostly asked questions instead of always telling his anecdotes. I never knew him to pitch a temper tantrum if he did not get his way. Once in a while, he would have what he humorously referred to as "old-timer's disease" and forget someone.

The Virtue of Mentoring

Forry not only mentored this author, he mentored William F. Nolan, Ray Bradbury, Joe Dante, Terri Pinckard, Donald F. Glut, Joe Moe and many, many others. The list goes on and on. "Mr. Sci Fi" enjoyed helping people who expressed an interest in classic horror films and science fiction film and literature. He enjoyed showing people around his Ackermansions and the Ackerminimansion. Forry knew that when he scattered his jewels some would not land before an appreciative audience, but many would land before appreciative persons who would do something with them. No matter that the museum in his house was slowly diminished bit by bit over time as pieces went to the Science Fiction Museum on 5th Avenue in Seattle, Washington, or to other collectors, or to storage. He had the same attitude he had always had: to encourage anyone who was interested in the arts and especially science fiction. We were content to sit in clusters alongside Forry's chair and listen to all of his accounts of this star or that author, of this trip to visit Mary Shelley's grave or that journey to Paris, France to see a museum where they had the beautiful costume used in the silent film *L'Atlantide*.

Forry was interested in seeing a healthy planet with productive people free of addictions to chemicals, and urged his readers and fans not to get intoxicated for fun, smoke or become part of the drug scene. He offered the alternative of movies and movie history, mummies and invisible men, werewolves and dinosaurs, space stations and trips to Antares.

Perhaps I saw a quality in Forry that non-biologists have somehow missed, or, if they did notice, did not mention to me. Perhaps it is the biologist in me that saw this. We biologists have discovered something in nature called "neotenic characters." This pertains to qualities present in juveniles persisting to adulthood and being passed on. At first glance this may appear to not be advantageous, but in fact is. The tunicate is a squat little soft-bodied creature that looks like a pepper pot and which lives on the shallow sea floors. Its larval form looks a bit like a fish with a tapered body and a "notochord," a rod surrounded by musculature and which protects the primitive nervous system cord that runs from head to tail. When it grows up it loses most of this feature and becomes completely quiet and unmoving. Scientists surmise that in the remote misty past of prehistoric time some never lost their notochords when they matured and when these matured they mated and passed on the notochord feature. We see the result in the "amphioxus" or yellow lancet, a species of primitive chordate living today in Jamaica and in some parts of Asia. It is a small yellow creature that spends a lot of time burrowed under the silts, but it does superficially resemble a fish and is, in fact, related to the ancestors of fish. Of course, fish are the ancestors of you and me. We also see neotenic characters in the domestic dog. Wolves bark when cubs but when they grow up they only yip and howl. The dog, a form of canid closely related to the wolf, barks as an adult.

What is a discussion of a squat little pepper pot and of cuddly cubs that keep barking when they grow up, doing in this book about Forrest J Ackerman? Well, sometimes the retention of some juvenile characters, like the penchant for collecting movie memorabilia well into late adulthood, or sharing outrageous puns, has an advantage. One can be childlike or one can be childish. We all know childish people and we all know childlike people, and we know the difference. Childish people possess the negative qualities of childhood: the stubbornness, the temper tantrums and the lack of responsibility; childlike individuals retain a sense of wonder about the world around them and are not afraid to play. The adults who retain this childlike sense of wonder and curiosity are the more evolved ones who have been the artistic and scientific pioneers.

My other observation is that here is a mind which was and always will be nonspiteful, clever, responsible, and having an almost nonstop wicked sense of humor. He made mistakes in his life, yes, and in that respect was like everyone. Even though there were some people who treated him shabbily, and people who disliked him even though he had tried to promote their work, Forry did not withdraw into cynicism the way some persons would. Despite the fact that "fans" would enter his home as part of the tours and, unnoticed, steal from his collection, Forry continued to conduct the tours. In his mind, he was doing more good than harm and did not want to stop the tours since he was helping the people who were not stealing from him.

Many others would have quit the program of tours because of the actions of these few. Forrest J Ackerman did not want to have a collection of interesting film artifacts that no one but a select few trusted persons could view. He wanted to share, and share he did. For a man who claimed that he was nonspiritual, Forry was very introspective and interested in the world of consciousness. For several years he even kept a dream journal in which he recorded some of his ordinary and extraordinary dreams.

Without being a member of any particular order or religious or spiritual organization, he thought of life as something to live well and, in so doing, leave happier beings in one's wake. He did not think he would be rewarded in an afterlife for being good, and that is not why he was good. Nor did he do good to avoid punishment after death, as some religions of the world maintain. He simply did good things because it seemed like the right thing to do. Perhaps this is Forry's greatest gift. Forry showed his fans and admirers that the source of goodness is us. We can make the decision to be good and to do the right thing. Being generous paid off for Forry and so he served as an example that we do not always impoverish ourselves when we give.

Some people like adventure fiction, escapism and popular culture. Might it not be good that someone who teaches a better way of living be a leader in those areas to inspire and influence? Forry is one of those leaders. What could be harmful or detrimental about being interested in our science fiction heritage, including film and television? Is being interested in motion picture history and its artifacts any different from being interested in preserving and perpetuating Chinese armor from the 1300s, or cookware used by 18th century North Carolina colonists? People often threw those very objects away 150 years ago, because they thought they were outmoded and it was foolish to keep them. Only a few "eccentrics" kept such things for posterity. Now we of the 21st century place these objects in museums and hire specially trained conservators to keep them from deteriorating. Forry was smart enough to know that one day film props and materials would be terribly valuable to historians, and he was correct — even though he was ridiculed for wanting to keep them.

It was all right, in fact, it was good, said Forry, not to want to kill animals for sport. It was all right not to curse, take drugs or smoke or become ill or injure one's self or others as a result of alcohol abuse. It is better, he said, to be interested in the arts. It is better to acquaint one's self with the literary achievements of Goethe, Shelley, Stoker, Wells and Weinbaum. This not only improves one's vocabulary, it can provide enough mental stimulation and pleasure to substitute a hundredfold for intoxicants.

He was a leader to millions of persons. People who consider themselves different because they like science fiction and fantasy films, who often feel ignored or even scorned by the larger society for their interest, look upon him as their mentor, someone grand and fine who understood them. Forry lived a life that showed that he was a normal, intelligent and healthy individual. He had a mate, he had thousands of friends; he had careers and a home. Some collectors are reclusive; he was not. Some film historians are guarded; he was not. Someone who literally stood tall, who loved science fiction and classic monster films, told them that it was all right to be interested in motion picture history, the acting realm, and film technology. He also showed them how much he cared about them by sharing what he had with them.

I close with these words, one observation taken from Sam Sackett's 1952 interview of a 36-year-old Forry published in *Fantastic Worlds*. "And that, after all, is Ackerman. Not this: 'If I get rich, think of all I can buy for myself.' But this: 'If I get rich, think of all the help I can be to science fiction and my friends.' Anybody who can live for any length of time on the planet Earth and still look on life that way has not been unsuccessful."[8]

Five Personal Reminiscences (Powell, Knight, Atkins, Hawk, Morrow)

Some admirers and friends of Forrest J Ackerman have consented to publish their thoughts in this biography.

MARTIN POWELL is a writer and a huge admirer of Forry.

My goodness, I suppose to begin with I should say that Forry helped me learn to read. My first issue of *Famous Monsters* was number 34, when it was new on the stands. I was about six years old and had just visited the doctor. Not long before I'd seen *Bride of Frankenstein* on TV, and I begged my mother to buy the magazine for me. She did. I was mesmerized by it, then and ever-after. It was simply the greatest thing ever. I didn't understand all the words, but I sure wanted to. I'm certain that I became such a skilled reader soon afterward mainly so I could fully experience the pages of *FM*.

Forry also frequently recommended various sci-fi authors in his editorials. I discovered the likes of Jules Verne, H.G. Wells, Edgar Rice Burroughs, and Ray Bradbury due to him. Amazing inspirations.

Many years later, after I'd begun my own professional writing career, I wrote a graphic novel adaptation of Mary Shelley's *Frankenstein*. I dedicated the book "To Forrest J Ackerman and the gentle ghost of Boris Karloff," and sent a copy to Forry. He graciously responded to me by letter, thanking me. I remember feeling that I'd really "made it" now that one of my own books had been added to the famous Ackerman library.

Some years after that, I finally met Forry in person. It remains one of the greatest thrills of my life. I could hardly express to him how much he had meant to me. I honestly feel that Forry had a much more positive influence on me than my own father (who's a great guy). Forry himself plays a cameo in the third issue of *Martians, Go Home*. The entire series is devoted to him and his legacy.

Forry's passing pains me still. I continue to think about him every day, wishing I'd had a better opportunity to show my appreciation.

Five Personal Reminiscences (Knight)

PAUL S. KNIGHT, a writer for *Scary Monsters Magazine*, wrote of Forrest J Ackerman.

Forrest J Ackerman ... what can I say about this gentleman that hasn't been so eloquently stated already in books and articles before and after his passing? Unfortunately I have also read unfounded rumors, innuendos and speculations on the Internet that I and others feel need to be cleared up. I believe this book written by Miss Painter will give you the facts and be a proper tribute to this amazing human being!

I assume like myself, many of us first became familiar with Dr. Acula (his pun pen name) when we picked up our first copy of the original *Famous Monsters of Filmland* by Warren Publishing Co. I started a little late with the *F.M.* craze beginning in issue number 120 of this fun and frightening fanzine fellow Forry fans. It had an underwater picture of the *Creature from the Black Lagoon* (Universal Pictures, 1954) on the front cover that got the attention of this (at the time) eight-year-old boy. To shamelessly quote Mr. Ackerman, the magazine also said to me, "Take me home, little boy; you will love me"! This publication and Uncle Forry spoke volumes to we Monster Kids that has also influenced many now-famous actors, authors, directors, make-up, special effects artists and other related crafts in the industry. Not only was he a brilliant editor, agent and historian but a great writer as well. My colleague Deborah Painter had her first article in *Famous Monsters*, number 160 (January 1980) with her "Tyrannosaurus Wrecks" article. Like many of us, also, our now high priced back issues probably ended up in the trash or given away in the foolishness of our youth and the struggle to give up the last vestiges of our childhood. Thanks to the help of our local comic shop, the Trilogy, I've been able to locate some of these old treasures for a decent price and Gerry the local proprietor is cool enough to give me a discount to boot at times. I remembering reading Deborah's contribution when it first came out and thinking, "COOL, a girl wrote this"! If you had told me some 20 years later that she would become a dear friend, collaborator and writing mentor, I would have thought you were crazy. I would have again thought you were nuts if you also had told me I would be writing and doing photography for a horror magazine entitled *Scary Monsters Magazine* (Dennis Druktenis Publishing) that began for me in 1999. One of the nicest compliments I hear from time to time is readers coming up to me at a convention and stating, "This reminds me of the old *Famous Monsters of Filmland*." Dennis has tried hard to give his magazine that old *F.M.* feel yet, at the same time, add his own unique style to this labor of love. I also have Forry to thank for my use of alliteration and a plethora of puns people. It has amazed and saddened me that the so-called "intelligentsia" has always looked down on this style of writing and the horror and sci-fi genres in general. While getting my muse motivated for these Ackermonster memories, I delicately removed some of my mint issues from their plastic prisons in order to once again enjoy their wonderful content, and to inhale that intoxicating old pulp paper smell that brings back the remnants of a much happier time.

Most of you have probably read of the visits to the Ackermansion and meeting him at various functions for the first time. It is hard to be original and not redundant in that aspect regarding Forry stories. I'm hoping my reminiscences will bring more memories and perhaps a feeling of *déjà vu* for those who had met him and convey the mood and feeling to those who wished they had. The FJA tale that I will regale is seeing him again at the Monster Rally in 1999, in Virginia. It was a hot and muggy Saturday morning in August when I left with my friend Debbie from Norfolk. We met our friend Pam Truesdale halfway to carpool with us from her home near Richmond. The drive to the Arlington area wasn't too bad. Not only was the Ackermonster there but also Christopher Lee, Ray Harryhausen, Victoria Price (Vincent's daughter), Sara Karloff, Bela Lugosi, Jr., Ron Chaney, Conrad Brooks (Ed Wood films), D.C. horror host Count Gore De Vol (Dick Dyszel) and many others who I apologize for having forgotten to mention. I tried to dig up the old program book but to no avail since time and many trips to various conventions over the last 25 years may make things a little fuzzy at times. Our focus is on Forry, my friends, so I'll try my best to stay on the subject.

The FJA at the rally is one my favorite memories because he was a younger and healthier man back then — a chubby-cheeked and cheerful person with that certain gleam in his eyes that was so appealing to everyone. This meeting happened shortly before that horrendous incident with Ray Ferry's lawsuit. Not only do I feel what Mr. Ferry did was inexcusable on so many levels, but I and others feel that the stress of this travesty was a contributing factor to the downward spiral of Uncle Forry's health. I have a few choice words for Ferry that probably wouldn't be proper to publish in this book as well as risking a libel lawsuit. In my defense, not only am I thinking what most of us probably feel about this subject, but technically speaking it's not libel if what you're feeling and expressing is the TRUTH!

We arrived in time to hear Dr. Acula speak about his experiences and his first encounter with *Amazing Stories* and the famous line he quoted regularly about the magazine calling to him as a little boy and how it all started with his love of Science Fiction and Horror. I had heard his legendary "Take me home, little boy" speech numerous times before but I don't think I will ever tire of it.

After his talk he came up to us and gave Deborah a big hug and I shook his hand saying "Mr. Ackerman." He corrected me with a smile and said, "Please call me Forry." I started to get a swelled head by this but realized later that he says that to everyone. That was just the kind of guy he was. I asked him if we could take a picture together and he said yes without hesitation. I don't think he has ever turned down a fan's request for an autograph or picture. Those pictures of moi and the Ackermonster are probably some of my most prized possessions. Debbie invited him to lunch and I was stoked knowing we were going to eat with a living legend. On our way to the hotel's dining room people would yell out "Uncle Forry" and he would try to wave and Ack-knowledge (misspelling on purpose) everyone that did so. Lunch was great and he kept us entertained with his humor and wit. I had a hard time finishing my lunch for fear of missing some of his dialogue. Folks would occasionally come up to him or try and get his attention from another table. Forry was always gracious even when he was eating and I don't know how he got in a bite or two. Lunch ended way too quickly for me. He had to leave and attend to other things, but we later got to see him in the dealer's room peddling his wares. I was fortunate enough to get his autograph, Ray Harryhausen's and Sara Karloff's that day making me a happy Monster Kid. We said our goodbyes later and I really didn't want to leave but "all good things." I was still on an adrenaline rush by the time we pulled back into Norfolk later that night and couldn't sleep with my "inner ten-year-old" still hopping up and down inside my head. It wouldn't be till several years later I got to see him for the last time.

The Monster Bash 2005 held in Pennsylvania would be my last Ackermonster memory. Deborah Painter, David Hawk and I had a little longer drive this time from our respective homes in Virginia. I was looking forward to seeing several folks including Ben Chapman, Bob and Cathy Burns, Basil Gogos and, of course, Forry again. One of the projects we were working on was getting several of the guests to wish our local Tidewater horror host, Dr. Madblood (Jerry Harrell), a happy 30th anniversary. A funny coincidence happened when I talked to Craig T. Adams, director, writer, producer, prop meister, Uncle Felonious, the voice of the Brain and too many characters to list of Dr. Madblood's Movies. The day before on the phone, I asked Craig if there was a hard-to-find movie I could pick up at the Bash that he and his wife, Debra, might like. If you can't find it at the internationally known Bash you may not find it anywhere. Craig responded, "No, but I would like you guys to do me another favor." I knew where this was going since we had planned this months before. I normally don't try to be rude and finish people's sentences but my response was, "You want us to go around and get several of the guests to wish Dr. Madblood a Happy 30th Anniversary as a horror host?"

There was a moment of silence and a chuckle on Mr. Adams's end. At the convention we had Ben Chapman (Creature from the Black Lagoon) who was a very nice man (R.I.P.). Bob and Kathy Burns who are always wonderful and, of course, Forry gave "well witches" to the Doctor. I knew about Forry's numerous health problems since I had last seen him and had sent him numerous get well cards over the years. During those short years legal and medical bills began to take their toll on this gentleman. Although Forry had won his day in court I don't believe he ever received any of the awarded judgment from the man whose name leaves a bitter taste in my mouth every time I speak it. Forry had to move from the well-known Ackermansion to a smaller home and had to part with a large chunk of his priceless collection. I had seen him in pictures over the years since the convention in '99 and was saddened by how thin he looked, but it was still kind of a shock to see him in that condition from when we last met. I guess it's unfair to expect any of our idols to always remain young and immune to the ravages of time and illness. Forry was a fighter, and I don't feel a lesser man might have fared so well with as much as he had to endure in those couple of years. He still had that flicker in his eyes but it didn't burn as brightly as before. It appeared he had to keep his energies in reserve, but when he released them—"watch out"! There were several instances when this held true. When we approached FJA about wishing our friend a happy 30th it was like someone had turned on a switch and the old Uncle Forry we knew so well came back to life. That flicker grew into a flame with him saying, "Dr. Madblood... this is Dr. Acula." I was thrilled to see this side of him come alive again. Later that evening he surprised me once again. The folks from *Scarlet Street* magazine invited Mr. Ackerman to dinner at a nice restaurant in town. Unfortunately, Richard Valley, their publisher and editor, has passed away also. My kudos to the folks who help keep it going! Debbie, David and I were at another table across from the group. Forry would occasionally look our way and I waved back to him. After we finished we wanted to say goodnight to him and the *Scarlet* gang. I approached him and said, "Forry, it was nice seeing you again." I once again saw that gleam in his eyes and that devilish grin and he replied back, "It was ... wasn't it?" I laughed as well as the others in earshot at the tables. I thought to myself, "You still have it, Uncle Forry." He also mentioned to me that he was glad he wasn't the only one wearing a jacket to dinner this evening. Maybe I shouldn't mention the fact that I was wearing a monster T-shirt under mine but if I remember correctly FJA was wearing a tropical print under his (laugh). It was a "pun-derful" evening, and I was happy to see him still so sharp.

Joe Moe kept us informed on Mr. Ackerman's health and of various gatherings and convention appearances on different message boards, which was nice. I was fortunate enough also to get some first hand information from my friend Deborah Painter. Unfortunately, when I talked to Debbie in 2008, the prognosis seemed very serious this time. Joe Moe and Forry's friends and caregivers were getting very concerned about his heart condition and various other complications. I think a lot of us folks in the horror and sci-fi community were getting a little stressed at this point. Dr. Acula had problems in the past and always bounced back like the fighter he was, but I think it finally hit home for many of us that this might be "it" for the Ackermonster. We tried to be positive and Forry was inundated with words of love and well wishes for a quick recovery. I sent my last get well card to Forry in early October of that year. I signed the card "Beast Recovery Witches, Paulzilla" hoping that he would appreciate the pun (probably used by him) and being able to give him a chuckle and return a small amount of joy in exchange for the huge amount of happiness he had given to so many of us. It seemed those cards, phone calls and visits were helping him to bounce back and the community was keeping their fingers crossed. Deborah, sensing urgency, went to see him before his birthday for fear Forry might not make it. One of my biggest regrets was not being able to afford a fair-priced flight to Hollyweird, California, with Ms. Painter. I was happy to hear his spirits were better from someone who had actually spent some time with him.

The Ackermonster held in there and made it to his 92nd birthday on November 24. They had a celebration for him that he couldn't attend but they televised the event for him at the mini-mansion, and he was surrounded by friends at home for the event. On December 4, 2008, Forrest J Ackerman left us ... but not in spirit. What a mundane world this would have been without him. Uncle Forry will forever live in our hearts and minds!

Five Personal Reminiscences (Atkins)

RICK ATKINS, author of *Let's Scare 'Em! Grand Interviews and a Filmography of Horrific Proportions* and *Among the Rugged Peaks: An Intimate Biography of Carla Laemmle*, is a longtime friend of Forry.

Six days ago (December 4, 2009) Forrest J Ackerman would have turned an earthly 93 years of age. However, ten days after Forry's 92nd birthday he was summoned to death's domain.

Thirty-five years ago, the tall red doors of his Mexican hacienda, located near Griffith Park, in Los Angeles, were opened to this 15 year old, another in thousands of young avid readers of the times and a fan of Ackerman's now legendary monthly magazine, *Famous Monsters of Filmland*. The purpose for my meeting with Mr. Ackerman was to interview him.

Since his passing, many tributes have been written and published throughout the media regarding, in numerous names and spellings, "Forry," "The Ackermonster," "Ack," "4SJ," "4E," "Forrie," and "Mr. Sci-fi," "Uncle Forry," and "Uncle Pun."

When I first met Forry, I knew him as Mr. Ackerman. His home near Griffith Park was referred to as "Son of Ackermansion." It was located on Glendower Avenue. Forry, his wife, Wendayne, Forry's mother, Carroll, and her sister inhabited it. Before I arrived in Los Angeles that May Day in 1974, I quickly asked, without repeating the address that I had, if his address stayed the same. He said, "Yes." Once arriving, I had the address 915 Sherbourne Drive. I went there in a taxi. The house looked rather abandoned and I almost walked away. However, I made it to the front door and knocked on the front window. Suddenly, an elderly woman stood at the window, shaking her fist and motioning me away. I later learned after returning to my motel, Forry said by phone that he and his wife, Wendy, had relocated from the original "Ackermansion" on Sherbourne Drive some years before. He told me, "That poor woman! If she had a nickel for every stranger who has come to her door, she'd be a rich woman."

Forry Ackerman and I became friends, first in "fandom" and later in a more personal nature. Over the years, I realized that Forry was more internal, suppressing his true feelings to others. On the other hand, it was his classic memorabilia collection (that he began collecting in 1930) that enabled him to externalize the years of experience. This realization began for me a few years after his wife passed away.

I could go on with numerous experiences that Forry Ackerman and I have shared down through the years, but that would be overshadowing my initial feelings about him. I believe that Forry Ackerman loved people. And people really loved him. Forry's infectious personality is known the world over and some seem to be emulating him today.

There is only one Forrest J Ackerman. He is the same Mr. Ackerman whom I looked up to when I was a teenager, and the same Forry who I got to know personally. The last time I spoke with Forry in his living room he shared much with me regarding his parents and his late brother. His was most sincere as he speculated on how they would all see him today, as he is. Soon after, he simply shrugged his shoulders and grinned his familiar grin. His was peaceful like no other.

Five Personal Reminiscences (Hawk)

Forry left behind no surviving family members. However, he does leave behind his legions of fans from all over the world (honorary nieces and nephews).

Thank you, Debbie Painter for this privilege.

DAVID HAWK is a freelance writer and photographer and knew Forry since the 1980s.

I "met" the Ackermonster one Saturday when I went down into the pharmacy under the Mayflower Building in Virginia Beach, Virginia. In a dark corner of the pharmacy were old wire racks where they displayed comic books and magazines. I found a wondrous surprise and an unusual magazine called *Famous Monsters*. It was issue number 65 with a fantastic cover painted in cool greens, talking about Boris Karloff starring in Fu Manchu. The use of grisly greens set the perfect mood for reading a monster magazine on a bright cheery, sunny day in May 1970. Soon after, I was hooked, searching the oceanfront stores and friend's houses for more and more issues of this fantastic magazine. I acquired more magazines and I first learned of an actor called Lon Chaney. He quickly became my favorite actor, and every issue of *Famous Monsters* I found I would scan to see if there was any mention of him. *King Kong* was my favorite film at the time, and finding issues 25, 26 and 27 (Forry's ultimate filmbook of *King Kong*) blew me away. I had started attending a local event called Sci Con and that led me to other local conventions. At one of these, Atlanticon II, I had heard that their special guest was going to be the editor of *Famous Monsters* himself, Forrest J Ackerman. I had also met a girl who said she knew him and would introduce me to the Master.

The date of the convention was some weeks off when I went through my collection for one perfect item for Mr. Monster to sign. I did not wish to bother him with a pile of magazines like some common fan. I selected *Lon of 1000 Faces!*, the pride of my collection of Lon Chaney books I had managed to find on my cherished actor, compiled and written by Mr. Ackerman himself. Debbie, my friend, introduced me casually to the Ackermonster. I have never been shy around actors and sci-fi icons, but this was different. Mr. Ackerman was a creator of words which, having been raised to love reading, made me feel taken aback. I handed him my book and told him how much I enjoyed it. I had just wished it had more text. It is a mostly photograph collection book. Mr. Ackerman rightfully pointed out that Lon was a man of few words (a silent movie actor) so he had based the book on that premise. Few words, many photographs. Little did I know how rare those pictures were at the time.

I also saw Mr. Ackerman when he was a guest at the Rising Star convention in Salem, Virginia, back in 1995.

Year later I was invited to go with Miss Painter to visit Mr. Ackerman at his home on Glendower Avenue in Los Angeles. We flew out there on a United Flight. I was so happy to see Mr. Ackerman and his fabulous collection that I think I might have managed the flight myself. I was very impatient with all the crap that the airlines had us do. Little did I know what was to come! But finally we left LAX and got our rental car. I then found out why Miss Painter brought me along. She hates L.A. traffic. We had reached a certain intersection and Miss Painter was reduced to tears trying to make a left turn with no advance green arrows. Los Angeles later started installing left-turn lights.

We pulled up in front of the house I had only seen in blurry photographs in *Famous Monsters* magazine. I was expecting to hear, "Who dares disturb the Ackermonster" phrase that Debbie had told me he used when greeting guests. Instead, a tall young man named Sean Fernald answered the door, recognized Debbie and greeted us. We were told that Forrest was sick, but could come on in. Inside we were met by a strange sight. The house was being used for a location of a film. We carefully wriggled in amongst lights, cameras and young actors. It seemed that William Shatner's daughter was doing an Internet broadcast of a horror film using Mr. Ackerman's kitchen for the climatic scene. They filmed their project as we watched, fascinated. Soon they wrapped and we were alone in the Ackermansion. Sean had given Debbie the keys to the house. I was overwhelmed by the immensity of his collection. Everywhere one looked there were rare paintings, the originals of old pulp magazine covers, published before I was born. A Cylon warrior stood guard in the hallway. Lobby cards that would have driven dealers crazy with desire were taped here, there and everywhere there was a space. To say the walls were covered would have been an understatement. Many places you could not tell what color the wall had been originally. The living room was saturated with awards, all to Mr. Ackerman, from every conceivable organization in horror, science fiction and fandom. On the outer wall, backed by a magnificent view of Los Angeles, was Forry's pride and joy: the Ultima Futura Automaton, decorated with Christmas ornaments and tinsel from the previous holiday. To the left was a large chair, which I later learned was a piece of history in itself. It had been used by Forry's ancestor to take Abraham Lincoln's portrait.

The room was filled with history of film and writings. There was the lever from *The Bride of Frankenstein*, Stephen King's first story, and oh, so many cover paintings from science fiction pulps. Debbie led me into the dining room. A corner was covered with every possible figure ever made of the Frankenstein monster and toys, dolls, collector's figures. Forry had them all. On the opposite corner, Debbie reverently showed me Forry's rarities. Kept in a special glass case was his original copy of *Dracula*, signed not only by Bram Stoker, but by every actor who had played the part. An original large emerald ring worn by Uma Thurman when she played Poison Ivy in the *Batman and Robin* movie was in the case. And the "holy icons of horror," the ring with the Crest of Dracula and the Mummy's ring. Both were from the '30s films and were worn by Bela Lugosi and Boris Karloff, respectively. Passing the kitchen door I saw the original artwork in the first story of *Vampirella* and the costume worn by the actress in the filmed version of the comic was nearby. This led us into the Lon Chaney room. I had now entered the holy of holies of horror fandom. There were original posters and lobby cards lining the wall except where a gargoyle model of the Hunchback hung from a light fixture. On a table was a glorious model of Chaney at his makeup table, and there was the top (beaver) hat and teeth actually worn by Chaney in *London After Midnight*. It was a total sensory overload and I have wondered what happened to these treasures when he died. Where did they go?

That night we were told that we could stay upstairs in the Karloff/Lugosi room. A Karloff/Lugosi room? We dragged our luggage up the stairs lined with even more paintings from the old pulps and turned right into the room. It was lined with pictures and posters from many of their films. *The Bride of Frankenstein* and *Frankenstein* were framed with those wonderful lightning mats specially made for their frames. And there was Lugosi's cape. Succumbing to temptation, I put it on for a moment.

There was a sofa, where I was supposed to sleep (sleep in this wonderland?). But eventually I did. I fell off it during the night and awoke next to the coffee table (a real coffin). It gave one a surreal awakening.

The next day Debbie, worried about Forry, consented nevertheless to give me the grand (grander?) tour of the house. We went down into what was the basement level of the house where Forry kept his office. It was one of the busiest places on Earth. There was a string of filing cabinets where Forry kept his 30,000 plus stills and his desk, chair and books. I thought my own six to seven thousand books were an unwieldy mass! Forry had something like 50,000 to 80,000 books. Luckily they were kept very dry due to L.A.'s very dry climate and the house's location, built up on a hill. Going further through the basement, there were several shelves of masks, mostly by Don Post, of every horror character known to man. And mixed in with the books were Forry's joys: his pulp magazines. He had complete runs of many magazines. Behind these shelves were his tributes to his old friend Ray Harryhausen. My God, was there no end to his collection? He had the steel skeleton of most of the creatures from *King Kong*, some still having remnants of the latex and sponge rubber so laboriously applied by Marcel Delgado. And Ray's projects were well represented with the portion of the Golden Gate Bridge from *It Came from Beneath the Sea*, the U.S. Capitol dome from *Earth Vs. the Flying Saucers*, rarities from *Mighty Joe Young*, and the brontosaur from Ray's aborted *Evolution*. This was a treasure trove beyond price! In another room there was the Tingler from the Vincent Price film, Indiana Jones's golden idol and a full size Gremlin. There were many other items which memory has failed to recall.

In the sub-basement, which Forry called "Grislyland," were kept objects that were beyond categorizing. There were various mummies and torn body parts from many horror films apparently carelessly stacked and piled down in what looked like a dark ancient crypt. I felt a bit like Indiana Jones down there, not knowing what next was to surprise me.

I did not see Forry that trip. He was staying in the hospital and was soon to undergo surgery. We did stop at the hospital but hung back because he could not receive visitors so soon.

Unfortunately, Forry's failing health and Ray Ferry's legal actions forced the Ackermonster to sell the property that year and so many of his carefully collected pieces of film history. Why, the City of Los Angeles should have been on their knees, begging to put these objects in a museum.

These are just a couple of my Forry memories that Debbie has asked me to record for her labor of love. If you see me at a convention I will probably share more with you.

Five Personal Reminiscences (Morrow)

JIM MORROW shared a long friendship with Forrest J Ackerman.
IN THE BEGINNING ...

Never in my wildest dreams did I ever think I would become friends with Forry Ackerman. Yet ... he did become my friend, my best friend of 34 years!!

I had known of Forry through his magazine, *Famous Monsters of Filmland*. I was four years old when I saw someone with the magazine. I remember the excitement I had looking at the magazine throughout my years in elementary school. While I was not able buy the magazine, I looked through and read my friends' copies.

In January of 1966, while my father was in the Air Force, the family was stationed at Tripoli, Libya. After a long flight, he took us to our new home. Once he took us to our new home, he had to go to the base and took me with him. He told me whatever I wanted, he would buy for me.

Arriving at the base, he took us to get ice cream at the restaurant on base called The Mirage. Inside the restaurant was a room in the back that was a newsstand that sold newspapers, magazines and paperbacks. This little magical room was my link to the outside world, especially to home!

I still remember the magic after I walked into that room filled with magazines galore. Seeing covers to paperbacks painted by the amazing Frank Frazetta and James Bama was a treat indeed. Looking at all of this was like being in a candy store!! Now remember, my father had told me he would buy anything I wanted. So what did I see? I was looking at all the magazines, when FM #36 just popped out and that was what I wanted. My father promptly bought it for me. I still remember the excitement and to this day can remember all of the contents of the magazine.

However ... my mother was so worried when she saw that mummy — and a one eyed one at that — on the cover!! So, she made me throw that magazine away in the trash can. "You'll have nightmares!" she explained.

In 1974, my mom, who had long realized that Forry's magazine did not harm me in any way, bought me most of those issues of *FM* available in the magazine that year. (She finally got a chance to meet him in 2004 when, in a cross-country trip, we dropped by and surprised him with a pie from House of Pies.)

I wrote to Forry and told him about this. He printed the letter in the *King Kong* issue #108. I then got a phone call from him that same week and I was beyond excited!! We talked for a long time. I was on cloud nine!! You could have heard me yelling from excitement that night!!

Every day the following week, I started to get bright neon colored envelopes with Xeroxed copies of articles by and about him. I also got a large package with a personally inscribed program book of the recent Luna Con 74 where he had just been honored.

He had published my name along with my brother Jeff in the "You Axed for It!" section in the 100th issue of *Famous Monsters*. He published my picture a few years later in the letters section.

Famous Monsters of Filmland was just the most amazing magazine. The secret, of course, was that Forry edited the magazine with love. That is why we were all enthused by it.

I would eagerly await the magazine and just devour the whole thing. It gave me history of the movies. It helped me to read, as I read it all the time. More than that, it gave me a deep love for the actors, actresses, writers, directors, special effects people and make-up geniuses in the business. I had a vast knowledge of these things.

But this one phone call was the beginning of a long journey with an amazing man. A man I loved for 34 years.

Say 2495 Glendower Avenue to anyone who is a fan of horror, sci-fi or fantasy and I guarantee you that most will equate that with Forry. I wish I had a copy of Forry's phone message when you called his home, with directions and all. Ever since I had been a fan of FM, I had always dreamed of going to visit Forry's home. I actually dreamed of it many times.

But let me tell you ... no words can describe your first visit to the original Ackermansion. When I finally went in 1986, I was beyond excited when I got there. It was even better than I had even imagined it. Everywhere you looked it was a smorgasbord of delicious goodies. You would see something that you remembered from a movie that you loved. You saw the actual item. You recognized it. It was like finding the Holy Grail! Lon Chaney's make-up kit, an autographed picture of Boris Karloff, items from *King Kong*, a first edition of *Dracula* signed by Bela Lugosi, Christopher Lee, Vincent Price, Bram Stoker and many others!

I was in L.A. for a week. I went there every day and most days I stayed there from early morning till late at night. Even helped out Brian Forbes to get things ready for Forry's birthday party, my first of many in the years to come. I found it fascinating that no matter how many times you went, you saw something you didn't notice before. So many books. So many pictures. So many cinematic memories in front of your eyes.

Probably my favorite memory is when one morning, I was there when Ray Bradbury came by. What a thrill to be with him as we both looked around admiring Forry's treasures. He marveled like a young kid when he saw a newspaper of Buck Rogers. Here we were talking and enjoying the visit—certainly something that I will never forget. Ray is someone who I have loved since childhood and still love. Forry gave me the love of the movies and Ray gave me the love of books. Forry made it possible for me to start corresponding with Ray. If you had told me all those years ago that I would be able to call him a friend, I never would have believed it. I have known Ray since 1983—he is such a dear and sweet man. There were three people who meant so much to me over the years: Forry, Ray and Bob Bloch. Bob, the author *of Psycho*, and I became friends from 1974 till his death in 1994. Such a delightful man with a wicked sense of humor. All because of Forry! He made it happen. That is the kind of person he was. In 1986, at Forry's birthday party, I sat with Ray Bradbury, Steve Jones, Walt Daugherty, Dr. Donald Reed, Gary Dorst, Wiktor Burkato (Mr. Science Fiction from Poland) and the amazing writer Brad Linaweaver.

I would be remiss if I did not mention Wendy, who was Forry's biggest treasure.

She was the sweetest woman, delightful in every way. And you could just see how much Forry loved her.

I met three of Forry's personal assistants over the years. Brian Forbes in the '80s, Lee Harris from the '90s and Joe Moe from the '90s till the end of his life. Brian was a young go-getter who could always be dependable. I met him a few times. I often wonder how he is doing nowadays. Lee was and is a delight with a diabolical sense of humor. He also loves puns as much as Forry did. He has remained a friend all these years later. He did love Forry and I would see him from time to time at Forry events. Always kept Forry and others laughing with his jokes.

Dear Joe will always have my undying gratitude for taking care of dear Forry during the last years of his life. I worried about him at the end, but felt so much better knowing that Forry was in good hands with Joe. Forry would tell me many times when we were alone, "I don't know what I would do without Joe." Joe did an amazing job with making sure Forry got the care that he needed. Made sure he was able to go to conventions when he was able to. He was just a jack of all trades with Forry. He and I had many conversations about Forry, so he knows how much I loved him. Of course, he also kept me up to date towards the end when ... But mainly he just made Forry happy and comfortable. I was so saddened when Forry had to sell the Glendower Ackermansion. It was like losing a part of your childhood. I can't even imagine how Forry felt.

But I will say this. The mini–Ackermansion on Russell Avenue was a nice little home for Forry at the end. Very quaint place. I liked it. Forry liked it because he told me it was much like the bachelor bungalow he had many years before. He seemed happy there. I give full credit to Joe Moe who did an amazing job fixing it up. Hanging up all of the items that Forry kept from the sale a few years before. He was able to keep the things that mattered most to him. And frankly, it was much easier to keep up than the larger place. As much as I missed the other place, this was, in the end, more practical for Forry. He still had the life masks of Karloff, Lugosi, Price, Tor, Lorre, Carradine and, of course, himself. He had the *Dracula* book. He had the Lugosi/Dracula ring. He had his Hugo award. He had the cream of the crop!

He still had his tours every Saturday as always. Was there quite a few times. And as always, I loved looking at his treasures. It was a comfortable place and it was down the street from the House of Pies, which he loved. We both went there many times over the years. Oftentimes with a group. Fun times for sure.

I cannot tell you enough about Forry's amazing kindness over the years. He was, simply put, next to my father, the kindest man I ever knew. I know because I was able to witness his kindness to so many people over the years.

He was extraordinarily thoughtful. Not just with people he knew, but with fans. He had amazing patience with each and every fan, no matter how old or young they were.

I think the reason for this was because he remembered what it was like to be a fan. The fact of the matter was ... he never stopped being a fan himself. I have fond memories

Forry clowns around singing an Al Jolson song in the forecourt of the famed Grauman's Chinese Theater on Hollywood Boulevard.

of his interaction with the fans who loved him. He always had the time to listen to the heartfelt thanks that they would say to him.

Watching him reach out to those who loved him would bring me smiles when I was with him because he truly was in his element being the "Uncle" to all of his nieces and nephews, so to speak. Watching him recite all the answers that I had come to memorize over the years was still fun for me. As a matter of fact, I am going to confess something for the first time. There was many a time that I would purposely ask him a question at a panel just to hear him recite the answers for those who may not have had the pleasure of hearing it. Seeing the sheer delight in the eyes of those who reached out to talk with him is something that I shall not forget. As I would look at them, I could not help but remember how special I felt when he would talk to me. He was the first adult who befriended me at the young age of 17 years after I wrote that fan letter in the King Kong issue in 1974. He never once talked down to me, but as an equal. He always made me feel that I had something of worth to say.

I never saw Forry be rude once to any of the fans who went up to him. Even when he was pressed for time, no matter how many were gathered around him, he always took the time to sign items, or answer a question for the millionth time, or chat with them. For example, the two *FM* conventions in the nineties ... being the obvious special guest, everywhere he and I would go, like the pied piper, people would follow him in droves. After each panel in which he participated or was an audience member, people would go up to him and ask him to sign items or just talk to him. Never turned anyone down. As a matter of fact, I remember that if he was needed at another panel, he would kindly tell them to walk with him out the door. Then he would proceed to mingle with them.

The love was just immense wherever he went.

One of the things that stands out in my mind — and I saw this countless times. He was such a ham in a fun way. He loved to make your visit to the Ackermansion a most memorable one. Down at the basement he had an exhibit known as "the Dungeon." He would take the guests outside, walk them down a small flight of steps and with a serious ominous voice say ... "Are you brave enough to enter the Dungeon? Well, you have been warned." At this point, he would be "ack"ting out as if he was struggling from some monster from the dungeon. Always fun to watch and I do miss seeing him do that.

I took my younger brother, Jeff, with me to the Atlanta Fantasy Convention in the early '80s. I wanted him to meet Forry. He went and to this day, he will tell you that he was a very nice man and so interesting.

Forry let me try on his Bela Lugosi ring one time. As I put it on my finger, he said with a wicked grin, "Of course, if you can't get it off ... that will be another finger added to my collection."

On his 85th birthday party, he was honored with a roast at the L.A. Shriner's Roast Club, a fascinating place of history. I was asked to speak there.

Anyway, towards the end of the night, as it was late and some of the people had left, some of us were milling around shooting the breeze. I stood by the door quietly soaking up the scene of Forry just happy with those who came. Suddenly, to my side, a tall man came up to me with a shy smile. It was John Philip Law who came by long after most of the people left. He was watching Forry with sheer respect, telling me how much he loved the man. Just saying how much he had enjoyed knowing him and how much he loved him. Just the most pleasant conversation.

He had a Kodak instamatic camera and said he wanted his picture taken with him and handed me the camera and asked if I would take his picture with Forry. I told him I was happy to do it. Took a picture of him with Forry and a few group shots. I had my picture taken with him. Very kind man. Gentle soul and still handsome. Very pleasant smile. I am forever glad I had the chance to meet him.

But I have to tell you, it was the small things that he did that made me love Forry Ackerman dearly. At the *Famous Monsters of Filmland* Convention in 1993, he found out that I had to request a volume-control device for the telephone during my stay there. I was born with a hearing loss due to German measles (rubella) in 1957. I have worn a hearing aid since the age of four.

Two of the early members of the Los Angeles Science Fantasy Society — Forry Ackerman and Ray Bradbury — celebrate being friends for many decades (Jim Morrow).

Shortly after the convention, I received a package from Forry in the mail. Always excited when I would get a little surprise from him, I eagerly opened the package. Inside, was the hearing-aid amplifier that I used at the hotel. He had remembered it and sent me my very own. I cannot tell you how much that simple act of kindness truly helped me over the years. I still have it as a reminder of his kindness. Such were the little things that were big things to me!

His little gifts were many. Many Xerox copies of articles by and about him were sent when they were published. Books that he wrote or had a part in were sent inscribed by him. I have hundreds of them.

Yet, of all the things he did for me, the thing that truly meant the most to me occurred in 2003. On December 12, 2002, as I was getting out of my car to go to a store, I had a terrible dizzy spell. Within two hours I lost all of my hearing. I was totally deaf for the next several months. Of course, Forry knew of this as well as Joe Moe and all of my Forry friends.

I was recommended as a perfect candidate for a cochlear ear implant. On June 4, I had the implant and on July 7, had it turned on. When they turned it on, everyone sounded like Minnie Mouse! But what an amazing thing to hear again. The next day, I had to go back for some more adjustments and afterwards, everyone sounded like Darth Vader. This went away within a few days and immediately I was able to hear sounds that I had never heard before. Forry was extremely excited and happy for me. So much so, that he flew me out to L.A. to stay with him at his house and be his guest at the 50th anniversary of *War of the Worlds*. Now this was such an emotional thing for me because this was the first real movie that I watched after the surgery with any success. I had seen this movie dozens of times over the years but I can truthfully say that it was like I had never seen it before. I heard sounds that I never knew were in the movie, subtle things that I am sure not many would notice. I remember being just amazed at the clarity of the film. The little things such as hearing the car door lock. For this, I will be forever grateful to Forry. He gave me a wonderful gift. He was just fascinated by this and talked about it at length. He was truly happy for me and he made sure I knew it. I told him it truly was sci-fi that came to life.

A few years ago, I went ahead and had another cochlear ear implant in my left ear, the one in which I had never heard anything. For the first time, I hear in that ear as

Friends for many years. Forry Ackerman (left) and Jim Morrow smile for the camera in 2004 (Jim Morrow).

well. It is still a work in progress as I write this. Forry knew of this surgery and was happy about it.

Such was the amazing generosity of dear Forry.

Forry's later years are special memories for me because I went to visit him a little more often. I tried to fly out to L.A. once or twice a year. Went to the 50th anniversary of *War of the Worlds* that I mentioned earlier. Went to many of Forry's birthday parties. I wasn't able to do that in 2008. I wish I had. Just couldn't do it. Oftentimes, he would put his arms around mine to help him walk more steadily. And nothing made me feel better than knowing that I could help him in some way.

As much as he loved the parties with all of the guests, my favorite times to see him was during the summer when we could spend quality time alone together. Those are the times that really mattered to me. We would talk endlessly about many things. Some very personal. But what a delight he was. And how we laughed.

But the last several years saw many health issues for Forry. He told me often, lamenting the problems he had. Yet, the one that he probably hated the most was his loss of taste. He was a man who loved to eat food and desserts. Many of my favorite memories are of us eating at various places. Many times it was just the two of us. Other times it was with a group. It didn't matter, because what really was important to me was being with him. I loved that man. He was just a fascinating man with the keenest wit. He was a master at puns. Now some do not like puns, but I do. And Forry could come up with some hilarious ones. The cornier they were, the better they were. And the twinkle in his eyes ... ohhhh ... priceless.

He talked slower than when I first met him, but his mind remained sharp as a tack. And whenever we talked on the phone, it was like 20 years just melted away. We would have wonderful conversations on a wide variety of subjects. He had the heartiest laugh whenever I said something funny to him. Of course, he could make me laugh harder. In the last year and a half there were fewer phone calls. How I missed those monthly phone calls that we had over the years.

The last time I saw him I only stayed a very short while as he had just had his physical therapy. Joe had told me not to be alarmed if he looked so bad. But the therapy did take a lot out of him. I was shocked at how thin he was. Of course, no longer having a sense of taste didn't help either. Kevin Burns was there as we were all cheering him on.

My concern must have shown because Kevin came up to me privately afterwards and told me that he looked better than the last time he saw him, two weeks before, so he was getting better. I will always be grateful to Kevin for making me feel much better. (I must also say that Kevin does a dead-on imitation of Forry's voice.)

I sensed that, at the end of his life, Forry appreciated his friends that much more. My hugs from him were a little tighter and a little longer.

IT WAS A WONDERFORRY-FULL LIFE!

Joe contacted me and told me that Forry took a turn for the worst and that he may not make it through the night. These were words that I so dreaded. I remember

I immediately wrote to him via email for Joe to read. I poured my heart out in the email. I basically told him how much he meant to me. Just mentioning all the happy memories I had of him. Every year, on his birthday, I would mail or email a tribute to him. Just telling him how important he was — not just the world of horror, sci-fi or fantasy — but to me.

Well, shortly after that, Joe posted that he was not doing well and for people to write to him. It was certainly medicine for him because I really do believe that he lived just a little while longer for them.

I would email him every day or every other day cheering him on. Always telling him I loved him. Joe told me that he appreciated them so much.

The day he died, my world just grew a little darker. I knew it was coming. As much as always thought that he would live to be 100 years old, I knew that the end was coming. But you are never prepared.

I cried rivers of tears that day and several days after that. I was so beyond sad about it. He was, next to my father, the finest man I ever knew. And I wasn't going to see him anymore!

Joe Moe assured me that Forry died very peacefully. I take much comfort in that. I also take comfort in the fact that as much as I wanted to be there, he surely knew how much I loved him and appreciated him, plus he had people around him who loved him as well.

Joe Moe put together an amazing tribute to Forry in 2009. It was an amazing event with so many people at the Egyptian Theater in L.A. I went and sat in the reserved seats with many of his close friends. I sat next to the lovely Lydia van Vogt, widow of A.E. van Vogt.

So many of the famous who had been touched by Forry were there. Ray Bradbury, John Landis, Joe Dante, Rick Baker, Kevin Burns, Tim Sullivan (who did an outstanding job hosting the event!), Oscar-winning director Del Toro, Brad Linaweaver and, of course, Joe Moe.

It had been a short while since Forry died when I went to the tribute. I would still get emotional whenever I would talk about him. But it was almost like I still had not wrapped my head totally around it. Just didn't want to totally accept it.

I thought I had my emotions in check but once Ray Bradbury gave his eloquently moving speech, telling us it was okay to cry, that he was giving us permission to cry ... well the dam burst at that moment. All the tears just came down like rain. All the happy memories flooded my soul at that moment. I would wipe the tears away as the tributes were being told. There were laughs as well, remembering funny things he said or did.

When Joe Moe got up to address the group, I was totally shocked when he sang. In all the years I had known him, I had not realized that he had such a beautiful voice. He led the whole theater in singing "Forry Boy" sung to the tune of "Sonny Boy," a song that Forry loved to sing.

I tried but when I opened my mouth, my throat tightened and nothing would come out. All that came out were sobs of grief. The tears just flowed.

At the end, Joe introduced us to a video that totally took my breath away. It was Forry telling all of us his last goodbyes. I looked at him and that gentle smile and just cried. There wasn't a dry eye in the place. After it was over, I went to Joe and hugged him and just cried. I hugged Pam Keesey, who was crying at well. I saw Terry Pace. I was just at a loss for words. I had to walk off to the side behind the curtains and just cried my eyes out and wiped away the tears as best as I could. That night, some of us were invited to a dinner down the street to celebrate Forry. It was a wonderful night. So many faces that I knew. So many wonderful memories being shared. So many laughs and smiles. Exactly the way Forry would have wanted it.

Final Thoughts

I was extremely lucky to have known the man. I got to see the man and not the personality. He was a dear man. There are so many memories I have of him. It is funny. Now, for every one memory I have of him, I remember several more that I had forgotten. One of my favorite memories that I just thought of was at the Ackermansion. I, along with Gary Patti, his sister Susan and Anne Hardin were at his house when we went upstairs and got a large trunk and brought it downstairs. When we opened it, it was filled with tons of photos of Forry with his family. It was a poignant moment, seeing Forry talking about those pictures. It was fascinating to see what his life was like. A memory that I was privileged to have been a part of. I miss his mail with copies of articles by and about him. I miss his little gifts that he would send to brighten my day. I miss our monthly phone calls. I miss his puns. I miss his laughter. I miss our desserts that we ate together, sometimes in the wee hours of the morning. I miss that twinkle in his eye when he would say something witty to you. I miss our long talks not just about his life but life in general. I miss his total enthusiasm for life. I miss his love of everyone. I miss his childlike wonder in life. The secret of his longevity was that he never lost his sense of wonder. He never grew up. I miss how he would show you his collection and talk about it. I miss his singing of the old songs. He had a wonderful voice.

A gift that Forry gave me was the gift of so many people I have met over the years and many becoming friends with. John Agar, Angus Scrimm, Ray Bradbury, Kevin Burns, Bobbie and Frank Bresee, Verne Langdon, Robert Bloch, Lee Harris, Joe Moe, Ron Chaney, Sarah Karloff, Fritz Leiber, George Clayton Johnson, Richard Matheson, Tim Sullivan, John Landis, Joe Dante, Ray Harryhausen, Brad Linaweaver, Pam Keesey, Debbie Painter (the author of this book), Gary Patti, Anne Hardin, the wonderful Terry Pace and his lovely family, Ann Robinson, the talented Casey J. Wong, Frank Dietz, Vincent Price and so many others. When I see them, I smile because I have special memories of Forry. We have a common bond.

At first, he was "Uncle Forry" to me. Then, as we became closer, I began to see him as the older brother I never had. Yet, he will never be gone because he will always be in my heart. Whenever I need a lift, I will think of him and, with a tear in my eye and a smile on my face, I will think of him. I loved him so much. I wish I could go in that time machine from the movie *The Time Machine* and just go back 34 years ago when It all started! I would gladly relive those moments all over again. But I can't. I just have the wonderful memories.

Weren't we lucky to have had him in our lives even if for such a little while?! I just miss him. I miss him dearly. Every day.

Chapter Notes

Preface

1. Munn. *Strange Horizons,* http://www.strangehorizons.com.

Chapter 1

1. Thomas Cridland page. http://www.ohiohistory.org.
2. Bellamy, *Looking Backward,* p. 44.
3. Conkling family history, Roots Web page. Rootsweb.ancestry.com.
4. Los Angeles City Directory, 1915.
5. Ackerman, *Amazing Forries,* p. 24.
6. Los Angeles Census pages, p. 1922.
7. Sackett, *Fantastic Worlds,* p. 33.
8. Ackerman, *Amazing Forries,* p. 11.
9. Ackerman, *Amazing Forries,* p. 11.

Chapter 2

1. Ash, *The Visual Encyclopedia of Science Fiction,* p. 30.
2. Siegel (as Herbert S. Fine), "The Reign of the Superman," *Science Fiction* #3, 1933, pp. 7–8.
3. Ash, *The Visual Encyclopedia of Science Fiction,* pp. 272–273.
4. Alex Paige, personal communication, May 20, 2009.
5. Ackerman, *Amazing Forries,* p. 10.
6. Ackerman, *Amazing Forries,* p. 25.
7. Dorf, taped interview with Forrest J Ackerman, 1985.
8. Ackerman, *Expanded Science Fiction Worlds of Forrest J Ackerman and Friends, PLUS,* pp. 36–41.
9. de Camp, *Lovecraft: A Biography,* 88.
10. Pohl, Frederik, *The Way the Future Was,* 42.
11. Ackerman, *Famous Monster of Filmland Vol. 2,* .9.
12. Harryhausen, *Harryhausen: The Early Years* (film).
13. Ackerman, *Famous Monsters of Filmland* 149, pp. 6–13.
14. Ackerman *Gosh! Wow! Sense of Wonder Science Fiction,* pp. 381–382.
15. Tomomatsu, personal communication, August 8, 2009.
16. Ackerman, *Mimosa* 17, pp. 32–33.

Chapter 3

1. Ackerman, *Amazing Forries,* p. 9.
2. Ackerman, *Amazing Forries,* p. 27.
3. van Hise, *Edgar Rice Burroughs' Fantastic Worlds,* p. 177.
4. Porjes family tree.
5. Pacificon Program Book, 1946, p. 4.
6. Complaint for Divorce, 1958.

Chapter 4

1. Harris, personal communication, September 22, 2009.
2. Sheffield, "Lugosi's Last Years," *Famous Monsters of Filmland* #133, pp. 46–51.
3. Ackerman, "Scientifilm Marquee," *Imaginative Tales,* p. 97.
4. Trimble, personal communication, August 9, 2009.
5. *Virginia Creepers: The Horror Host Tradition of the Old Dominion* (film).
6. Daniel, *Famous Monsters Chronicles,* p. 14.
7. Daniel, *Famous Monsters Chronicles,* pp. 15–16.
8. Daniel, *Famous Monsters Chronicles,* p. 18.
9. Daniel, *Famous Monsters Chronicles,* p. 20.

Chapter Notes

10. Daniel, Famous Monsters Chronicles, p. 20.
11. Ackerman, "Ces Amours de Monstres," pp. V59, 77.
12. Editors, *Science Fiction Awards Watch*, 615.

Chapter 5

1. Ackerman. *Gosh! Wow! Sense of Wonder Science Fiction*, p. xviiii.
2. Ramsey, personal communication.
3. Ackerman, *Spacemen* 1, p. 3.
4. Ackerman, *Spacemen* 1, p. 67.
5. Kirk, *Scary Monsters Magazine*, pp. 70, 54.
6. Ackerman, *Famous Monster of Filmland* Vol. I, p. 21.
7. Program Book, *The 27th Annual Saturn Awards*, June 2001.
8. Paige, personal communication, May 27, 2009.
9. McDaniel, *The Man from U.N.C.L.E: The Vampire Affair* (No. 6), p. 78.
10. Langdon, personal communication.
11. Daniel, *Famous Monsters Chronicles*, p. 14.
12. Dorf, Taped interview with Forrest J Ackerman, 1985.

Chapter 6

1. University of Kansas, *Science Fiction Films: A Lecture* (film), 1970.
2. Ackerman, *Famous Monster of Filmland* Vol. II, p. 58.
3. Paige, personal communication, May 28, 2009.
4. Chaney, personal communication, June 26, 2009.
5. Paige, personal communication, May 30, 2009.
6. Ackerman, "Dr. Frankenstein, the Ackermonster and the Wolf Man," *Famous Monsters of Filmland* #133, pp.14–21.
7. Paige, personal communication, May 27, 2009.

8. University of Wyoming, Preliminary Inventory, letter dated March 17, 1987.
9. Ackerman, *Amazing Forries*, 30.

Chapter 7

1. Daniel, *Famous Monsters Chronicles*, p. 144.
2. *Famous Monsters of Filmland* #178, pp. 60–70.
3. Daniel, *Famous Monsters Chronicles*, p. 8.
4. Ackerman (as Paul Linden), "The Ackermonster Quits Famous Monsters!," *Fangoria* 24, 1983, pp. 24–27.
5. Roach, et al., *The Warren Companion: The Definitive Compendium to the Great Comics of Warren Publishing*, p. 13.
6. Ackerman, et al. Panel on Science Fiction Film, 42nd World Science Fiction Convention, 1983.
7. Dorf, taped interview with Forrest J Ackerman, 1985.
8. Ackerman, *Famous Monster of Filmland* Vol. II, p. 58.

Chapter 8

1. Ferry, *Life Is But a Scream!*, p. 268.
2. Ferry, *Life Is But a Scream!*, p. 275.
3. Harris, personal communication, September 19, 2009.
4. Ferry, *Life Is But a Scream!*, p. 124.

Chapter 9

1. Moe, personal communication.
2. Zimmerman, personal communication.
3. Porjes family tree.
4. Knowles, *Ain't It Cool News*, September 2004. http://www.aintitcoolnews.com.
5. Harris, personal communication, December 28, 2009.
6. Flycon web site.
7. Ackerman, *Amazing Forries*, p. 6.
8. Sackett, *Fantastic Worlds* 1952, p. 33.

A Brief Bio-Bibliography

In compiling this bio-bibliography, I have provided the reader with a representative sampling of the body of work Mr. Ackerman accomplished in a variety of categories, rather than a comprehensive listing of his books, articles and films.

Some of His Books

Amazing Forries. Hollywood, CA: Metropolis, 1976.
(as Paul Linden). "Ackerman Quits Famous Monsters!" *Fangoria* (Issue #24), pp. 24–27.
"The Ballad of Berta." Unpublished poem from late 1940s.
Corupe, Paul, Gene Simmons, Jovanka Vuckovic, Joe Moe, Tim Sullivan, Dave Alexander and Rob Bottin. "Famous Monster." *Rue Morgue*, #83, October 2008, pp. 16–29.
"Dr. Frankenstein, the Ackermonster and the Wolf Man: The Night *The Tomorrow Show* Became the Tomb-Morrow Show." *Famous Monsters of Filmland*, #133, pp. 14–21.
"Editorial." *Forrest J Ackerman's Monsterland*, Issue #6, December 1985, pp. 2–25.
Expanded Science Fiction Worlds of Forrest J Ackerman and Friends, PLUS. Florence, SC: Sense of Wonder Press, 2002.
Famous Forry Fotos: Over 70 Years of Ackermemories. Florence, SC: Sense of Wonder Press, 2001.
Famous Monster of Filmland # 1: A chronicle of issues 1 through 50. Denver: Imagine, 1986.
Famous Monster of Filmland # 2: A chronicle of issues 50 through 100. Los Angeles: Hollywood Publishing Company, 1991.
Forrest J Ackerman, Famous Monster of Filmland, Volume I. Pittsburgh: Imagine, 1986.
Forrest J Ackerman, Famous Monster of Filmland, Volume II. Hollywood, Universal City, New York and Canada: Imagine, 1991.
Forrest J Ackerman's Fantastic Movie Memories. Canoga Park, CA: New Media, 1985.
Forrest J Ackerman's World of Science Fiction. Toronto: Stoddart, 1997.
Forrest J Ackerman's Worlds of Science Fiction. Los Angeles: General Publishing Group, 1997; Florence, SC: Sense of Wonder Press, 2001.
The Frankenscience Monster. New York: Ace Books, 1969.
Gosh! Wow! Science Fiction: Nineteen Nostalgic Knockouts Compiled by Forrest J Ackerman. Bantam, Ontario and New York: Sense of Wonder Press, 1981.
Keesey, Pam (co-author). *Sci Fi Womanthology.* Toronto: Sense of Wonder Press, 2003.
Linaweaver, Brad (co-author). *Worlds of Tomorrow: The Amazing Universe of Science Fiction Art.* Portland, OR: Collectors Press, 2003.
Metropolis by Thea von Harbou; Introduction and "Stillistration" by Forrest J Ackerman. Florence, SC: Sense of Wonder Press, 2001.
Metropolis by Thea von Harbou, with Illustrations from the 1927 Fritz Lang Film; Edited and with an Introduction by Forest J Ackerman. Florence, SC: James A. Rock, 2001.
Rainbow Fantasia: 35 Spectrumatic Tales of Wonder. Toronto: Sense of Wonder Press, 2001.
Reference Guide to American Science Fiction Films, 1930–1945. Bloomington, IN: Tichenor, 1983.
Riley, Phillip J. *A Blind Bargain.* Ackerman Archives Series, Vol. 2. Chesterfield, NJ: Magicimage Filmbooks, 1988.
"Scientifilm Marquee." *Imaginative Tales.* September 1956, pp. 95–99.
Stine, Jean (co-author). *Reel Future: The Stories That Inspired 16 Classic Science Fiction Movies.* New York: Barnes and Noble, 1994.
Strickland, A. W. (co-author). *Reference Guide to American Science Fiction Films 1900–1929.* Bloomington, IN: Tichenor, 1982.
"Through Time and Space with Forry Ackerman."

Mimosa 17, pp. 32–33. http://jophan.org/mimosa/m17/ackerman.html.

Waite, Ron (co-author). "The Night We Invaded the Earth." *Famous Monsters of Filmland*, #149, pp. 6–13.

Some of His Anthologies

Ackermanthology: Millennium Edition: 65 Astonishing Rediscovered Sci-Fi Shorts. Florence, SC: Sense of Wonder Press, 2002.

Best Science Fiction for 1973. New York: Ace Books, 1973.

Dr. Acula's Thrilling Tales of the Uncanny. Florence, SC: Sense of Wonder Press, 2005.

Expanded Science Fiction Worlds of Forrest J Ackerman and Friends, PLUS. Florence, SC: Sense of Wonder Press, 2002.

The Gernsback Awards (Vol. 1), 1926. Rockville, MD: Wildside Press, 2003.

Keesey, Pam. *Sci Fi Womanthology*. Florence, SC: Sense of Wonder Press, 2003.

Martianthology (with Ann Hardin). Florence, SC: Sense of Wonder Press, 2003.

Rainbow Fantasia: 35 Spectrumatic Tales of Wonder. Florence, SC: 2001, Sense of Wonder Press, 2001.

Stein, Jean (co-editor). *Reel Future: The Stories That Inspired 16 Classic Science Fiction Movies*. New York: Barnes and Noble, 1994.

Weist, Jerry. *Original Comic Art* (with a foreword by Forrest J Ackerman). New York: Avon Books, 1992.

Some of His Short Stories

"Atoms and Stars"
"Count Down to Doom"
"Dhactwhu!—Remember?"
"Earth's Lucky Day"
"The Great Gog's Grave"
"Letter to an Angel"
"A Martian Oddity"
"Micro Man"
"Sabina of the White Cylinder"
"The Shortest Story Ever Told"

Some of His Awards

Bram Stoker Award for Lifetime Achievement, 1997
First International Science Fiction Film Festival, 1951
Honorary doctorate in literature from St. Andrews University, 1970
Horror Hall of Fame (nicknamed the "Grimmy" Award), 1990
Hugo Award, Number One Fan Personality, 1953

Some of His Film Appearances

The Aftermath (Nautilus Films, 1982): curator of the last museum on Earth.

Amazon Women on the Moon (Universal, 1987): president of the United States.

Beverly Hills Cop III (Paramount Pictures, 1994): a bar patron.

Bikini Drive-In (American Independent Productions, 1995): man with insect repellent.

Dinosaur Valley Girls (Frontline Entertainment, 1996): man on the street.

Dracula Vs. Frankenstein (Independent International Pictures, 1971): Dr. Beaumont.

The Farmer's Daughter (RKO, 1947): man at political rally.

Frankenstein and Me (France Film for the Disney Channel, 1996): minister.

Hey, Rookie! (Columbia Pictures Corporation, 1944): Sergeant Ack Ack.

Hollywood Boulevard (New World Entertainment, 1976): party guest.

The Howling (Avco Embassy Pictures, 1981): bookstore patron.

Kentucky Fried Movie (KFM Films, 1987): juror.

Michael Jackson's Thriller (Optimum Productions, 1983): movie theater patron.

Oscar (Touchstone Pictures, 1991): wedding guest.

Queen of Blood (Cinema West, 1966): lab assistant.

Red Velvet (Ulalume Films, 2009): himself.

SadoMannequin (Popgun Productions, 2001): Dr. Acula.

Schlock! (Gazotskie Productions, 1973): movie theater patron.

The Sci-Fi Boys (Yellow Hat Productions, 2006): himself.

That Little Monster (Ottermole Moving Picture Company, 1994): Edward van Groan.

The Time Travelers (American International, 1964): robotics technician.

The Vampire Hunter's Club (Doodle Barnett Productions, 2001): vampire hunter.

Vampirella (Concorde-New Horizons, 1996): nightclub patron.

The Winner's Circle (20th Century–Fox, 1948): horseracing spectator.

The Wizard of Speed and Time (Medusa Productions, 1989): man at garage sale; sign holder.

Some of His Documentary Appearances

Attack of the 50 Foot Monster Mania (interviewee), 1999.
Flying Saucers over Hollywood: The Plan 9 Companion (interviewee), 1990.
Goolians: A Docu-Comedy (interviewee), 2006.
Heartstoppers: Horror at the Movies (interviewee), 1990.
Hollywood Goes Ape! (interviewee), 1994.
Huell Howser's *Visiting...* with Huell Howser (interviewee), 2001.
Keepers of the Frame (interviewee), 1999.
Lon Chaney: A Thousand Faces (interviewee), 2000.
Lugosi: The Forgotten King (host), 1985.
Mr. Science Fiction's Fantastic Universe (writer and host), 1989.
Texas Chainsaw Massacre: A Family Portrait (interviewee), 1989.
The True Story of Frankenstein (interviewee), 1994.
Universal Horror (interviewee), 1998.

Special thanks, *Future by Design*, Open Edge, 2006. William Gazecki, Director/Producer.

Bibliography

"About the Big Heart Awards," *Science Fiction Awards Watch*, http://www.sfawardswatch.com/?page_id=615.

Ash, Brian, editor. *The Visual Encyclopedia of Science Fiction*. Harmony, NY: Crown, 1977.

Astrella, Al, and James Greene. *A Forbidden Look Inside the House of Ackerman: A Photographic Tour of the Legendary Ackermansion*. Baltimore: Midnight Marquee Press, 2010.

Bellamy, Edward. *Looking Backward*. New York: Oxford University Press, 2007.

Brooks, Ned. *What Is Science Fiction Fandom?* Boston: National Fantasy Fan Federation, 1944.

Chaney, Ron. Personal communication, June 26, 2009.

Clute, John, and Peter Nicholls. *Encyclopedia of Science Fiction*. London: Orbit, 1993, pp. 3–4.

Constellation, the 41st World Science Fiction Convention Program Book. Baltimore, 1983.

Daniel, Dennis, with Jim Knusch. *Famous Monsters Chronicles*. Albany, NY: FantaCo Enterprises, 1991.

de Camp, L. Sprague. *Lovecraft: A Biography*. New York: Doubleday, 1975.

diMassa, Cara Mia. "Historic Clifton's Struggles to Sustain Itself." *Los Angeles Times*, August 5, 2009.

Dorf, Shel. Taped interview with Forrest J Ackerman on the subject of the origin of Vampirella, 1985.

Fantastic Worlds, Fall/Winter, Vol. 1, #3 (fanzine). Los Angeles: Sam Sackett, 1953.

Ferry, Ray. *Life Is but a Scream*. North Hills, CA: Karmanirhara, 2000.

47th World Science Fiction Convention, Noreascon Three 1989; 47th Anniversary Worldcon Program Book. Boston, 1989.

Gilbert, Elizabeth. "My Favorite Martian." *Gentlemen's Quarterly*, March 2001, pp. 331–335.

Gilstrap, Peter. "Monster Magnate." *New Times* (Los Angeles), July 25–August 4, 1999.

Harris, Lee. Personal communication, September 19 and 22, 2009; December 28, 2009.

Harryhausen, Ray. *The Early Years*. DVD documentary, 2005.

"History of the 42nd Tank Battalion." http://www.11tharmoreddivision.com/history/42nd_tank_battalion_hist.htm

Hufnagel-Giba, Johnathan. "That Little Monster, or So You Want to Make a Movie." *Cult Movies* #20, 1996, pg. 62.

James van Hise Presents Edgar Rice Burroughs' Fantastic Worlds (fanzine), 2002.

Jones, Stephen. *The Essential Monster Movie Guide*. New York: Watson-Guptill, 2000.

Kirk, Daniel. "How I Met the Man Behind *Famous Monsters of Filmland!*" *Scary Monsters Magazine*, #70, April 2009, pp. 54–55.

Knowles, Harry. *Ain't It Cool News*. http://www.aintitcool.com

Kramer, Edward E., and Peter Crowther. *Tombs*. White Wolf, Canada: Pacificon, 1996.

McDaniel, David. *The Man from U.N.C.L.E.: The Vampire Affair* (#6). New York: Ace, 1966.

Munn, Vella. "Homer Eon Flint." *Strange Horizons* (http://www.strangehorizons.com), March 19, 2001.

Pacificon 1946 Program Book. http://www.fanac.org/fanzines/Pacificon/Pacificon/pb-00.html

Paige, Alex. Personal communication, May 20, 27, 28, and 30, 2009.

Perret, Patti. *The Faces of Science Fiction*. New York: Bluejay Books/St. Martin's, 1984.

Pohl, Frederik. *The Way the Future Was: A Memoir*. New York: Random House, 1978.

Porjes Family Tree. http://www.porges.net/FamilyTreesBiographies/Porjes.html.

Roach, David A., and Jon B. Cooke, editors (consultant: James Warren). *The Warren Companion: The Definitive Compendium to the Great Comics of Warren Publishing*. Raleigh, NC: Two Morrows, 2001.

Roots Web page. rootsweb.ancestry.com http://wc.

Bibliography

rootsweb.ancestry.com/cgi-bin/igm.cgi?op=GET&db=geolarson2&id=I228468.

Sackett, Sam. *Fantastic Worlds* (fanzine). Fall/Winter 1952. Vol. 1, No. 2, 1952.

Sheffield, Richard F. "Lugosi's Last Years." *Famous Monsters of Filmland*, #133, April 1977, pp. 46–51.

Siegel, Jerry (as Herbert S. Fine). "The Reign of Superman." *Science Fiction* #3, 1933, pp. 1–8; reproduced at the Superman Through the Ages web site, http://superman.nu/seventy/reign/.

Strickland, A. W., and Forrest J Ackerman. *A Reference Guide to American Science Fiction Films Volume 1*. Bloomington, IL: T.J.S. Publications, 1981.

"Tales of Future Past." Hugo Gernsback Page. http://davidszondy.com/future/Gernsback/gernsback.htm

27th Annual Saturn Awards Tuesday June 12, 2001, The (Program book). Los Angeles: The Academy of Science Fiction, Fantasy and Horror Films, 2001.

Timpone, Tony, ed. "The 100 Most Important People in Science Fiction" *Starlog* #100, November 1985.

Tomomatsu, Tadao. Personal communication, August 8, 2009.

University of Kansas. "Science Fiction Films: A Lecture" documentary, 1970.

University of Wyoming Division of Rare Books and Special Collections, Preliminary Inventory, #2358-86-00-00, letter dated March 17, 1987.

Virginia Creepers: The Horror Host Tradition in the Old Dominion (documentary film). Horse Archer Productions, 2009.

White, Alan. 4SJ: "A Jovial Tribute to the Ackermonster." *Delineator*, pp. 64–97. 1988.

_____. *Mr. Monster: Another Time, Another Place*, 2008, pg. 33.

Wingert, Wally, and Daniel Roebuck. *Goolians: A Docu-Comedy* (DVD). Entertainment Rights, 2005.

Index

Abel, Alfred 21
Academy of Motion Picture Arts and Sciences 41, 83
Ace Books 77, 82, 84, 92, 203, 204
Ackerman, Alden Lorraine 16, 23, 26, 29, 43, 44, 47, 49, 53, 186
Ackerman, Forrest J: agenting career 49–53, 55–59, 66–67, 86, 108, 119; ancestry 11–15; Army career 41–45; awards 7, 51, 71, 117, 120, 128, 155, 174; books 84–90, 92, 96, 102, 106, 146, 148, 155, 159–162; childhood 15–27; coining of the term "sci-fi" 55; columns 54, 122; conventions 8, 35, 37–40, 47, 50, 52, 55, 79, 92, 93–94, 118, 140, 194; death 171; death of brother 43; death of father 49; death of maternal grandfather 40; death of maternal grandmother 48; death of mother 96; documentaries 87–88, 108, 117, 122, 162; editorships 28, 34, 43, 60–103, 107, 108, 118–120, 122; fan activity 18–48; films 42–54, 71–76, 81–87, 90, 93–94, 108, 111–112, 112–121, 124, 148, 162; influences 15–31; marriage 48; story 27; travel 20, 51, 55, 66, 90, 106, 111, 117
Ackerman, Joe 23
Ackerman, Wendayne Wahrman: birth of son 47; college teaching career 66; death 113; fleeing Nazi regime 47; life in Poland 47; marriage 47, 48; translation of *Perry Rhodan* series 82, 92–93
Ackerman, William Schilling 15–16, 26, 29, 31, 47, 49, 176

Ackerman Science Fiction Agency 48, 67, 124
Ackermanthology: Millenium Edition; 65 Astonishing Rediscovered Sci-fi Shorts (book) 204
Ackerminimansion see 4511 Russell Avenue
Action Comics (comic) 28
Addams Family (television series) 75
Aelita, Queen of Mars (film) 19, 122
After Hours (magazine) 58–59
Aftermath 111
Aint It Cool News (web site) 168
Aldrin, Buzz 85, 140
Algol (film) 18
All-Story Weekly (magazine) 18, 46
Allen, David 112
Amateur Press Association 35
Amazing Forries (book) 43, 99, 124, 176, 203
Amazing Stories (magazine) 9, 15, 24–25, 37, 51, 66, 98, 124, 159, 162, 167, 183
Amazing Stories 35th Anniversary Issue (magazine) 66
Amazon Women on the Moon (film) 112, 172
American Cinematheque 20, 160, 171, 173, 193
American International Pictures 57–58, 71, 75–76, 112
American Weekly (newspaper) 38
An American Werewolf in London (film) 102
Analog (magazine) 104
Anders, Merry 72
Anger, Kenneth 109, 112, 122
Ann Radcliffe Award 71, 174
Anthony, Brian 155
Apollo 11 Moon Landing, 1969 84

Appelbaum, Jacqueline (Jacie) 142–143, 171
Arkoff, Samuel 57
Armstrong, Neil 85
Arsenic and Old Lace (radio drama) 96
Ashton, Eric 96
Asimov, Isaac 37, 49, 55, 104, 122, 151
Associated Oil 31
Astrella, Al 16
Atkins, Rick ix, 44, 154, 181, 186
Atlanticon II science fiction convention, Virginia Beach 105
"Atoms and Stars" (short story) 204
Attack of the 50-Foot Monster Mania (documentary) 205
Authentic Science Fiction (magazine) 151
Avalanche (film) 34

Balboa High School 31, 45, 54, 57
Banana Monster (film) see *Schlock!*
Bannister, Reggie 124
Barkett, Christopher 112
Barkett, Steve 111
Barnett, Buddy ix, 122
Barrymore, Lionel 19
Battlestar Galactica 140
Baum, Melissa 124
Beast from 20,000 Fathoms (film) 52, 57
Beaumont, Charles 57
Bellamy, Edward 17
Bellamy, Ralph 108
Bergmann, Michael 117
Bernhardt, Kurt 81
Best Science Fiction for 1973 (book) 90, 204
Beyond the Pole (short story) 24
Biemiller, Carl L. 159
Bikini Drive-In (film) 204

Index

Billows, Dennis 96, 160
Binder, Eando 119
Bixby, Jerome 49
Bjo Trimble's Sci-Fi Spotlite (magazine) 122
Bjo Trimble's Space-Time Continuum see *Bjo Trimble's Sci-Fi Spotlite*
The Black Cat (film) 128; see also *The Vanishing Body*
The Black Sleep (film) 53–54, 58
The Blackbird (film) 19
Blade Runner (film) 14
Blair, Patricia 53
Blaisdell, Paul 64–65
A Blind Bargain 19, 132, 203
Blind Spot (novel) 8
Bloch, Robert 47–48, 52, 55, 78, 102, 104, 105, 112, 118, 139, 199
Blood Feast (film) 83
Blood of Dracula (film) 58
Bloom, John 90
Blown (novel) 84
Bond, Nelson S. 37, 57
Bonnie Barker 108
Boris Karloff's Thriller (television series) 77
Borland, Carroll 98, 108, 112
Boulanger, Jamieson 123
Boxleitner, Bruce 147
Boys' Ace Library (magazine) 17
Boys' Cinema (magazine) 65
Boy's Scientifiction Club 27
Bradbury, Ray 2, 33, 36–37, 49, 52, 57, 83–89, 106, 109, 112, 128, 121, 146, 151, 158, 160–161, 163, 168, 171, 177, 181, 191, 198–199
Bradbury Building, Los Angeles 14, 129–130, 161
Bradley, Tom 111
Bresee, Bobbie 117–118, 199
The Bride of Frankenstein 29, 95, 102, 126, 127, 181, 188–189
Brooks, Larry 96
Brooks, Paul 96
"Brother Theodore" 112
Brundage, Margaret 111
Brzezinski, Anthony 125
Bunnell, Paul 124
Burks, Arthur J. 148
Burns, Bob 112, 144, 147–148
Burns, Kathy 147, 184
Burns, Kevin J. 146, 157, 171, 197–199
Burroughs, Edgar Rice 39, 45–46, 181
Burroughs Bibliophiles 127, 174
Butler, Octavia 106

By Rocket to the Moon (film) 34
Byrne, Stuart J. 92

California State University, Fullerton 98
Caloric Appliance Corporation 58
Camacho, Juan 96, 152, 171
Campbell, H.J. 51
Campbell, John W., Jr. 37, 82
Carey, Phillip 72
Carnell, E, J. 47
Carradine, John 54, 108, 192
Carroll, Regina 88
Castle of Frankenstein (magazine) 64
Chaney, Creighton see Chaney, Lon, Jr.
Chaney, Jaclynn ix
Chaney, Lon, Jr. 19, 53–54, 68, 88–90, 126, 138
Chaney, Lon, Sr. 8, 15, 19, 26, 60, 80, 83–84, 95–96, 98, 104, 106, 111, 126–127, 132, 187–188, 191
Chaney, Ron ix, 90, 112, 183, 199
Chapman, Ben 184
Chapman, Edward 37
Chekhovich, Dimitri Victorov 106
Chicon (Chicago World Science Fiction Convention), 1940 39–40
Chiller conventions 140
Ciak! (magazine) 122
Cinema 57 (magazine) 59
Clarke, Arthur C. 106
Clay, Cassius M. 12
Clifton's Cafeteria, Los Angeles 36, 39, 52
Clive, Colin 26, 29
Close Encounters of the Third Kind (film) 105, 138
Coe, Frank 65
Colorado Fantasy Society 32
Columbia Pictures Corporation (film production company) 42–43, 58, 104, 140
"Confessions of a Sci-Fi Addict" (article) 31
Conkling, Rebecca D. 15
Conquest of Space (film) 84
Constellation, 41st World Science Fiction Convention, Baltimore 104
Copner, Michael 122, 151
Cosmic Report Card: Earth (short story) 32
Cosmos (fiction serial) 82
Coulter, Eli 148

"Count Down to Doom" (short story) 204
Count Dracula Society 71, 117, 128, 174
Cox, Arthur Jean 152, 163
Cozzi, Luigi 92
Crazy Ray (film) 18
Creation (film) 136
The Creature from the Black Lagoon (film) 59, 86, 182, 184
Creepy (magazine) 98, 103
Cridland, Thomas W. 11–13, 129
Crosby, Bing 20, 170
Cult Movies (magazine) 122, 151
Cummings, Ray 37, 88
Cushing, Peter 80, 94, 96

Dalton, Bob 58
Daltrey, Roger 81, 121
Danforth, Jim 112, 134
Daniels, Gray 96
Dante, Joe 65, 112, 138, 171, 177, 198–199
Darlton, Clark 57
Daugherty, Jessie 27
Daugherty, Mary Ellen ix, 33, 36, 44, 48, 50, 62, 71, 73–74, 82, 97, 114, 132, 134, 151, 156, 176
Daugherty, Walter J. 27, 33, 36, 40, 43, 44, 48, 50, 56–57, 62, 71–74, 82, 97, 101, 102, 114, 121, 134, 142, 151, 156, 162, 176, 191
Daughters of Bilitis 45
Davids, Paul 16, 161, 163, 171
Davis, Sammy, Jr. 94, 146
The Day the Earth Stood Still (film) 54, 105
Deall, John 149
Deane, Jameson 19
Death Kiss (film) 131
De Brullier, Nigel 19
De Camp, L. Sprague 32, 37, 38
Decca Records 78
Decla/Bioskop UFA 22
Del Toro, Guillermo 5, 171
Deluge (film) 28, 102
Denvention (Denver, Colorado World Science Fiction Convention), 1941 39–40
Devil Commands (film) 131, 136–137
"Dhactwhu! Remember?" (short story) 204
Dickson, Gordon 92
Dietrich, Marlene 26, 34
Dietz, Franklin 56
Dinosaur Valley Girls (film) 123–124, 204

Index

"The Discovery of the Future" (speech) 40, 56
Dr. Acula's Cardiac-Cards 142
Dr. Acula's Thrilling Tales of the Uncanny (book) 160, 204
The Doctor Prescribes Death (radio drama) 96
Doherty, Tom 92
Domkowski, Arlene ix, 122, 171
Dorf, Shel 34, 59, 107, 156
Double Indemnity (film) 14
Douglas, Myrtle 33, 37, 38
Dracula (theatrical production) 26
Dracula versus Frankenstein (film) 88, 204
Draculina (character) 80, 81
Draculon 79–80, 121
Druktenis, Dennis ix
Dune (film) 104
"Dwellers in the Dust" 35

E. Everett Evans Big Heart Award 63
Earth versus the Flying Saucers 57, 134–136, 189
Earth's Lucky Day (short story) 27, 204
East Los Angeles Junior College, Los Angeles 66
Edison film studios 18
Eerie (magazine) 98, 103
Eisley, Anthony 88
Electric Lemon Record Company 78
Electrical Experimenter (magazine) 24
1115 East 18th Street, Los Angeles 15
Ellison, Harlan 80, 92, 109, 146
The Empire Strikes Back (film) 103
Employee's Entrance (film) 42
Engel, Roger 88
Ennis-Brown House, 2655 Glendower Avenue, Los Angeles 139, 150
"Ermayne, Laurajean" (Forrest J Ackerman pseudonym) 45, 53
Ernsting, Walter *see* Darlton, Clark
Esper, Dwain 26
Esperanto 30, 38, 45, 66
Evolution (film) 134, 189
Expanded Science Fiction Worlds of Forrest J Ackerman and Friends PLUS (book) 8, 203
Expanded Worlds of Forrest J Ackerman and Friends (book) 148

The Fabulous Fantasy Films (book) 96
Famous Forry Fotos (book) 160, 203
Famous Monster (documentary) 161
Famous Monsters Chronicles (book) 101
Famous Monsters of Filmland (magazine) (Dynacomm Publishing) 108, 118, 119, 120, 121, 140, 142–143, 146, 194
Famous Monsters of Filmland (magazine) (IDW Publishing) 172
Famous Monsters of Filmland (magazine) (Warren Publishing) 54, 58–61, 64–67, 69, 71, 79, 82–84, 88, 90, 92, 94–95, 96, 98–103, 107, 125, 146, 148, 152, 166, 175–176, 181–182, 186–188, 190, 194
Famous Monsters of Filmland convention, Burbank, 1995 119
Famous Monsters of Filmland convention, Crystal City, 1993 118, 194
Famous Monsters of Filmland convention, Indianapolis, 2010 172
Famous Monsters of Filmland convention, New York, 1974 94–95
Famous Monsters of Filmland convention, New York, 1975 94
Famous Players–Lasky Film Corporation 18
Fangoria (magazine) 103
Fantascience Filmart (column for *Voice of the Imagi-Nation*) 28
Fantastic Film Festival, Ambassador Hotel, Hollywood 90
Fantastic Monsters of the Films (magazine) 64
Fantastic Voyage (film) 104
Fantasy Book (magazine) 35
Fantasy Fan (fanzine) 30, 32
Fantasy Fiction Field (fanzine) 32
Fantasy Foundation 41, 47, 176
Farkas, Phyllis 60
Farley, Ralph Milne 119
Farmer, Phillip José 84
The Farmer's Daughter (film) 43, 204
Fearn, John Russell 159
Fernald, Sean 161
Ferrari, Andrea 122

Ferry, Ray 39, 117–120, 140, 142–144, 146, 148, 183, 189
Fiend Without a Face (film) 67
5327 Virginia Avenue, Los Angeles 15, 18
Filmfax (magazine) 111
"Filthy Pierre" 63
Finlay, Virgil 38
First International Science Fiction Convention, London 51
First International Science Fiction Film Festival, London 51
First National (studio) 35
530 Staples Avenue, San Francisco 26
Flagg, Francis 27, 42, 45
Fletcher, Louise 123
Flint, Homer Eon 8
Fluor Drafting Company 41
For Monsters Only (magazine) 64
Forbes, Brian 101, 121, 143, 191–192
Forbidden Planet (film) 105
Ford, Ron 8
Forrest J Ackerman, Famous Monster of Filmland #1 (book) 203
Forrest J Ackerman, Famous Monster of Filmland #2 (book) 33, 203
Forrest J Ackerman's Amazing World of Science Fiction and Fantasy (documentary) 117
Forrest J Ackerman's Anthology of the Living Dead (book) 161
Forrest J Ackerman's Monsterland (magazine) 35, 107, 110, 203
Forrest J Ackerman's Wide Webbed World (website) 159
Forrest J Ackerman's World of Science Fiction (book) 122, 140, 203
Fort MacArthur 41–42, 44–45, 120
Fort MacArthur Bulletin/Alert 42, 44–45, 120
4511 Russell Avenue, Los Angeles 78, 151, 155, 167, 169, 171, 196, 192
43rd World Science Fiction Convention, Melbourne, Australia 111
Four Sided Triangle (film) 57
Foyt, John 93
Frame-Gray, Nola 111
Francesco-Valente, Silvio 117
Francis, Kay 42
Franken, Steve 72
The Frankenscience Monster (book) 84, 203

211

Index

Frankenstein (1931 film) 26, 29, 88, 94–95, 102, 124, 131, 189
Frankenstein and Me (film) 123, 204
Frankenstein; or, The Modern Prometheus (novel) 17, 60, 61, 88, 96, 99, 122, 125, 126, 127, 181, 188
Frankenstein's Aunt (book) 125
Freehafer, Paul 27, 39
Friars Club 120, 121
Fröhlich, Gustav 21
Frye, Dwight 26
Frye, Dwight, Jr. 118
Futura Award for Multimedia Science Fiction and Fantasy 152, 174
Future by Design (documentary) 161
The Futurians 37

Gambling with the Gulf Stream (film) 18
Garage Mahal 138
The Genie (film) 54
George Arents Library, Syracuse University, Syracuse 98
Georgia Institute of Technology, Atlanta 98
Gernsback, Hugo 15, 23–24, 30, 51, 66, 82, 153
The Gernsback Awards (book) 204
Get Off the Earth (proposed film) 96
Getty Oil 26
Ghost of Slumber Mountain (film) 131
Ghost Stories Magazine (magazine) 16–17
Ghostbusters (film) 134
Gilman, Mark S., Jr. 108
Glasser, Allen 34
Glen or Glenda (film) 52
Glut, Donald F. 123, 177
Gods and Monsters Lifetime Achievement Award 155
Gogos, Basil 60–61, 125, 184
Golden Library of Eastern New Mexico University 98
Golden Scroll Award 82
Golden State Mini Comic-Con 86
Goolians: A Docu-Comedy (documentary) 205
Gordon, Alex 108
Gore Creatures 64
Gosh! Wow! Science Fiction; Nineteen Nostalgic Knockouts Compiled by Forrest J Ackerman (book) 203
Goss, John 159
Gough, Michael 165, 172
Grant, Cary 34, 136
Grauman's Chinese Theater 193
Grauman's Egyptian Theatre *see* American Cinematheque
"The Great Gog's Grave" (short story) 204
Greene, James 16
Griffith, Raymond 96
Guernsey's Auctions 111

Haldeman, Gay 106
Haldeman, Joe 106
Hallind, Kristina 92
Hamilton, Edmund 82
Hanke, Ken 122
Hardin, Ann 148, 199, 204
Harrington, Curtis 54, 66, 75, 112
Harris, Lee ix, 20, 51, 77, 121–122, 155, 170–171, 192, 199
Harrison, Harry 37
Harryhausen, Ray 35, 36, 39, 52, 57, 100, 112, 117, 126, 134, 136, 140–141, 167, 183–184, 189, 199
Hawk, David ix, 29, 61, 115, 121, 148, 160, 170, 172, 173, 181, 184, 187
Hays, Will H. 23
Heartstoppers: Horror at the Movies (documentary) 205
Hefner, Hugh 58, 150
Heinlein, Leslyn 33
Heinlein, Robert A.: co-creator with Forrest J Ackerman of the term "sci-fi" 55; disagreements with Forrest J Ackerman 53, 57; early writings 39, 56, 88, 122; guest lecturer at the Denvention 39–40; involvement in the Los Angeles Science Fantasy Society 33, 39; positive attitudes toward minorities 57
Heller, Berndt 22
Helm, Brigitte 21–22
Herbert, Frank 104
Hey, Rookie! (film) 42–43, 204
High Treason (film) 19–20, 28, 139
Hines, Desi Arnaz 117
Hirscher, Ingrid 155
Hirscher, Joe 155
Hoganmiller, Linus 27
Hollywood Boulevard (film) 204
Hollywood Goes Ape! (documentary) 205
Honorary Doctorate in Literature, St. Andrews University 120, 204
Hooray for Horrorwood (documentary) 39, 117
Hopper, Dennis 75
Hornig, Charles D. 30, 32
Horror Hall of Fame 117, 126, 204
House of Frankenstein (film) 90
House of Horror (film) 107
House of Pies 1, 147, 151, 160, 162, 167, 190, 192
The Howling (film) 204
Hubbard, L. Ron 49
Huell Howser's Visiting... (documentary) 205
Hugo Award, #1 Fan Personality (1953 World Science Fiction Convention, Philadelphia) 7, 51, 174, 192, 204
Hume, Benita 20
The Hunchback of Notre Dame (1923 film) 19, 111, 188
Hunt, Roy V. 32
Huppertz, Gottfried 22

I Was a Teenage Werewolf (film) 58
Illustrated History of the Horror Film (book) 64
Image of the Beast (novel) 84
Imaginative Tales (magazine) 54, 69, 203
Independent International Pictures (film production company) 88–89
The Indestructible Man (film) 14
International Geophysical Year 65
Intolerance (film) 23
The Invasion of the Body Snatchers (film) 155
Invasion of the Saucer Men (film) 54
Ishida, Hajime 121
It Came from Beneath the Sea (film) 57, 134, 189

Jackson, Peter 159–161
James A. Rock & Company Publishers 146, 148, 152, 160, 203
Jarman, Peter J. 92
The Jetsons (television series) 66
Jittlov, Mike 112, 152, 163
Johnson, George Clayton 151, 156, 160, 163–166, 171, 199
Johnson, Tor 53–54, 138, 157
Johnston, Ian 161

212

Index

Jolson, Al 20, 42, 151, 170–171, 193
Jolson Sings Again (film) 42
The Jolson Story (film) 42
Jones, Franklin 49
Jones, Stephen 191
A Journey to the Center of the Earth 99
Just Imagine (film) 28

Kable News 59–60
Karloff, Boris 26, 68, 71, 77–79, 80, 84, 94–96, 103, 112, 120, 126, 128, 131, 136–137, 151, 187–179, 191, 192
Karloff, Sara 117–118, 183–184, 149
Katz, David B. 121
Keepers of the Frame (documentary) 205
Keesey, Pam 155, 170, 199, 203–204
Keller, David H. 119, 160
Kelly, Ken 125
Kentucky Fried Movie (film) 204
Kim, Phillip 172
King Kong (1933 film) 26, 35–36, 86–87, 90, 96, 126, 134, 136, 151, 159–160, 187, 189–190, 191, 193
King Kong (1976 film) 96, 98, 100
Kirk, Daniel 67–70
KISS (rock band) 146
Klein-Rogge, Rudolph 21
Kline, Otis Adelbert 119
Korda, Alexander 36
Kornbluth, Cyril 37–38, 56
Kuttner, Henry 122
Kyle, David 52, 55–56, 112

L.A. Shriner's Roast Club 194
Laemmle, Carl 28–29, 126
Laemmle, Carla 112, 152, 154, 171, 186
Lamb, Janie 63
The Land That Time Forgot (novel) 46
Landis, John 93–94, 108, 112, 121, 138, 140, 152, 155, 161, 171, 198–199
Lang, Fritz 22, 42, 75, 78–79, 96, 100, 106, 112, 120, 126
Langdon, Verne ix, 77–78, 151, 156, 157, 199
Larrinaga, Mario 126
Larsen, Milt 78
The Last Godling (manuscript) 8
Latté, Lily 42
Law, John Philip 194

Lee, Jenny 51
Lee, Walt 163
Leeds, Ron 99
Leinster, Murray ix, 49
Lennig, Arthur 91
"Letter to an Angel" (story). 8, 204
LeVey, Anton 61–63, 112
Lewis, Hershel Gordon 83
Life magazine 51
Lilley, Jessie 122, 166
Linaweaver, Brad 165–166
Lincoln, Abraham 12–13, 129, 188
"Linden, Paul" (pseudonym of Forrest J Ackerman) 54, 103
Lininger, Hope 52
Lon Chaney: A Thousand Faces (documentary) 205
Lon of 1000 Faces! (book) 106, 187
London After Midnight (film) 96, 127, 151, 161, 183, 188
Long, Amelia Reynolds 67
Long, Harry 122
Long, Julius 119
Looking Backward from 2000–1887 (novel) 14, 17
Lorre, Peter 42, 68, 138, 192
Los Angeles Science Fantasy Society 7, 32–35, 39, 43, 54, 61, 71, 111, 157, 163, 195
Los Feliz Theater, 1822 North Vermont Avenue, Los Angeles 151, 167, 175
The Lost World (1925 film) 20, 35, 54, 64
Lovecraft, H.P. (Howard Phillips) 32, 155
Lovsky, Celia 112
Lugosi, Bela 26, 52–54, 96, 108, 112, 122, 126, 128, 131, 138, 183, 188, 191, 194
Lugosi, Lillian 52, 91
Lugosi: The Forgotten King (documentary) 108, 205
"The Lure and Lore of 'The Blind Spot'" (magazine article) 8

M (film) 42
MacDonald, Michael 161
The Mad Brain (manuscript) 38
Magic and Myth of the Movies (book) 64
Magid, Ron 107
Mahr, Kurt 92
Malone, Bill 22, 132, 159
The Man from U.N.C.L.E.: The Vampire Affair (novel) 77

Mand, Cyril 119
Maniac (film) 26
March, Fredric 95, 126
Marly, Florence 75–76, 90
M.A.R.S. (film) 18, 34
Marshall, William 123
"A Martian Oddity" (short story) 204
A Martian Odyssey 38
Martianthology (book) 159–160, 203
Marvel Tales (magazine) 35
Massey, Raymond 37, 41
Master of the World (film) 138
McDaniel, David 77
McGee, Mark 65
Melchior, Ib 71, 112
Méliès, Georges 96
Mercury Theater on the Air (radio program) 37
Merritt, A. (Abraham) 38, 82
Metropolis (film) 6, 19, 21–22, 34, 42, 54, 79, 88, 100–102, 126, 129, 132, 146, 151, 159
"Micro-Man" (short story) 204
"Midnight Mail Goes to Mars" (illustration) 124
Midnight Marquee (magazine) see *Gore Creatures*
Mighty Joe Young (1949 film) 57, 120, 136, 138, 189
The Mike Douglas Show (television series) 91
Miller, Ann 42–43
Miller, Patsy Ruth 19, 111
Mills, Nancy 107
Mimieux, Yvette 80
Miracle Science and Fantasy Stories (magazine) 124
Mission Stardust (film) 76, 90
Mr. Monster's Movie Gold (book) 106
Modern Electrics (magazine) 24
Moe, Joe ix, 1–3, 78, 103, 138, 142, 146, 149, 151, 155, 156, 160, 161, 166, 170–171, 177, 185, 182, 195, 198–199
Monster Bash conventions, Pennsylvania 140–141, 158, 159, 161, 162, 172, 174, 184
Monster Parade (magazine) 64
Monster Rally convention, Crystal City, Virginia, 1999 140, 142, 183
Monster World (magazine) 55, 83, 140
Montgomery, Frances Trego 17, 129
The Moon Pool (novellette) 38

Index

Moore, Catherine 112, 122, 123, 148
Morgan, Bassett 148
Morrow, Gray 92
Morrow, Jim 118, 164–165, 167, 190–200
Morse, Samuel F.B. 11
Movie Monsters Magazine (magazine) 96
The Munsters (television series) 75, 76, 160
Murders in the Rue Morgue (1932 film) 29
Music for Robots (record album) 65
My Lovely Monster (film) 117
The Mysterious Island (1929 film) 19
Mystery of Life (film) 34

Naish, J. Carroll 88–89
Nebula Science Fiction (magazine) 54
Neill, Noel 118
Neville, Kris 57
New Media Publishing 107
New Wave science fiction 90, 99
New York World's Fair of 1939 38
Newman, Rick 104
Nicholson, Jim 57, 112
Night of the Living Dead (film) 84
915 South Sherbourne Drive Los Angeles 51, 62, 78, 110, 186
1939 World Science Fiction Convention, New York 38
Ninotchka (film) 52
9th World Science Fiction Convention New Orleans 49
Nolan, William F. 177
Norton, Andre 63
Novotny, Norbert 79, 92, 96
Nudist Colony of the Dead (film) 112
Nuetzell, Charles 49, 60, 75
Nuetzell, Albert 60

O'Brien, Darlyne 112
Ogilvie, Kevin 170
Ogre, Nivek *see* Ogilvie, Kevin
Old Mother Riley Meets the Vampire (film) 52, 108
On a Lark to the Planets (book) 17
Once Upon a Time (film) 136
One Glorious Day (film) 15, 18, 151
Orick, George 55

Original Ackermansion *see* 915 S. Sherbourne Drive
Original Comic Art (book) 204
The Origins of Continents and Oceans (book) 132
Oscars (awards) of 1939 41
The Outer Limits (television series) 75, 126
The Outlaw of Torn (novel) 46

Pace, Alexandra 168–169
Pace, Anita ix, 168, 171
Pace, Forrest Phillips Bradbury 168–169
Pace, Terry ix, 163, 168, 169, 199
Pacific Electric Building 39
Pacific Western Oil Corporation *see* Getty Oil
Paige, Alex ix, 29, 77, 92–93, 96
Painter, Floyd Eugene v, 106, 114
Pal, George 57, 66, 80, 82, 98, 106, 112, 114, 136, 147
Palmer, Randy 96, 103
Palmer, Raymond A. 34–35, 119
Parks, Larry 42–43
Partch, Virgil 42
Paul, Frank R. 24, 37, 66, 124–125
Paxton, Bill 147
Perry Rhodan (book series): Ace Publishing imprints 82, 92; clubs and fandom 92, 93; convention 92; German imprints 77, 167
Petaja, Emil 57
Peter (book) 64
Peters, Luthor 14
The Phantom of the Opera (1925 film) 19, 60, 95, 100, 127, 148
Phelps, Dennis ix
Philbin, Mary 127, 148
Philcon (Philadelphia World Science Fiction Convention), 1953 8, 51
Photoplay Magazine (magazine) 28
Pickford, Mary 77
Pinckard, Terri 106, 177
Pinckard, Tom 106
Plan Nine from Outer Space (film) 53, 136
The Planet (fanzine) 34
Planet of the Apes (film) 96, 138
Planet Stories (magazine) 159
Planeta Burg (film) 138
Playboy (magazine) 56, 58–59
Poe, Edgar Allan 17
Pohl, Frederik 33, 104, 120, 122
Pointer-Ford, Paula 8
Polanski, Roman 80

Porjes, Frederic 47
Porjes, Michael 47, 84, 140, 168
Porjes, Wendy 140
Powell, Martin 181
Presio, Vic 60
Puddinhead Wilson (novel) 17
Pursuit to Mars (novel) 82

Quarry, Robert 96
Queen of Blood (film) 75, 76, 204

Rabogliatti, Mary Ellen *see* Daugherty, Mary Ellen
Radio-Mania (film) *see* M.A.R.S.
Rainbow Fantasia: 25 Spectrumatic Tales of Wonder (book) 148, 160, 204
Rains, Claude 26, 65, 95
The Rains Came (film) 41
Ralph 124C41 + (novel) 24
Ramsey, Michael ix, 13, 79, 91, 102, 119, 125, 127, 128, 130, 131, 133, 135, 136, 137, 139, 142, 143–144, 146, 147, 149, 152–153, 160
Rathbone, Basil 5, 53, 75, 138
Ray Harryhausen: The Early Years (documentary) 36
Rector, Jeff 123, 147
Red Velvet (film) 3, 161, 166, 204
Redford, Robert 166
Reed, Donald A. 71, 82–83, 106, 146, 191
Reel Future: The Stories That Inspired 16 Classic Science Fiction Movies (book) 203
Reference Guide to American Science Fiction Films 1900–1929 (book) 102, 203
Reference Guide to American Science Fiction Films 1930–1945 (book) 102, 203
The Resuscitated Monster (film) 57
The Return of Dr. X (film) 107
Return of the Ape Man (film) 108
Reynolds, Burt 123
Reynolds, Gene 117
Riley, Phillip J. 96, 132
Rising Star Science Fiction convention, 1990 114
Rising Star Science Fiction convention, 1995 115, 120, 187
RKO Production 601: The Making of Kong, Eighth Wonder of the World (documentary) 160
RKO-Radio Pictures 35, 57, 96, 160

214

Index

"The Roads Must Roll" (short story) 39
Roberts, Jeff ix, 147, 171
Robinson, Ann 82, 152, 163, 171, 199
Robinson, Beth ix
Rock, James A. 146, 148, 152, 203
The Rocketeer (film) 134
Rocklynne, Ross 57, 159
Roebuck, Dan 146
Roesel, Earl 170–171
Rossito, Angelo 88
Rovin, Jeff 96
Rudley, Herbert 53
Rundfunk-Sinfonieorchester Saarbrücken 22
Russell, Marc Anthony 92

"Sabina of the White Cylinder" (short story) 204
SadoMannequin (film) 204
San Diego Comic-Con International 34, 59, 86, 151
Saratoga (film) 53
Saturn Awards 83, 117, 128, 147
Saxon, John 75
Scarlet Street (magazine) 122, 160, 185
Scary Monsters Magazine 182
Schallert, William 118
Scheer, K.H. 77, 92
Schlock! (film) 93, 108, 138
Schneer, Charles H. 57
Schnoeker-Shorb, Yvette 148
Schuster, Hal 107
Schwartz, Julius 27, 34, 37–38, 112, 156
Science and Invention (magazine) 17, 24
Science Fiction (fanzine) 28
Science Fiction Club Deutschland 57
Science Fiction Digest (fanzine) 35
Science Fiction Films: A Lecture (documentary) 87, 122
Science Fiction League 30, 32, 33, 39, 105
Science Fiction Monthly (magazine) 159
Science Fiction Museum, 5th Avenue, Seattle, Washington 159, 178
Science Fiction Records 65
Science Fiction Week, 1975 96
Science Fictioneers 33
Science Wonder Stories (magazine) 25, 66, 134, 162
Scientifilm 28
"Scientifilm Marquee" (column for *Imaginative Tales Magazine*) 54, 203
Sci-Fi (aborted magazine) 55
The Sci-Fi Boys (documentary) 36, 161, 204
Sci-Fi Womanthology (book) 155, 160, 204
"Scream-O-Scope Is Here!" (article for *After Hours Magazine*) 59
Screen Gems (film production/distribution company) 58
Screen Thrills Illustrated (magazine) 61, 65
Scrimm, Angus 112, 171, 199
Sense of Wonder Press 152, 155, 159, 203, 204
Serling, Rod 49, 86
Serviss, Garrett P. 82
Seven Footprints to Satan (film) 107
Seven Footprints to Satan (novel) 38
Sheffield, Richard 52–53
Shelley, Mary Wollstonecraft 16–17, 99, 122, 126–127, 178, 180–181
Shinnick, Kevin 122
Shock Theater (television syndicated package) 58, 60, 75
Shorb, Terril 148
"The Shortest Story Ever Told" (short story) 204
Shuster, Joseph 28
Siegel, Jerome 28
Siegfried (1924 film) 22
Silverberg, Robert 109
Simak, Clifford D. 106
Simmons, Gene 146
Siodmak, Curt 90, 112
Skerchock, John 146
Slan (novel) 88
Slater, Ken 8, 51–52
Smart Money (magazine) 55
Smith, Clark Ashton 32
Smith, E.E. ("Doc") 33, 63, 77
Snyder, Tom 94–95
Son of Ackermansion *see* 2495 Glendower Avenue
Son of Blob (film) 90
Son of Dracula (film) 90
Son of Frankenstein (film) 5, 52
Son of Kong (film) 160
S.O.S. aus dem Weltraum (film) *see Mission Stardust*
Soto, Talisa 81, 121, 126
Space Boy (film) 90
Spacemen (magazine) 66
Spacemen and Spacewomen (magazine) 122
Spicy Mystery Stories (magazine) 18
Stapledon, Olaf 31, 29, 122, 132
Star Trek (television series) 55, 103, 106–107, 122, 138, 140, 151
Star Trek III: The Search for Spock (film) 104, 106
Star Wars (film) 102, 104–105, 138
Stark Mad (film) 107
Stevenson, Robert Louis 99
Stewart, Don 121, 144–145
Strange Illusion (film) 42
Strickland, A.J. 102, 203, 208
Stuart, Gloria 118
Superman (character) 28, 39, 102, 105
Superman II (film) 102–103
Supernatural (film) 108
Swisher, Robert B. 37
Sykora, Will 37

Tamblyn, Russ 88
Tarzan (character) 18, 45–46
Tarzan and the Golden Lion (film) 46
Tarzan, Lord of the Jungle (novel) 46
Tarzan of the Apes (serialized novel) 46
Tarzan of the Movies (book) 64
Tarzana, California 45
The Terror (film) 108
Test, Roy 30
Test, Wanda 30
Texas Chainsaw Massacre: A Family Portrait (documentary) 205
That Little Monster (film) 124, 204
Thea von Harbou's Metropolis: 75th Anniversary Edition (book) 146, 203
Them! (film) 110
Thief of Bagdad (1924 film) 128
The Thing from Another World (film) 128
Things to Come (1936 film) 28, 36, 38–39, 41
This Island, Earth (film) 54, 57
The Thought Monster (short story) 67
Thrilling Wonder Stories (magazine) 25, 29–30, 37, 50–51, 119
The Time Traveler (fanzine) 27, 34, 102
The Time Travelers (film) 71, 172, 204
Tinnell, Robert 123

Index

To Tell the Truth (television series) 87
Tomomatsu, Tadao ix, 61
The Tonight Show (television series) 62
Tourist Trap (film) 138
Train, Oscar 37
Trimble, Bjo 54–55, 90, 112, 122
Trimble, John 54–55, 90
The True Story of Frankenstein (documentary) 205
Turkeys in Outer Space (film) 112
2495 Glendower Avenue, Los Angeles 90, 108, 139, 165, 191
20,000 Leagues Under the Sea (film) 136
20,000 Leagues Under the Sea (novel) 17
Twitter 35
236½ North New Hampshire Avenue, Los Angeles 45
2001: A Space Odyssey 84, 105, 138

Under the Moons of Mars (serialized novel) 46
The Unholy Three (1930 film) 26
Universal Horror (documentary) 205
Universal Pictures Corporation 19, 28, 34, 52, 86, 88–90, 96, 109, 110–111, 149, 152, 182
University of California at Berkeley 31
University of Kansas 87, 98
University of Wyoming at Laramie 98
The Unknown Purple (film) 34

V (television series) 104
V26 (magazine) 43
V59 (magazine) 61
Valley, Richard 122, 161, 185
The Valley of Gwangi (film) 126, 140
Vampira 53, 58
The Vampire Hunters Club (film) 148, 204
Vampirella (film) 81, 121, 126, 204
Vampirella of Draculon (character) 79–81, 103, 120

Vampirella's Feary Tales (comic) 81
Van Hise, James 45, 107, 110
The Vanishing Body (film) 58; see also *The Black Cat*
van Vogt, A.E. 49, 71, 88, 92, 105, 163–167, 198
van Vogt, Lydia 163–168, 198
Verne, Jules 17, 19, 99, 122, 181
Verrill, A. Hyatt 24
Vertex Science Fiction (magazine) 32, 56
Vice Versa (magazine) 45
Vista Theater, 4473 Sunset Drive, Los Angeles 140, 167
Voice of the Imagi-Nation (fanzine) 28, 43
Voltz, William 92
Vukovich, Jovanka 171, 203

Waite, Ron 96, 203
War of the Worlds (1953 film) 152
War of the Worlds (radio dramatization) 37
The Warner Brothers Museum, Warner Brothers Studios Burbank 166
Warren, Bill 65, 69, 151, 171
Warren, James 58, 59–61, 66, 76–77, 79–81, 83–84, 94, 96, 99–101, 103, 120, 146, 151–155, 172, 176
Warren Publishing Company 6, 61, 65–66, 80, 94, 103, 107, 118, 175, 182
WCAU TV (Broadcasting station) 58
Weinbaum, Margaret 38
Weinbaum, Stanley G. 38, 88, 180
Weird Tales, the Unique Magazine (magazine) 18, 33, 67, 108, 111, 119, 134, 160
Weisinger, Mort 27, 34, 37
Weiss, George Henry see Flagg, Francis
Welles, Orson 37, 94
Wellman, Manly Wade 37
Wells, H.G. (Herbert George) 8, 37, 41, 82, 84, 117, 166, 180, 181
West of Zanzibar (film) 127
Westercon 1953, San Francisco 50–51

When Dinosaurs Ruled the Earth (film) 134
Where East Is East (film) 127
White Zombie (film) 52
Wholesale Oil Company 15
The Wide Awake Library (magazine) 17
Wildest Westerns (magazine) 61, 65
William, Warren 42
Williams, Monty "Two Gun" 27
Williams, Robin 109
Williamson, Jack 88
The Winner's Circle (film) 204
The Wizard of Speed and Time (film) 112, 152, 204
Wolf, Leonard 94
Woman in the Moon (film) 22
Wonder Stories (magazine) 27, 30, 32
Wonderama (aborted magazine) 59
The Wonderful Electric Elephant (novel) 17, 131
Wong, Casey 165
Wood, Edward D., Jr. 49, 52–53, 136
Wood, Larry 104
World Famous Creatures (magazine) 60
Worlds of Tomorrow 160
Wrede, Shirley 30
WRNY Radio (broadcasting station) 23
WTOP TV (broadcasting station) 58
Wyman, Belle 11–12, 14, 16, 45
Wyman, Carroll Cridland 14, 26, 47–48, 96–97, 186
Wyman, George 12, 14, 16–17, 40, 45, 129, 161
Wyman, Mark 14, 130

The X-Files (television series) 140

Yano, Tetsu 50–51
The Young Diana (film) 19

Zacherle, John 58
Zamenhof, Ludovic Lazarus 30
Zimmerman, Troy 165

www.ingramcontent.com/pod-product-compliance
Ingram Content Group UK Ltd.
Pitfield, Milton Keynes, MK11 3LW, UK
UKHW050529150426
5217IPUK00026B/1855